The use of computers for profit
A businessman's guide

*Other titles in the McGraw-Hill European series
in Management and Marketing*

Foster: Automation in Practice
Gage: Value Analysis
Goodman & Whittingham: Shop Stewards in British Industry
Humble: Improving Business Results
Morse: The Practical Approach to Marketing Management
Singer & Ramsden: The Practical Approach to Skills Analysis
Wright: Discounted Cash Flow

The use of computers for profit

A businessman's guide

Laura Esther Tatham

McGRAW-HILL · LONDON

New York · St Louis · San Francisco · Sydney
Toronto · Mexico · Panama

Published by

McGRAW-HILL Publishing Company Limited

MAIDENHEAD · BERKSHIRE · ENGLAND

07 094213 7

Dedication

This book is gratefully dedicated to the many executives,
managers, computer users, and computer specialists who
have allowed me to pick their brains during the past ten years

Contents

Preface   ix

Chapter 1: Introduction   1

Chapter 2: First definitions   5

Chapter 3: Computers and men at work   28

Chapter 4: The impact of computers on commercial
             and industrial management   52

Chapter 5: The computer as a management tool   82

Chapter 6: The computer on the factory floor   138

Chapter 7: Choosing and installing a computer   163

Chapter 8: Computers and people   217

Chapter 9: Why computer installations fail   252

Chapter 10: Computer service bureaux   263

Index   283

Contents

Preface

This book has been written for lively business managers. That is, I have assumed that you, like me, believe that in aiming to run a commercial or industrial enterprise as profitably as you can, you are engaged in an absorbing, challenging, and worth-while activity.

My principal purpose, therefore, is to try to show how you can employ computers to enhance the profitability of your business.

As a business man (or woman), you, like other intelligent and thoughtful people, are almost certainly interested in many aspects of automation. You may, for example, be concerned with the impact of computers upon our society, or be excited by the new possibilities their use opens up in the arts as well as in the sciences.

These and many other aspects of computerization are of profound importance and I would do you no service as a whole human being if I did not at least touch upon them in these pages. At the same time, I have tried to confine the discussion to these topics as they affect business and to emphasize that for you, in your capacity of business-man, there is only one valid reason for installing or using a computer: to increase the profitability of your enterprise. Unless you recognize this, you will regard a computer as a toy, a hobby, or a status symbol, in which case this book is not for you.

As a motivation, profitability can be pretty pedestrian. Indeed, it has its humdrum aspects, but so does writing a book or even a symphony. On the other hand, the job of running an organization for maximum profit is also intensely creative and calls as much for imagination and vision as for common sense and good housekeeping.

These two aspects of the managerial function are inseparable and of equal importance. I have therefore discussed computers in a down-to-earth way as a subject for hard-headed, meticulous calculation, careful planning, and as a powerful influence on the profit-and-loss account. At the same time, I have attempted to stir your imagination by indicating how these immensely powerful tools can be used to implement new and better solutions to the human and technical problems met in business management.

Perhaps the moment has come to describe in a little more detail what kind of people I think you, my readers, are: I see some of you as having been in business some years before computers appeared on the commercial and industrial scene; some of you have started your business career with an organization that already has a computer on the premises; others of you may be thinking for the first time about the possibility of installing or using a computer; yet others may not have taken their first job in business.

I see you as people who are either in top or senior managerial positions or as eventual aspirants to these. On the whole, I envisage you as working in medium-size or small organizations rather than the giants. But I have referred to what is done in the big corporations because it is within these that many of the most important ideas are born—ideas which later, suitably modified, are applied in much smaller enterprises.

One thing you have in common is little or no first-hand knowledge of computers. You may have had some formal instruction, have done some background reading, but your knowledge is rather patchy and unco-ordinated. From time to time, you find yourself itching to ask some very basic questions, but you hesitate to speak because you feel somehow you *ought* to know the answers. Some of you are not completely *au fait* with all the latest management techniques, so I have included some explanation of the principles of these before describing how computers permit or contribute towards their implementation.

Most of you will encounter in this book some statements that are, to you, blindingly obvious, some explanations that seem superfluous. I make no apology for this. Your commonplace is another man's discovery. And since no two people's pattern of acquired knowledge is identical, one must approach the subject systematically for only in this way can one hope to present a complete and coherent picture.

Several friends who knew I was writing this book implored me to avoid jargon and I have followed their advice to the best of my ability. Jargon is the legitimate shorthand of any technology. But its use, except between technicians, is often an excuse for laziness, a cloak for imperfect understanding, or the result of a rather naïve attempt to impress. Apart from this, it makes reading uninviting and laborious.

On the other hand, one must avoid what Fowler has called 'elegant variation'—the contrived use of alternatives. Sometimes the use of specialist computer terms is inevitable because of their neatness, because standard English offers no precise synonym ('input' and 'output' are cases in point here), or because correct use of them is essential for satisfactory communication between the computer specialist and the businessman. In these cases, I have explained the terms fully at their first use and have included them in end-of-chapter summaries.

Finally, I should like to emphasize my conviction that there is nothing mysterious about computers. A computer extends the effectiveness of the thinking processes in the same way that a machine amplifies the power of human muscle. A computer is no more mysterious than a machine tool. In each case, the mind of man has contrived an ingenious device that only he can utilize—a device that lacks life or motivation of its own.

This, then, is a book about a tool. A tool that, used intelligently and exploited ingeniously, can relieve the mind from drudgery and thereby set free its creative powers for initiating progress and innovation.

Laura Tatham

1. Introduction

If you constantly associate with the people who manufacture, sell, program, operate, manage, and use computers, you find it difficult to believe that only a decade or so has elapsed since they were regarded as awesome curiosities—particularly in a business environment. And if your job takes you mainly to wherever computers are to be found, it is quite easy to gain the impression that the non-user is a comparative rarity.

As soon as you break out of this comparatively small circle you appreciate you are suffering, if not from an obsession at least from myopia. For it soon becomes clear that most people are scarcely aware that computers exist except as highly specialized aids for scientists and accountants.

Yet it is no exaggeration to state that today very few aspects of our daily lives remain untouched by computers. The design and structure of many of the buildings, bridges and roads we use owes much to them, and the cars we drive are manufactured with their help. Without a computer, the aircraft in which we travel would probably not yet have come off the drawing board and its chances of a safe landing would be very much smaller.

The lenses in your holiday camera have probably been designed by a computer—at least if you bought it within the last few years. The electricity you use in your home comes from a power station that may well be wholly computer-controlled. A computer probably monitored the production of the paper on which this book is printed and could have set the type. The food that fed the pig whose flesh appears as a pork chop on your dinner table was quite possibly formulated by computer while yet another maintained records that allowed the farmer to breed an animal that grew only an acceptable proportion of fat and yielded him a maximum profit. A computer watches over our bank accounts, keeps track of our hire-purchase payments, maintains our National Health and private insurance records. Computers can help lawyers thread their way through a tangle of legislation, and doctors to diagnose our diseases, and are used by hospitals to ensure that adequate supplies of drugs and bandages are available.

Computers are employed by historians, economists, local authorities, literary researchers, archaeologists, architects, chemists, accountants, engineers, biologists, manufacturers of all kinds, administrators, mathematicians, advertising agencies, meteorologists, statisticians, launderers, salesmen, astronomers (and, for all I know, astrologers): in fact, by almost every type of person whose job at some time or another necessitates the handling and manipulation of a large volume of facts and figures.

How is it, when only a decade or so ago computers were regarded almost exclusively as tools for scientists and accountants, they today exercise such a pervasive influence on our lives?

Briefly, because very big and very significant advances have been made in three main directions during the past few years. First, in the design of the computers themselves, which have become far more powerful and versatile than they were even five years ago. Second, in the evolution of methods that have simplified and speeded communication between man and machine. Third, in the development of our ideas about how computers can be used, the widening of horizons at first bounded by the limits imposed by traditional methods of thought.

I have discussed all these developments in detail in chapter 2. Here it is necessary only for me to say that together they have combined, not only to increase and broaden usage of computers until now but to ensure that this trend will continue.

Why should this be so? The speed with which developments in the design and application of computers have occurred during the recent past might reasonably suggest that the time has arrived to pause for breath. Would it not be realistic to assume that the upward rush will slacken off and that we have reached a plateau on which we may gratefully rest for a while?

There are strong indications that the opposite is true. It would be more accurate to compare the past few years with human childhood, the present with adolescence. We are, if you like, in the position of a boy who, tied to a school desk, has always regarded lessons as a necessary evil because one day he must earn a living and then realizes with a shock that the knowledge he has acquired changes his relationship to the world. Suddenly, the learning that looked like drudgery is the key to self-fulfilment. The theorems of Euclid or the rules of perspective are disciplines which allow creativity and self-expression in engineering or art.

Businessmen once regarded a computer simply as a means for speeding up the mechanics of the job, a faster way of handling historical data, of churning out routine documents. Today, it emerges as a means for implementing entirely new management techniques, for throwing new light on how business and industry operate. A computer system can revolutionize our concepts of what is and what is not possible in business management; it can offer to the controllers of a huge enterprise the sensitivity and flexibility, the clarity of purpose, that until now have been the prerogative of the one-man business; it can provide a means for exploiting the exclusively human attributes of judgement and creative thinking that have often remained submerged under a flood of drudging routine work. Computers can foster creativity by making it possible for the first time to try out new theories, bold experiments, without the financial risk that has precluded adventurousness in the past.

I think it is only fair to state that, at the time of writing, most of these concepts have got no nearer to realization than a few, tentative experiments carried out in some large, long-sighted organizations. Nevertheless, they are immensely important, and so exciting that only time is needed before they are translated into practical reality. It has been very truly said that without vision the people perish—and this applies at least as much to businessmen as to the rest of the population.

Returning to the needs of the moment, there remains the necessity for simple survival in an environment that is growing daily more competitive. This survival must, initially, be heavily dependent upon an ability to employ successfully existing techniques that make for more efficient management in its most pedestrian sense—the handling of workday routines with speed and accuracy.

In this context alone, the computer has already overwhelmingly proved its value, not only to large and medium-size organizations but to the many small concerns who regularly use the facilities of computer service bureaux. Present developments are moving fast to create a situation which will make the use, even of a very powerful computer, an economically realistic proposition for even the smallest business.

The factors I have named in this chapter add up to show

unmistakably that any businessman who is concerned with the present profitability and future survival of his enterprise can ignore computers only at his peril. This does not imply that he should attempt to become a computer expert: few people are suited by natural ability and qualifications to perform this role and the company manager has another, though equally specialized, function to perform.

What the business or industrial manager needs is a background of broad knowledge of the subject. He should know what computers are, how work for them is organized, what they can do—and in what areas they are ineffective. He must understand very fully how the introduction of a computer into his organization will affect people —his colleagues and employees who are indirectly as well as directly involved. He will also, if he is wise, avail himself of the considerable body of experience already accumulated so as to profit by the hard lessons learned in this way.

These topics are covered in the following pages.

2. First definitions

As managers, now or in the future, few of you will find it either necessary or desirable to acquire any really detailed technical knowledge of the workings of computers. On the other hand, you can neither intelligently discuss the possibility of using a computer within your own organization nor guide the efforts of a computer team until you have a good general idea of what a computer is, the functions played by its various parts, and the significance of programming and other purely human supporting functions.

The purpose of this chapter is to fill in this background.

Electronic computers fall into two distinct types: *analogue* (the American spelling, *analog*, is frequently used) and *digital*. It is the second of these two that concerns us in this book since analogue computers, though useful tools for scientists and engineers, are not used in the management aspects of business or industry.

The fundamental difference between analogue and digital computers lies in the form in which information is received, processed, and emitted. An analogue computer deals with information expressed in the form of a continuous electric current whose fluctuations form the basis of calculation. A digital computer, on the other hand, accepts, processes, and emits information expressed as discrete electric pulses. In other words, the information it deals with must be described by figures or alphabetical characters translated into numerical values.

Perhaps the easiest way to understand this difference is to contrast two commonly used types of domestic clock. There is the kind whose hands move continuously round the dial without a pause—an analogue movement; and the type whose hands jerk forward every half-minute, remaining stationary the rest of the time—a digital movement. Since business transactions and information can be expressed only in digital terms, it is digital computers that are used.

B

Computer hardware

Computing today consists of two major elements: the machines themselves; and the programming and other human work directly associated with causing the machines to perform. These two elements are of equal value. When speaking of computer operations, it is customary to differentiate between these two elements by using the terms *hardware* to describe the machinery and *software* to cover the human aspect. Software, however, is a term used in connection with the rather specialized kind of human contribution that makes the computer function as opposed to the writing of applications. I will explain this in more detail later. The term *liveware* has been coined to cover the people who are concerned with development of a computer project. But this is rather contrived and not often used, so I shall not employ it in this book.

WHAT IS A DIGITAL COMPUTER? There is a good deal of controversy among computer manufacturers and users as to exactly what equipment can be described as a computer and what is not eligible. The Board of Trade, who at the time of writing offer investment grants to cover 20 per cent of the purchase price of a digital or analogue computer to be used for certain specified aspects of commercial and industrial management, describe a digital computer in part as being capable of:

accepting data, processing it, putting out results and restarting the cycle without operator intervention; that is not to say that the equipment must always be used in this way or that, when it is so used, an operator may not intervene in the event of errors or emergencies arising, but simply that the configuration of equipment should be such that this mode of operation can be employed; storing instructions in such a way that under programme control it can operate on instructions as though they were data and can subsequently execute these modified instructions; this would normally mean that programmes and data should both be held in the same kind of store and that the instruction code should provide for address modification.

The definition goes on to state that a computer installation normally includes a range of essential ancillary equipment, names typical items and states that these too qualify for a grant.

Many people, however, maintain that much of the equipment that qualifies for a Board of Trade grant cannot be called true computers but can more accurately be described as electronic accounting or invoicing machines. There is some force in this argument. Some of the systems that are eligible comprise no more than an electric typewriter with a punched paper tape reader, a small electronic calculating and storage unit and perhaps a paper-tape punch which between them cover no more floor space than a couple of office desks and have a very limited speed and capacity. Manufacturers and users of equipment that can indisputably be described as 'electronic computers' are apt to look down their noses at these far smaller, far less sophisticated systems.

For the purposes of this book, an electronic digital computer is a group of machines with the following capabilities and characteristics.

(a) It is designed to accept the bulk of incoming data in machine language—e.g., in the form of punched cards or perforated paper tape—as distinct from being operated through a typewriter or other keyboard. It reads this data automatically.

(b) It incorporates a storage device in which it retains operating instructions and information while these are in use.

(c) It processes information according to a program of instructions that has first been fed into its internal store; and performs these instructions without human intervention.

(d) It automatically communicates the results of its processing (which can broadly be described as calculation and the manipulation of data) by printing these and/or producing new material in machine language; or, in process control alone, by initiating instructions that result in some physical action at a distant point.

(e) It has, in addition to the internal storage device, some form of external store (which is part of the computer system but not part of the central processor) on which it alone can 'write' and from which it alone can 'read'.

This definition excludes electronic accounting machines and electronic invoicing machines but also excludes what are known as 'visible record computers'. These are, in fact, a kind of hybrid as they possess most of the characteristics listed above but accept a good deal of data fed in through a manually operated keyboard and use magnetic-stripe cards as an external store. These incorporate strips of magnetic tape upon which the machine can write and from which it can read 200 or so alphabetic or numeric characters; but they are also used for printing in the same way as are conventional ledger cards.

None of the information given in this book therefore relates to visible record computers unless I specifically state otherwise.

WHY SYSTEMS? Computers are almost always described by the initiated as *computer systems*. This term is used, not to confuse non-specialists but because it is an accurate description. A computer is not a single machine but, as I have mentioned already, a group of discrete units which perform separate and clearly defined functions. Each of these units is usually, though not invariably, housed in a different cabinet.

All modern computer systems permit the user to choose which he wants from a selection of different units. Normally, for example, there is an option of a basic or larger (basic plus one or more increments) internal store. One may always choose from a range of units for feeding in data and for printing or otherwise recording the results of processing. All the units, other than the central processor and the control console through which the operator communicates directly with the system and vice versa, are described as *peripherals*.

The precise combination of central processor and peripherals chosen by the individual user is known as a *configuration*. Thus it does not mean much to a knowledgeable person if you refer to an IBM System/360, Model 40, or a Univac 490. Only when he knows what the configuration is does he gain some idea of the scope of the system.

THE CENTRAL PROCESSOR. The central processor is to a computer system what the brain is to the human body. That is, it acts as the ultimate controller of every part of the system as well as performing the calculations that are required of it.

Though we are not normally aware of it, our brain performs several different types of control function within our bodies. These include issuing instructions to our limbs to move as we desire, keeping our glandular system in balance and shifting information from our subconscious to our conscious memory as the result of receiving information through our senses.

The control functions of a computer's central processor are somewhat analogous to these and in this sense alone it is accurate to refer to an 'electronic brain'. The processor is responsible for issuing instructions to the peripherals—e.g., 'print out the results of the calculations I have just done' or 'feed me some more basic information'; and it controls the movement of information from one part of the system to another—from the internal store to external store, for instance.

Just as the memory is an integral part of the human brain, the internal memory is an integral part of a computer's central processor. This memory is often referred to as a *core store*. This describes the actual physical structure of the memory which comprises an interlacing network of fine wires with little rings (cores) at the intersections. It is not, however, always accurate today as there are various other methods for constructing internal memories.

The function of the computer's internal memory is very much like that of your own. When you are, say, dialling a telephone number or doing mental arithmetic, you use your memory to store information temporarily. In the computer, the internal memory also provides the most quickly accessible store for information needed during calculation and other forms of processing.

The internal memory also stores the computer program—the series of steps that defines exactly what must be done to carry out any given task. This program (the American spelling is now universally used) is not permanently retained in the internal memory any more than you retain in the forefront of your mind details of the route to Dover when you are driving to Manchester. A computer program is therefore retained in internal memory only while it is in use.

Human mental capacity is determined to some extent by the power and scope of the memory. The capacity of a computer is also governed partly by the efficiency and size of its internal memory. Central processor capacity is normally expressed in terms of the maximum amount of information (i.e., data, program instructions, and so on) it can retain in store at any given moment—a figure numbered in thousands of 'store positions' each of which can hold a number of digits. The letter K is used as an abbreviation for thousands, thus capacity is expressed as 8K or 64K and so on.

You should know, however, that this figure is only a very approximate guide and does not mean much to a computer man until it is qualified by a much more detailed description that relates partly to the format in which these digits are stored. This is pretty technical and need not concern us directly. But it is important to appreciate that, say, the 4K store of one central processor may be significantly more or less effective than the 4K store of another when certain applications are being considered.

(These figures are, in fact, approximate, total capacity being slightly larger, but are always rounded off for convenience.)

In modern computer systems, you are offered a choice of memory size. Though every system has a predetermined minimum, this can be stepped up by the addition of extra increments. This stepping-up cannot, however, continue indefinitely but is restricted according to the innate capacity of the central processor. The first additional increment of memory is usually equal in size to the basic minimum so that a computer with a basic memory of 8K cannot have less than a further 8K added to it. After this (assuming further increase is possible) the next size memory would be double again—32K—and the one after, 64K.

Computer systems are now designed in such a way that it is possible to add extra increments of memory at any time after installation. This means that you may start your system in a modest way with basic memory capacity (which will seldom be less than 8K for business data processing and frequently 16K) and add one or more units as your requirements expand. The problems which may arise from this expansion and in the transition from a small central processor to a larger when expansion on the first has reached the limit are discussed in chapter 6, 'Choosing and installing a computer'.

Another basic statistic relating to central processor capacity is the speed with which calculations can be performed. In early systems this was measured in thousandths of a second (milliseconds); in later systems, in millionths of a second (microseconds); and in many of the third-generation systems in use today it is quoted in nanoseconds. A nanosecond is one thousand-millionth of a second in British terminology, one billionth in American usage. This figure is perhaps a little less difficult to grasp when one is told that a nanosecond is to a second as one second is to 32 years!

Computer men bandy about a good many statistics that are quite meaningless to the businessman and sometimes irrelevant even in their own terms. It is chiefly the memory capacity and calculating/ data-handling speeds that contribute to give *power* to a computer, though today this term usually also implies versatility and good internal organization within the system.

THE BINARY BOGEY. One of the things that seems greatly to worry people is the fact that computers operate in binary arithmetic. That is, instead of using the kind of numerals we recognize they express figures and letters as combinations of ones and zeros.

If you wish to find out how binary arithmetic works there are plenty of books on the subject. But to you as a businessman the subject is irrelevant. A computer works in binary arithmetic because this method permits a simpler and more compact construction than would otherwise be feasible. Since the data you put into the computer and the results you get out of it are expressed in standard numerals and letters, it is quite unnecessary to know what goes on inside the calculator unit.

THE CONTROL CONSOLE. The purpose of the control console is to provide programmers and operators with a means of seeing what is going on within the system at any given time and to give them a quick, simple method of immediate communication with the system—and vice versa. The console normally comprises a display board with a few lights and switches and a typewriter which constitutes the medium of communication.

The operator or programmer may use the typewriter keyboard to intervene while a program is actually in progress. Such intervention may become necessary in program testing and in some scientific applications where the computer is instructed to go through, say, an enormous number of equations. A print-out may indicate that further pursuit of a certain set of calculations is likely to prove fruitless and the operator will then intervene and instruct the computer to abandon these and proceed to the next step in the program. The keyboard may also be used to question the computer on some aspects of its operations.

Using the console typewriter, the computer chats back to the operator. Since the content of its 'conversation' has been pre-determined by the programmer who has chosen what words it shall print to report on various situations, the language is often endearingly informal or even rude. When one sees these dialogues between man and computer in progress one has no difficulty in understanding the rapport that appears to build up between them. Irrational though this may be, it is no more foolish than the affection many men and women feel for cars or other mechanical devices.

Reports put out by the system at the control console may vary from automatic notification of faults to a request to the operator to make ready certain external storage media, such as magnetic tapes, for the next phase of the program upon which it is working. The system will also often maintain a running log which informs the operator of what it is doing.

EXTERNAL MEMORY. The term 'external memory' suggests that this unit is not a true part of the computer. In reality, it simply differentiates between the internal memory, which is part of the central processor, and other media for storing information. Thus, the external memory devices are peripherals just as punched card readers or printers are.

The external memory devices of a computer fulfil the same function as files do for a human clerk and indeed are often referred to as files or magnetic files. They store large quantities of information that need not be retained constantly in the internal memory but must be available quickly for reference when needed.

Often it is not necessary for the computer to be able to reach all the filed information during any given program. For this reason the number of units designed for handling information files can be limited, though the files themselves may greatly exceed in number the total that can be handled at one time.

Typically, then, a small computer system might incorporate only four magnetic-tape handlers but the user might have a library of scores or even hundreds of magnetic tapes any combination of which he can place on the handlers to use with any given program. This, of course, is exactly the same principle as is used with a tape-recorder for voice or music.

Because today's computers are designed to fulfil a very wide range of functions for users whose requirements vary enormously, manufacturers offer alternative types of external memory equipment. These devices fall into two broad categories: those which handle information in serial order (magnetic tapes); and those which permit 'random access' to stored information (discs or drums). Incidentally, the term 'random access' is now disliked by some manufacturers, notably IBM who probably coined it. 'Direct access' has now been substituted, as this term, it is felt, excludes the implication of closing the eyes and stabbing wildly with a pin that was in the earlier expression.

MAGNETIC TAPES. Magnetic-tape handlers, or tape decks as they are sometimes called, operate on the same basic principle as is used in a magnetic-tape voice-recorder. That is, they record information or read it off as the tape moves past a single magnetic head known as the *read-write* head.

Both these functions are, of course, done infinitely faster on computer tapes than on a voice recorder and the data is so densely packed on the tape that one is reminded of the mediaeval conundrum: 'How many angels can dance on the head of a pin?'.

Nevertheless, the only feasible way to put information on magnetic tapes or read it off is in serial order. That is, if the file contains, say, details of customer accounts, these details must be recorded in account number or some other predetermined sequence, and retrieved or updated in the same way. Otherwise the computer would waste an enormous amount of time and energy running the tape back and forth past the read-write head searching for individual items.

Information to be written on magnetic tapes must therefore first be arranged in serial number order and must be processed in sizable batches to make the job worth doing. A procedure which involved, say, writing fresh information on only one in every 500 of the accounts held on a tape file would be ridiculously slow and wasteful.

I do not want to suggest that magnetic tape is an inefficient storage medium: in fact, it is very well suited to many business applications varying from the production of invoices to the compilation of sales statistics or the analysis of market research information. But it has its limitations which must be appreciated.

MAGNETIC DISCS AND DRUMS. Magnetic-disc storage devices comprise sets of thin, flat plates rather like long-playing gramophone records in size and shape. The sets of discs, placed one above the other and spaced apart, are sealed into units which cannot be broken into; but individual units may be exchanged in the disc-handlers in the same way that tapes may be exchanged in tape-handlers.

On the disc handlers there is a separate read-write head for each disc, so that when the disc unit is put on the handler its appearance is like that of a gramophone loaded with a pile of records with a player head for each. The discs revolve at high speeds beneath the read-write heads and each disc is divided into a number of tracks onto any of which the head can jump as ordered by the central processor.

This arrangement enables the computer very quickly to write information on any part of any disc in a set and very quickly to retrieve any data already recorded there. All it needs is a reference to the appropriate head and track. Like the data recorded on magnetic tape, information maintained on discs is densely packed to utilize available capacity as fully as possible.

Information is not actually recorded on the discs in random order. That is, one does not, so to speak, throw in anything in a carefree way and hope to find it without any difficulty later. But the fact that the file is sectionalized and any segment quickly available to the computer means that it is unnecessary to pre-sort new data for the file or requests for retrieval into serial order. It is therefore feasible to do with discs many things that are impracticable with magnetic tapes—make new entries in one in every 500 accounts, for example. It is this facility which is described as random or direct access.

Empty disc files are also very useful for the fast sorting of data by the computer since they provide a facility equivalent to a large number of pigeonholes in which it can place data temporarily prior to final collation. In a computer configuration which includes both disc and magnetic-tape files, the disc file is frequently used to sort data into serial order before recording it semi-permanently on tape— a cheaper, more compact medium for this purpose than the discs.

The cost of disc handlers and files is higher than that of magnetic-tape equipment but lower than that of a magnetic drum which is the fastest, in terms of accessibility, of the three main external storage media available to a computer.

A magnetic drum is designed to give the computer direct access to very large files of information. Cylindrical in shape, the drum is permanently enclosed inside its handling equipment. It revolves at very high speed beneath a large number of read-write heads and its surface, like that of the discs, is divided into a number of tracks which, though invisible, are distinct and identifiable to the computer.

It will be seen that the main point of difference between a drum and other forms of magnetic storage is that *all* the filed data are directly accessible to the computer at all times. This contrasts with other stores where only as much data as can be loaded onto the available handlers can be accessible to the computer at any given moment.

The storage capacity of a magnetic drum is immense. The Univac Fastrand II, for example, maintains 132,000,000 characters of information as against the few hundred thousand that can be stored on a set of discs or a magnetic tape.

You will appreciate more fully the significance of drum storage when we come to discuss data banks.

OTHER RANDOM-ACCESS DEVICES. The magnetic storage media mentioned in the preceding paragraphs are now standard, with individual variations of course, to all manufacturers. There are, however, a few other types, but whether these will eventually survive is rather doubtful. The best-known currently is probably NCR's CRAM (Card Random Access Memory) system—a file that comprises a pack of large, oblong plastic cards which, like a pack of discs, can be exchanged within a handler. Individual CRAM cards are 'pulled' by the computer from this pack when it wants to read from or write on them.

Though they cannot be placed in the same category as the fast, sophisticated devices I have described so far, the magnetic-stripe ledger cards used by visible record computers (see page 7) also constitute a form of random-access (though not direct-access) storage. Fed individually into the computer by hand through the front feed on its keyboard or automatically through a special reader, they store some data magnetically which is read by the computer which also prints on their surface. The random-access element lies simply in the fact that, as the cards are similar in size and format to conventional ledger cards, they are maintained in ordinary filing trays and can be selected in any order by hand. This system one might, I suppose, fairly describe as a poor man's random access.

Summing up a computer as described thus far, we have seen that it possesses a central processor with external memory and can be equipped with various external memories which file data that can be retrieved by the system in serial or in random order. The next point to examine is how information is put into the system.

Putting information into the computer

At the present stage of development, it is not possible, except in a very restricted way, to offer to a computer information in a format identical to that acceptable to ourselves. We cannot, for example, feed it with handwritten, typed or printed documents prepared on standard machines, nor can we offer it a sound-recording. As optical readers (see later in this chapter) are refined and improved, the time when these restrictions will be overcome is drawing near. Meanwhile, it is necessary to translate documents intended for use by a computer into a code that can automatically be read by a machine which, in turn, passes on the information to the central processor.

The function of translating standard documents into machine code is known as *data preparation* and this covers all methods. The information thus prepared is termed *input data*, the machines that read it into the central computer are *input equipment*. The complementary terms *output data* and *output equipment* are used in connection with the production of final results by the computer. Devices like automatic typewriters whose keyboards can be used manually to put data into the computer or operated automatically by the computer to print out information are described as *input/output* equipment. All these words are neat and self-explanatory.

PUNCHED CARDS AND PAPER TAPE. At the time of writing, the codes most commonly used for computer input are patterns of holes punched into paper tape or special cards divided into 80 columns. These patterns are simply abstract representations of individual alphabetical or numerical characters, so that to render the word 'account' into machine code one would punch a separate code for each letter of the word.

Punching is done by girls who perform a function similar to that of copy-typing. That is, they read the original or source documents and use a typewriter or adding-machine-type keyboard whose keys, when depressed, punch out an equivalent code in addition to, or instead of, printing.

Since it is vitally important that data fed into the computer shall be as error-free as is humanly possible, a second operation known as *verification* is performed. There are several methods of doing this, but broadly it involves the feeding of the first set of punched cards or length of paper tape through a machine operated by a different girl who, working from the same source documents, duplicates the punching motions of the first. Any discrepancy between the first and second punching is revealed by automatic stoppage of the machine, visual inspection reveals whether the mistake was made during the first or second operation, and any correction (by re-punching) can be made. Though this method is not completely foolproof, it eliminates many of the errors that would otherwise reach the computer and hold up operations or produce incorrect results.

In some cases, it is possible completely to obviate the slow, expensive process of manual data preparation by performing this operation as a by-product of some other routine work such as machine accounting. An automatic paper-tape or card punch can be attached to many types of office equipment such as add-listing, keyboard accounting, and invoicing machines.

All or selected parts of the information keyed in by the operator or calculated by the machine during, say, the routine updating of ledger accounts or production of invoices, is then automatically punched into paper tape or cards without any additional effort on her part. Often the punch has a check-digit, a device which, by automatically applying a simple arithmetical formula to selected incoming data, such as account numbers, rejects items that are incorrectly rendered by the operator. Though this process cannot, of course, obviate the placing of a totally incorrect amount under a given account number, it does at least ensure that the numbers used are acceptable to the system.

This method of by-product data preparation is particularly useful for organizations who, perhaps, do their own accounting or invoicing by conventional methods but use a computer service bureau (see chapter 9) to analyse information derived from these documents. In this way, they can obviate the delay and cost incurred by manual data preparation and can retain the source documents on their own premises, sending only the paper tape or punched cards to the service bureau.

CARD AND PAPER-TAPE READERS. Data prepared by punching is fed to the computer through a paper-tape or punched-card reader. This is normally a free-standing unit connected to the central processor by a cable. Most manufacturers offer alternative models of these readers, one operating at a slow speed, say 400 cards per minute or 400 characters per second, the other having a speed of 1000 or more cards per minute or characters per second. (Speeds of card devices are always given as cards per minute while those of paper-tape equipment are quoted as characters per second.)

Electro-mechanical in construction, paper-tape and punched-card readers operate far more slowly than the computer's central processor. As the processor's time is valuable, it would be uneconomic to waste it in waiting around while data was passed in at a comparatively slow speed. Information read from cards or tape is therefore first channelled into a small separate store called a *buffer store*. This (whose function I once heard a computer expert neatly—and unforgettably—compare to that of a lavatory cistern) accumulates data until the processor calls for it. The store then discharges its contents into the processor at electronic speed.

This technology of buffering is an important one in computer technology for it provides, as we have seen, an adaptive mechanism for the linking of machines that work at different speeds. In a computer system using remote terminals, for example (*see* page 34), it would be absurd if data could be transmitted at speeds no faster than a girl could type on a keyboard. Consequently, data entered manually is accumulated in a buffer which, when signalled by the computer, releases its contents at the maximum speed the system will allow. This, by utilizing the central processor effectively, allows it to service a larger number of terminals more frequently.

MAGNETIC-TAPE UNITS. A type of data-preparation equipment that seems fast to be gaining popularity utilizes magnetic tape. Operated from a keyboard similar to that of a typewriter, it records the data on a kind of magnetic tape that differs from that used in the computer itself. Data prepared in this way is read into the computer by special equipment whose speed is comparable to that of a fast paper-tape reader.

Among the advantages of this kind of data-preparation equipment are ease of correction and (it is claimed) higher operator productivity because the keyboards are simpler and lighter to the touch than those associated with punched-card or paper-tape equipment. One drawback is that, if it is desired to store 'raw' data in this form (as an alternative, perhaps, to keeping original documents), magnetic tape is far more expensive than paper tape or cards.

OPTICAL READERS. Optical readers automate the job of data preparation by performing a vastly simplified version of the human reading function. That is, they optically scan information contained in documents and either automatically punch it into paper tape or cards or feed it direct into the computer system.

At this point, I must digress for a moment to explain the useful jargon terms *on-line* and *off-line*. Any peripheral that is connected directly to the central processor is described as being *on-line*; any which is used independently is said to be *off-line*. These expressions refer to status rather than equipment design and many machines— optical readers are a case in point—may be used in both capacities. When this is true, they are usually referred to as on-line/off-line or on/off line equipment. You will meet these terms repeatedly when you are given details of how computer hardware is to be used.

To return to optical readers: work has been in progress in many research laboratories for many years, but so far no manufacturer has succeeded in producing a machine that can accurately read hand-written characters other than rather carefully formed numerals. This is hardly surprising, for the design problem is formidable and in many ways akin to that met in devising machine translation systems. First, it entails designing an artificial substitute for the intelligence you or I apply so effortlessly to recognize characters that are mal-formed, incomplete, or misaligned; and then translating any design into a machine that can be sold at an acceptable price.

Meantime, existing optical readers operate by one of three methods. Some read alphabetical and numerical characters imprinted in slightly stylized fount by such machines as cash registers and type-writers. Others accept codes made up of patterns of short bars. The third type reads marks made by hand on a pre-printed grid. Each part of the grid is assigned a value and a separate grid is printed opposite each item to be recorded. Handwritten marks on the appropriate parts of the grid are detected by the optical reader and evaluated. At present, the most frequent users of this type of reader are probably supermarkets who employ this system for recording grocery orders made on depots by branches. The name of each commodity is pre-printed and the manager simply marks the grid opposite the items he needs to indicate the quantity he requires.

Though considerable difficulties were met when many readers now in use were first introduced to the market, most of the problems have now been overcome. The machines are, however, very expensive. In consequence, the capital cost of an optical reader can normally only be justified by organizations who have a very high volume of input data that must be prepared with as little delay as possible.

MAGNETIC-INK CHARACTER RECOGNITION. Magnetic-ink character-recognition (MICR) equipment, which at present is used almost exclusively by banks, performs a dual function. The machines read numeric characters imprinted in a highly stylized fount (e.g., the E–13B code that appears on the foot of the cheques in your cheque-book) by picking up signals from the magnetic ink with which they are printed. Concurrently with this reading, the machines physically sort small documents like cheques and other bank vouchers into a number of separate pockets at very high speeds.

Typically, initial data such as your account number and bank branch number are imprinted in magnetic ink on the blank cheques before they are issued to you. When your cheque reaches the payee's bank it will be given to a girl who, using a keyboard machine with a magnetic ink ribbon, will transcribe onto the face of the cheque the date and amount you have entered. The cheque is then ready for automatic reading and sorting.

Most MICR equipment is designed for on-line and off-line use.

MARK SENSING. Developed for use with punched-card systems in pre-computer days, mark sensing, though a technique for automatic preparation of data, is very little used today and will probably become obsolete. The person who first records the data (that is, completes the source document) makes pencil marks on the actual areas of blank 80-column cards that are afterwards to be punched. The marked cards are then fed through a machine that, by picking up the minute deposit of graphite left on the card by the pencil, generates a signal that causes a hole to be punched in this spot.

The scope of this equipment is limited and it has the disadvantage that cards must be marked with considerable care if accurate results are to be obtained. It was, however, extensively used by the Post Office before the advent of automatic exchange equipment for the recording of telephone calls.

MICROFILM EQUIPMENT. Microfilm input equipment is used to convert data recorded in graphic form (drawings, charts, maps) into numeric data acceptable to a computer. A high-speed device scans negative 35mm microfilm, using a beam from a cathode-ray tube that follows a programmed scan pattern. Varying degrees of threshold sensitivity —the ability to distinguish various degrees of density—are pre-determined so that the machine will convert into numeric data only the outlines of the image and not unintended blemishes such as fingerprints.

This equipment is not, at the time of writing, available in this country.

OTHER INPUT EQUIPMENT. Much of the data used in computerized routines may be drawn from stores held in the various types of external memory described earlier in this chapter, and is called in during processing according to the demands of the program. External memory devices must, therefore, also be considered as input equipment.

Input devices used at points remote from the computer, though on-line to it through telephone wires, are described in later sections 'Remote terminals' (page 34) and 'Process control' (page 149).

Taking information out of the computer

The final stage in the mechanics of any computer operation is the communication to the outside world by the computer of the results of its processing. How these reports are presented is a matter of choice for the user. Most commonly they are printed out. But they may be drawn as graphs, displayed on a screen like that of a television set (see 'Computer communications'), rendered into machine language—punched into paper-tape or cards—or written onto magnetic files. Those in machine language or written onto magnetic files may ultimately be destined for use by the same computer or by another. Many routines will, of course, involve the use of more than one of these types of output.

Much output equipment is electro-mechanical and is, therefore, like its input equivalents, far slower-working than the central processor. Buffer stores are therefore used, this time to accept the data from the central processor and release it at a speed the output equipment can cope with.

OUTPUT PRINTERS. A high-speed line printer whose output may range from about 600 to 1,500 or more lines per minute is standard equipment on every business computer today. The term *line printer* is used to differentiate machines like this, which print out an entire horizontal line of type at one time, from *character printers* which, because they print only one letter or numeral at a time as a typewriter does, are far slower.

What the line printer produces and how this is laid out on the paper depends upon the requirements of the computer user as interpreted by the programmer. Ingenuity in this area can often save computer time and paper. Small forms, for example, can be printed side-by-side two or three up and later separated by automatic guillotine or form burster. Since no more time is required for the output printer to use the entire paper width, ideas like this can greatly cut print-out time.

Output printers may also be used for the compilation of elementary charts such as histograms (profile charts) or bar charts. This is done simply by having X's or some other characters printed in appropriate spots instead of listing the information in the ordinary way.

Information presented like this often has far more impact and is much easier to assimilate than a list of figures, as Figs. 2.1 and 2.2 show.

CARD AND PAPER-TAPE PUNCHES. Card and paper-tape punches perform the same function as that carried out by a human operator

c

at a keyboard but, of course, at much higher speeds and with complete accuracy. A typical card punch speed is 300 per minute and tape punch speed 300 characters per second. These are slow com-

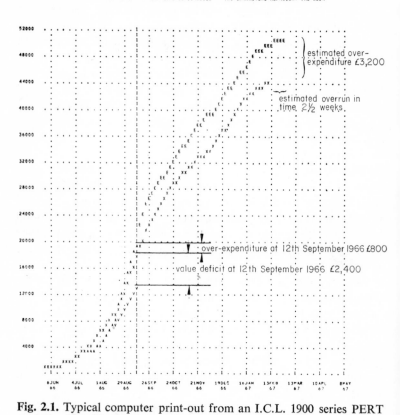

Fig. 2.1. Typical computer print-out from an I.C.L. 1900 series PERT analysis. The Figure shows the graphical representation of the cost analysis of the project. Such a print-out enables management to see at a glance the current status and future trends of project costs.
Key. X = planned cost. A = actual expenditure. E = revised estimated expenditure. V = value of work completed.

pared with those of high-speed readers for either medium, but it must be remembered that punching requires far more mechanical action than reading.

In computer configurations with no external storage medium, data files must be created by punching. In a payroll application, for

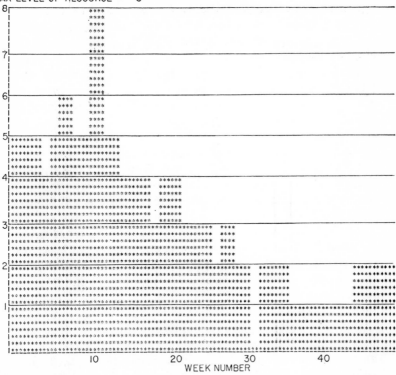

Fig. 2.2. Weekly manpower requirements expressed as a histogram on a standard computer line printer. Single digits are not used in computer systems, so week numbers 10, 20, etc. should be read as 1, 2, etc. The number of men and all the horizontal lines except the base were inserted by hand to make interpretation easier.

The proportions of the histogram are calculated by the computer, using the length of the horizontal axis as a base. Though the information could have been shown by using single rather than multiple lines of asterisks, this would have produced a very small diagram. The one shown here is easy to read and was big enough to use as a wall-chart. Alternatively – conveying, as graphically as it does, unevenness of manpower demand over a four-week period – it might be employed to draw management's attention to the desirability of smoothing requirements (if practical or desirable) by working overtime, thus shortening the time-span of the task.

example, one would normally maintain employees' basic details on magnetic files. Lacking these, the computer must punch out cards containing this detail and the up-to-date pay record for feeding in next week. Otherwise human operators would be involved in a great deal of work preparing data instead of having merely to record the latest figures each week.

Punched cards or paper tape, particularly the latter, is a convenient medium for the transmission by van or mail of data from one computer to another. Tape can also be used off-line in machines like typewriters with automatic paper-tape readers.

AUTOMATIC PLOTTERS. Pictorial presentations of a crude kind such as are illustrated by Figs. 2.1 and 2.2 may be produced by an output printer. It would, however, not be possible to use a printer to draw a fine, precise outline such as is required for an engineer's drawing or a contour map.

As people became more skilled in exploiting computers, it became clear that it would be immensely useful if a means could be devised of rendering data, which would eventually have to be translated into graphic terms, directly into this format. This would not only save a lot of human draughting but would eliminate the possibility of error that always lurks in a manual operation.

During the past few years, various types of automatic plotter have been evolved. The designer feeds information into the computer as alpha-numeric data and the computer makes the required calculations. Output data is translated into signals which, fed to one or more automatic pens (styli) poised over paper, are converted directly into drawings.

Plotters fall into two broad types. One is a more sophisticated version of a device that has been used for many years to record temperatures and other simple data—a pen or pens trailing over paper wound round a slowly revolving drum. In the other type, the paper is fixed on the surface of a table over which the styli, mounted on a carriage, move.

Though the speed of drawing by these methods is not spectacular, it is immensely faster than can be achieved by a human draughtsman. It also provides a method for direct translation of design ideas into graphic form—an exciting exercise for a creative mind. Automatic plotting also obviates pure drudgery of the kind that is involved in, say, the drawing of a large number of structural members that are almost but not quite identical in size and shape.

MICROFILM OUTPUT UNITS. These permit a computer to record drawings or other material direct onto microfilm without an intermediate paper stage. That is, data that might otherwise be fed to an automatic plotter is recorded direct onto microfilm.

Output data is fed to a cathode-ray tube within the unit. This tube emits a narrow beam which is directed by the computer program to trace the desired image onto a frame of standard size film. Film is automatically advanced during the recording process and an on-line developer renders it available for scrutiny within less than a minute.

This equipment, like the microfilm input unit briefly described earlier in this chapter, is not yet available in Britain.

OTHER FORMS OF OUTPUT. In process-control applications (see chapter 6), output is channelled by the computer through various intervening units into devices which physically control plant and machinery used by industry.

Logically I should, perhaps, insert here a description of the remote terminals such as automatic typewriters, teletype machines, cathode-ray tube display devices, and other equipment used as input/output media at points remote from the computer room. The objection to this is that the information will not mean much until you know something about the meaning and implications of real-time computing. I have, therefore, deferred a description of these until a later chapter.

This seems a good moment to pause for a brief summary of what I have so far told you about computer hardware.

(a) A computer may briefly be defined as a group of machines whose capabilities include the ability to read in information automatically, to process this according to a program of instructions which it holds in a memory, and to communicate the results of its work automatically to the outside world. Though it is possible and sometimes necessary for a man to communicate with the computer while this work is in progress, normally it will operate without human intervention.

(b) Because a computer is not a single machine but a group whose make-up is variable, it is always described as a computer system.

(c) A computer system must always include a central processor with a small but fast internal memory and a control console for use by its operator. But the remaining units, known collectively as peripherals, may be selected by the user as required. The user also has some degree of option as to the size of internal memory used by the central processor.

(*d*) The job of the central processor is to carry out calculations and manipulate data as dictated by the program; and to control the operations of all the other units so as to ensure that the entire system works as a single entity.

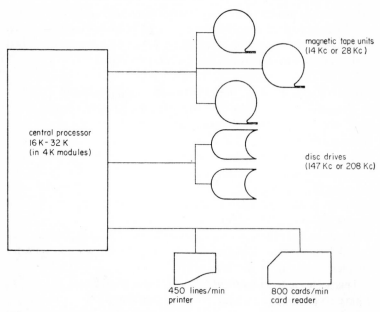

Fig. 2.3. This illustrates the way a computer configuration is represented on paper. It is intended merely to represent the components of the system, not to suggest how these should be physically placed on the computer-room floor. Symbols used to indicate the various types of unit are used internationally among all computer manufacturers and users. The system shown here (a Honeywell H.125) is typical of what might be ordered by a medium-size business.

(*e*) The functions of the peripheral units may be summarized under three broad headings.

To provide capacity for filing information which is too bulky to be stored in the internal memory but which must be quickly accessible to the central processor. This file-handling equipment or external memory is of two kinds: magnetic tape, which demands the handling of detail in serial order; magnetic discs, drums, etc., which, by dispensing with the requirement for serial order, permit faster writing and retrieval of the type called random or direct-access.

To provide a means for putting information into the computer system. This information must, however, first be rendered into some form of machine language.

To provide a method whereby the computer communicates the results of its work to the outside world.

(*f*) The following computer terms have been used in this chapter:

Hardware—computer machinery as distinct from the human contribution to computer procedures

Software—programming and other human effort which makes the machinery operate as required

Liveware (not much used)—the people involved

Input—as a noun, the information that goes into a computer; as an adjective, the equipment that performs this task

Output —as for *input* but referring to information emerging from the system

Central processor—see (*c*) and (*d*) above

Peripherals—see (*e*) above

On-line—an adjective applied to a peripheral indicating that it is directly connected to the central processor

Off-line—an adjective applied to a peripheral indicating that it is operating independently of the central processor

Both on-line and off-line are definitions of status, not equipment design.

Configuration—the collective noun for all the parts of a computer system.

Memory—an integral part of the central processor performing a function akin to that of human memory; or a peripheral providing a filing system for direct use by the central processor

Check-digit device—a mechanism that verifies input data by applying an arithmetical formula

Buffer store—a device that compensates for speed variations in different types of equipment operating together

Verification—data preparation in duplicate to obviate error

Line printer—a peripheral that prints an entire line at one time

Character printer—a peripheral that prints one letter or numeral at a time.

3. Computers and men at work

So far, I have given you an account, deliberately simplified and broadened as far as possible, of the principal items of hardware that make up a modern computer system, deferring only a discussion of remote, on-line terminals. In this chapter, I shall first describe in more detail how this hardware handles the demands made upon it by commerce and industry; and later outline the kind of human effort entailed in the preparation of the applications programs and other software without which the computer system cannot operate.

Early computers could handle only one part of any program at any given time. That is, when a paper-tape or card reader or printer was engaged on its task, most of the central processor and all the other peripherals stood idle.

At first, this did not matter. The computers were used for the solution of scientific and mathematical problems which are almost always characterized by having very little input and output, the main body of the work being calculation. The small hold-ups that occurred while the processor waited for the peripherals therefore did not seriously prejudice overall working speed.

As soon as computers began to be used for commercial and industrial applications it became apparent that this limitation imposed a very serious waste of time. Work of this kind involves a high volume of input and output and calculation that is quite small in amount and content. This meant that for long periods the system was operating at speeds no faster than those of the slowest peripheral, and the capacity and speed of the central processor were grossly under-utilized.

The problem was aggravated by the fact that no external memory devices were at first available. Data could be filed only in the form of cards or paper-tape prepared by hand or punched out by the computer itself during a previous run. All this had to be fed into the system through slow electro-mechanical peripherals each time a program was run.

This situation led manufacturers to design faster input and output equipment; and to invent magnetic files. It soon, however, became clear that if business users were to get maximum benefit from a computer it would be necessary to find a way to use the electro-mechanical peripherals simultaneously with one another and with other parts of the system.

The object was to allow the central processor to call in and process a batch of variable data from a peripheral like a card reader, pull out data relating to previous runs from magnetic external memory, process the whole in accordance with the program, and print out results while it was repeating this cycle. In a payroll application, for example, payslips could begin coming off the output printer as soon as calculations on the first set of details had been completed. When this was achieved, overall processing time was greatly reduced and throughput therefore significantly raised.

But even this was not enough. The increased speeds of central processors that were developed meant that work was gobbled up still faster, leaving processor capacity still badly under-utilized.

The only way to solve this problem was to devise a means of handling two or more programs concurrently. Clearly, the best way to achieve this was to feed into the system two complementary types of job, one scientific or mathematical, the other business data processing. Between them, these could use the system to best advantage, the scientific work soaking up most of the processor capacity but making little demand on the peripherals.

The flaw in this idea was that many business users had no scientific work and the scientists had no business-type applications. Machine designers therefore turned their attention to evolving systems that could handle more readers and printers. By doing this, they could load the central processor with more control functions and more calculations and increase overall throughput of the system even when it was used exclusively for business data processing.

Writing programs that could be run simultaneously was a difficult task, though. In effect, the programmer had to work out a kind of jigsaw of control and processing tasks whose overall demand did not add up at any given moment to a requirement for more capacity than the central processor had. How this problem was solved I have described later in this chapter under the heading 'software'.

Most modern computers are capable of handling several programs simultaneously—a function known as *multi-programming* or *time-sharing*. 'Simultaneously' is not, in fact, strictly accurate and is a practical rather than a literal description. What the computer actually does is to switch so rapidly from job to job and back again as to appear to be working on several simultaneously. Multi-programming is the term generally used when the programs involved are batch-processing ones (see below) fed in by the computer-room staff. Time-sharing refers to the processing of work fed in at random from a number of users of remote terminals (*see* page 32).

Batch processing and real-time

Patterns of thought change by evolution rather than by revolution. At the time computers became available to commerce and industry, mass production had abundantly proved itself an outstandingly efficient method of manufacture for certain types of goods. It was therefore quite natural that the computer, with its speed and accuracy, should be seen as a means of applying mass-production techniques to office work.

Successful exploitation of mass-production facilities depends upon processing as large a batch as is feasible. This was also true of business computing. To use a computer to prepare, say, only 50 invoices in one run was as absurd as to manufacture only 50 bars of soap at a time. When there was reorganization within offices, therefore, this was not mainly of routines—which were generally as nearly as possible carbon copies of those carried out previously by keyboard accounting machines or punched-card installations—but was intended to create a situation where large batches of work could be accumulated.

Thus, though the computer might be working on several programs at one time, each of these consisted of a single, homogeneous batch of work. You could not make up a mixed batch of, say, two dozen invoices, the payroll for one small department and a bit of stores accounting, though you could do all these jobs in parallel provided the individual batches of work were of economic size.

As time went by, it became clear that there was one big disadvantage of using computers—loss of flexibility. Certainly, a good many clerks had been eliminated (though by no means as many as had at first been supposed) and work was accomplished more quickly with fewer errors. But the need to collect large batches of work meant that, during the intervals between computer runs, information was effectively locked up. When you have a row of girls with accounting machines, you can generally find out, by asking one of them, the status of any particular customer's account even though this may involve a good deal of shuffling through paper. But between the time documents go to the punch room and the final emergence of print-outs, information is inaccessible. You cannot shuffle through the magnetic files of a computer.

An attempt was made to combat this drawback by inventing random-access files which provided a facility for interrogation of the computer on an item-by-item basis. Using a typewriter, you could, for example, ask what the present stock was of a certain item. Even this, however, was too limited because the record itself might well be out of date by at least a day during which, for all the computer knew, the items listed as in stock had yesterday been promised to a customer. New concepts of speed were introduced as a direct result of the wider use of computers, and delays which had seemed miraculously short only a few years earlier had begun to grow intolerable, especially in operations that are inherently tied to a time-factor—airline operations, for example.

In 1958, the first real-time computer was invented. The characteristic that most clearly differentiates a real-time system from batch-processing computers is its ability economically and efficiently to process isolated transactions and retrieve isolated items of data, instantly and on demand. Designed specifically for this purpose, the system can handle scores or even hundreds of these demands simultaneously without establishing any direct connection between them. The old necessity to make up batches is completely eliminated.

From a purely practical viewpoint, it would clearly be impossible to offer facilities like these if their use entailed a visit to the computer room or even a telephone call to the computer staff. In consequence, the system provides users with remote terminals. These, though directly linked to the computer by telephone lines, may be situated at any distance—even thousands of miles—away from it. Information or inquiries reach the computer through these terminals and answers are returned within a few seconds, either to the point of origin and/or to other terminals as circumstances demand.

A prerequisite for a system like this is that all relevant information on the organization's activities must be stored in a central file directly accessible by all terminals. (System design ensures that the range of access to each terminal is restricted when necessary so that the office boy cannot pull out details of the profit-and-loss account.) These huge, direct (random) access files are known as *data banks* and store hundreds of millions of characters of information.

You may well wonder why I have gone this far without giving you a definition of real-time. The fact is that almost every computer manufacturer and user offers a different definition and the easiest way to start a really fierce argument is to invite them to agree on one. For this reason, I have outlined the basic characteristics rather than provide a definition and will hope to show you what these facilities mean in practical terms by citing a couple of examples.

One of the best-known real-time applications in this country is by British European Airways who use Univac 494s. The system was originally set up to keep completely up-to-date lists of all seats booked on all passenger flights for months and even years ahead. This job could not successfully be handled by batch-processing methods because of the time factor and the random nature of the inquiries and reservations, and was previously handled with limited efficiency by manual methods.

The BEA system has hundreds of remote terminals, each with an operator. An intending passenger who rings up is put through to a terminal or, if he calls at a BEA office in person, speaks direct to the terminal operator. When he has stated his requirements the operator enters a code indicating the flight and number of seats required. Within not more than three seconds the computer indicates whether this accommodation is available. If so, the operator confirms the booking through the terminal and updates the record. If not, the operator interrogates for alternative possibilities. This system not only ensures that accidental over-booking cannot occur but permits the airline to sell seats up to the last possible moment before departure and also, of course, saves much time and clerical work.

Another real-time application employed by Westinghouse in the USA is designed for the immediate fulfilment of customers' orders for goods. A request for items is put to the computer through a terminal. The computer, referring to a zonal code provided by the operator, first interrogates the inventory of the warehouse geographically nearest to the customer. If the wanted item is not in stock, it searches the inventories of others in a widening circle until it finds what it has been asked for. Appropriate documents are then produced automatically at the chosen warehouse. At the same time the computer updates the inventory and enters a debit on the customer's account record. In consequence, goods are always delivered with the least possible delay.

These are only two applications but give some idea of the scope of real-time computing. Further details of these and of the implications of these for management are discussed in chapter 4.

Has real-time computing made batch-processing operations obsolescent? The answer is a firm 'no'. Batch processing remains—and probably always will remain—the most practical and economical method of handling much of the routine work that is done by a business but need not be completed in the shortest possible time. It would be ridiculous, for example, to use the real-time mode to produce thousands of dividend warrants for shareholders or a large payroll as there is no requirement for the immediate availability of these as individual documents.

Any real-time computing system therefore also has the capacity to handle batch-processing work, usually on a multi-programming basis. Real-time applications are, however, always automatically given priority and batch-processing applications cannot interfere. The computer is therefore organized so that the several batch-processing jobs that may be in progress at any given time can always momentarily be interrupted in order to fulfil real-time demands and resumed when these are satisfied. These interruptions probably last only for these tiny fractions of a second—but interruptions they are.

One vital statistic you will often hear quoted in connection with real-time computer systems is *response time*. This figure, normally quoted in seconds, is the *maximum* delay that is permitted to occur before the computer replies to a query submitted from a terminal or carries out a real-time transaction. Response time is not an inbuilt characteristic of hardware (in contrast to calculating time, which is) but is determined by the user. The decision about the response time required is one of the factors that determines what the capacity of the overall system must be, since provision must be made never to exceed this time however heavy the traffic at any given moment. Strict realism in setting the response time is therefore important. If circumstances are such that no user can conceivably be inconvenienced by waiting 30 seconds for an answer (and remember that response time represents the maximum wait), it is a needless extravagance to reduce this to 3 s. Similarly, lack of foresight in determining response time and installing appropriate hardware might result in delays of a length that made the full use of a busy terminal impracticable.

Remote terminals

Direct communication with a computer from a point distant from it in space is carried on through a device known as a remote terminal. Most commonly used of these is a variant upon an electric typewriter, for example a teletype machine, which enables a human operator to enter transactions or inquiries as though he were using an ordinary typewriter and on which the computer prints out responses. These machines have the advantage of being reasonably priced and simple to operate.

Some very large users of remote terminals, such as BEA or BOAC have special units manufactured for them. BEA, for example, have devices known as Unisets which, in addition to a typewriter keyboard, have a control panel set upright behind this. This panel, equipped with push-buttons and signal lights, also has a space that holds a removable plastic card. The card has printed on it in grid form details of one particular group of flights. By inserting a card and using the push-buttons, an operator eliminates much of the manual keyboarding that would otherwise be required to enter an inquiry or a booking; and the computer, by illuminating signal lights, obviates some of the printing that would otherwise have to be done.

Most spectacular of the terminals available at the time of writing is the cathode-ray tube (CRT) display device. This is a screen like that of a small television set and may be equipped with a keyboard and/or push-buttons for the entry of information. To enter data or an inquiry, the operator uses these keys, the result being shown not on paper but in illuminated alphabetical and numerical characters on the screen. Information returned by the computer will be displayed in the same way concurrently or after the first image has been dismissed. This type of terminal is very fast because no printing is needed. If, on the other hand, it is desired to print some information from time to time, this may be automatically produced on a separate typewriter terminal.

How precisely a CRT terminal is used by a manager depends upon the way the computer has been programmed. Typically, information is accessed in a hierarchical way so that, when searching for data on one particular subject, one might call out first a list of file groups, next a list of files within a selected group, then sub-heads within an individual file and so on until one reaches the wanted item. This can be done in almost as little time as it takes to read these words.

Let us suppose that a sales manager wants to ascertain the status of forward orders for the company. He first keys in a simple code to call in the computer which immediately displays a message indicating 'I am at your service'. A second code entered by the manager tells the computer what information he wants and within a split second this is displayed in tabular form on the screen.

He then decides he would like a more detailed breakdown of orders for one product. Again he keys in his request, the original table is replaced by the new one. He can repeat this process or ask for other information as long as he wants to. If at any time he wants a print-out, he can instruct the computer to produce this on another terminal.

This method not only gives a speed of access to information that was undreamed of only a few years ago, but should eventually obviate the need for much of the paper at present churned out by computers. The immediate availability of completely up-to-date information on call should make the production of statistical reports as a routine item completely unnecessary.

Even greater possibilities, particularly for people like engineers and designers who tend to think in terms of drawings, are opened up by CRT devices supplied with a *light-pen*. This is held in the hand like its manual equivalent and gives an effect like writing or drawing in light on the screen. In fact, the light pen does not itself generate light but enables the user to pull a spot of light across the screen. The spot leaves a trail wherever it has been (a bit like the vapour trail left in the sky by a plane, though a far thinner, finer line) and the user of the pen thus makes a drawing.

As this drawing is made, the computer automatically translates it into numerical data and, when instructed by the draughtsman via his terminal, can pull in detail already held in file, work on dimensions supplied by the draughtsman, and so on. It may thus, for example, straighten up the lines of a rough sketch, project certain lines, produce an amended version of the drawing or display an enlarged image of one part of it.

One of the most fascinating (and beautiful in visual terms) achievements is a program which causes the computer to rotate upon the screen an image displayed upon it. This facility allows the viewer to look at the image from all angles as it turns slowly before his eyes.

Facilities like these provide the designer with an entirely new way of creating and manipulating drawings. An idea, drawn roughly with a light-pen on the CRT, can immediately be exploited without all the manual labour normally associated with this process and without the problem that arises when a designer tries to convey a half-formed idea to a draughtsman. Its availability should not only greatly stimulate creative thought but encourage experimentation because this can be carried out at a fraction of the cost normally incurred with conventional methods.

Light-pen techniques can be used for the fast manipulation of any information that can be expressed in graphic form. One might, for example, express several interactive factors in company management in the form of lines on a graph and by changing one of these at a time with a light-pen see the effect on the others (see pages 130–133).

The name given to this constant communication between man and computer on an interactive basis is the *conversational mode*—a very apt term. Having had an opportunity to try it for myself, I can tell you that the effect is extraordinarily stimulating and remarkably akin to the exchange of face-to-face conversation with another, very bright person. If this sounds fanciful, I strongly advise you to have a go yourself at the earliest opportunity—and I shall be surprised if you do not share my feelings!

All the terminals I have so far mentioned are designed for establishing communication between man and computer. There are others, such as fast paper-tape readers, whereby the terminal communicates with the computer without human intervention. It is also feasible to use small computers as terminals, in which case they are generally referred to as *satellites*. A satellite computer may well perform a dual function, being employed as an independent, self-contained unit for local work and put on-line to a larger system only when it requires extra power or is used to transmit data direct to the larger system. Linked in this way, the systems exchange information in machine language. An arrangement of this kind may offer the best of two worlds, as the branch office or depot has an inexpensive system always at its disposal for handling local jobs but can tap the resources of a more powerful system whenever they are needed. It also obviates the need for a separate link when there is a requirement simply to transmit data to a central point.

Normally, the local computer will partly process work before passing it on to the big system so that the power of the latter is not wasted on elementary tasks that can more economically be done by the satellite. Results put out by the central system will probably be written onto magnetic files, if the satellite has them. This is faster than printing and permits the satellite to do its own printing after it is disconnected from the more powerful system. If, however, there are no local magnetic files, printing can be done direct.

I have discussed in more detail how terminals can be used on a bureau basis in chapter 10 'Computer service bureaux'.

Computer communications

The availability of facilities to establish direct, on-line communications between a computer and terminals of one kind or another situated many miles away is an important development. But it has faced managers with new problems as well as offering potential benefits. Before such communications were possible, the advantages of using a central computer to process the work of a geographically widespread organization were often dubious. When source documents are sent to a central point for processing and reports returned by the same means, there are considerable delays which may in the end cancel out the benefits of centralization.

Certainly it has been possible for some time to put punched paper-tape onto the reader of a teleprinter and transmit the data on it to a similar machine which will create a tape at the far end. Transmission from punched card to punched card is also possible. The trouble is that these methods used telegraph circuits (the Telex system or privately rented lines) that are too slow to permit the economical transmission of bulk data—or, of course, for direct linkage to the computer. All that is received at the computer centre, therefore, is punched tape or cards which might, in many cases, as well be sent by post, van, or train.

This left the managers of a scattered organization that desired to computerize in something of a dilemma. Either branch offices had to accept delays; or it was necessary to maintain tape- or card-punching keyboard accounting machines or separate small computers at these points. Consolidated results could then be obtained by collecting the output from these systems and processing them all together on yet another system at headquarters.

A set-up like this is expensive, both in terms of hardware and man-power, and is difficult to control adequately. There was clearly a big incentive for computer manufacturers to evolve hardware and software that would permit direct communication over long distances and at high speeds between a large central computer and relatively

D

inexpensive input/output terminals. This effectively places the power of the central system on tap when and where it is needed and at the same time permits the fast collection of information that must be handled at the central installation.

The difficulty that now faces managers, these facilities being available, is twofold. First, what degree of centralization is desirable; second, how much hold-up is likely to occur through non-availability of transmission facilities.

The first of these is at least as much a human problem as a technical one. In terms of pure theory, there may be much in favour of complete centralization, but the psychological effect of this may be disastrous since local managers who were at one time largely autonomous may lose initiative. It is almost inevitable that a man who has run his own show at a branch office will feel downgraded when even the everyday accounting is no longer under his supervision. In consequence, he may well be tempted to leave his job and seek something that uses the qualities for which he has previously been valued. This is a question I return to in more detail in chapter 7 when weighing the pros and cons of centralization.

Though the computer and communications hardware and software are already abundantly available for the employment of systems using remote, on-line terminals, the same cannot be said of transmission lines. Certainly the Post Office, who hold a monopoly of these facilities, are already offering several data-transmission services (this subject is discussed more fully in chapter 7 'Choosing and installing a computer'). But how much time will elapse before these transmission facilities become readily available in any quantity to actual users is another question.

Professor Stanley Gill, a prominent authority in the computer field, expressed both apprehension and pessimism in a public speech* he made in mid-1968. Existing facilities, he pointed out, are too few, too expensive, and will be inadequate when used much for data transmission as they were designed primarily for carrying speech. A national grid, whose function will include provision of data-transmission facilities for private users, is planned. But this, he said, is deplorably slow in getting off the ground and may not get going properly until as late as 1980. This will put Britain at a severe disadvantage vis-à-vis countries who have been more enterprising

* Speech given to members of the government, the civil service, and the computing industry, at a presentation of real-time computer systems at the Royal Festival Hall, 3 July 1968.

and far-sighted and have their data-communications facilities already well established.

It would be unbecoming for me to contradict Professor Gill. On the other hand, I think it is only fair to present another viewpoint. Computers still make news and it cannot be denied that new developments sometimes upset people's judgement. By this I mean that a new facility like fast data transmission is so exciting as to intoxicate computer specialists (who normally do not pay the bills) and so spectacular as to tempt management to regard it as a status symbol. Later, when it comes to counting the cost, a more sober appraisal is made.

I am not against technological or any other progress. But I am very wary of fashionable 'bandwagons' because they can be so very expensive and disillusioning. Many organizations who, in the early days, bought computers in a spirit of keeping up with the corporate Joneses lived to rue the day. Currently, there is an often indiscriminate rush for CRT terminals and some salesmen have told me they have had difficulty in restraining customers from ordering these wholesale.

It must be remembered that the provision of extensive high-speed data-transmission facilities demands the investment of very large sums of public money. If the high demand anticipated today does not materialize, much of this investment may be wasted. At present we have, I think, fallen in love with the idea of speed—sometimes at the expense of common sense. There can be no virtue in using high-speed data transmission when less sophisticated methods and slower speeds would be perfectly adequate.

Summing up, therefore, I would say that the prospect for the large-scale provision of high-speed data-transmission facilities in this country within the next few years does not look bright; but a shortage may not have such severely restrictive effects on progress as the pessimists fear.

User programming and computer software

Up to this point, I have written almost exclusively about computing machinery—the hardware as it is generally called. The time has now come to consider the complementary subject of the human contribution without which a computer is little more than an expensive heap of junk.

As I mentioned in chapter 2, *software* is the blanket term widely employed today to cover the human effort which, combined with hardware, makes a computer system a working reality. In fact, this definition is somewhat qualified since computer specialists generally use *software* to describe only those programs whose purpose is primarily to govern a computer system's internal 'housekeeping' functions. These programs have no direct connection with any actual application for which the system will be used.

Thus, a group (or *suite*, as it is usually called) of programs held permanently in store by the computer and which enables the system, say, to process a number of applications simultaneously, would be termed *software*; while a suite of programs written by a user to process his invoices and carry out sales analysis, for example, would be termed *user programs*, or *application programs*.

This difference may seem rather subtle and obscure now, but I think you will better understand it when you have read the remainder of this section. Meantime, let us consider the subject of programming in the broadest sense of the word.

PROGRAMMING. A computer system, like a car, is entirely useless without a human being at the wheel: until it is given specific and minutely detailed instructions about what to do and how to do it, it is an idiot that cannot do anything at all. These instructions are called *programs*.

Incapable of even the most elementary reasoning or the application of common sense, devoid of even rudimentary instinct and reflexes, a computer cannot recognize or act upon the obvious and is completely floored by faulty logic.

The most stupid man or woman told to walk from point A to point B and who sees an unexpected hole in the road will walk round it and resume his or her original path. A computer cannot perform this simple action spontaneously. Faced with an equivalent situation, it will either stop dead in its tracks or run round eternally in a loop between the starting point and the near edge of the hole. This sort of behaviour can be prevented only when the user has anticipated the situation and has either detailed the exact length and direction of every pace to be taken between the starting point and final destination or has, in effect, told the computer: 'If you encounter a hole, this is how you deal with it'.

Thus, though a computer is inherently capable of circumnavigating any number of holes in the road, the existence of these must have been anticipated by the programmer. A neat illustration of this point is provided by the experience of a friend who administers a small trust fund and pays its income tax in monthly instalments. One month he accidentally sent off a duplicate cheque and this innocent error caused considerable difficulty with the Revenue's computer. This arose from the fact that the programmers had incorporated elaborate checks to detect non-payment but had not anticipated the (admittedly unlikely) event of duplicate payments. In consequence, there was no routine for crediting my friend's account! Eventually, a small amendment was made to the computer program to cover this eventuality.

A computer program must, then, be absolutely comprehensive in scope. It must also be written in accordance with the rules of formal logic. This means, in effect, that one step must lead inexorably to another, and that where this other comprises alternatives each must be specified and evaluated. A typical alternative might be: If the weekly pay total amounts to less than £50, look up payee's tax record and tax table and apply appropriate rate; if total amounts to more than £50, reject.

No computer yet designed will accept instructions written in the ordinary languages used between one man and another. In consequence, it has been necessary to devise special codes. Each make, and sometimes each model of computer put out by the same manufacturer, has its own code which is generally known as *machine language*.

In the early days, there was no alternative for the programmer but to learn machine language. When computers were few in number, this did not matter too much, though machine language is elaborate and difficult to learn. Later, however, as more and more computers came into use and became more elaborate in design, it became clear that something simpler would have to be evolved so that communication between man and machine became easier.

Increased usage also caused a shift in emphasis. While it had been tacitly accepted previously that man should, to some extent, accommodate himself to the computer it now became apparent that this relationship should be reversed: the computer should be made to serve man. This meant that any evolution should be in the direction of making the computer itself do more work, the programmer less.

Since the computer's native language remains unchangeable, being indigenous to its engineering design, the only course that lay open was to evolve a translation process to be used by the computer. This would permit the programmer to use a language more approximating to his own tongue and throw on the computer the onus of rendering this into a form it could accept. This is, in fact, what is done today and machine language is almost never used.

Computer program codes in current use fall into two categories: *assembly languages* and *high-level languages.*

Assembly languages, or *autocodes* as they are sometimes called, are translated by the computer's hardware. Closely related to machine language, the assembly language can be used only for the make or model of central processor for which it was designed and is constructed on what is known as a one-for-one basis. That is, one instruction written by the programmer in assembly language is translated by the computer into one equivalent instruction in its own language.

On the face of it, this sounds as though an assembly language offers little advantage over machine language. But this is not true. Assembly languages are far easier for a man to learn and use than machine language. Thus, though the programmer must learn the rules of syntax and acquire a vocabulary, these have been simplified and reduced as far as possible. The programmer is thus in a position like that of an Englishman who wants to communicate with a Japanese and can avoid the complexities of that language by learning French which the Japanese also speaks.

High-level languages, as their generic name suggests, refine still further the communication process between man and computer. Not only do their terms approximate to those used in everyday communication between one man and another, but they are more compact than assembly languages. That is, a single instruction written by the programmer in a high-level language may be converted by the computer into a whole string of instructions. This conversion, or translation, is performed by software known as a *compiler*—of which more later in this chapter.

High-level languages are easily and quickly learned and may be used on any make or type of computer of suitable size provided a compiler is available. This feature is of immense importance, since it places within the grasp of almost anyone with a reasonable degree of intelligence and a logical mind a means of expressing his instructions to a computer. This, by implication, does much to dissipate the difficulty that arises when complex business systems or technical applications are to be computerized. A professional programmer may know nothing of the application and cannot, intelligent though he may be, learn it quickly. It is far easier to teach a mathematician, engineer, or accountant to program in a high-level language than it is to teach a professional programmer the intricacies of these users' requirements. Familiarity with a high-level language will often permit the use of a computer service bureau when the alternative (paying the bureau staff to write the program) would be too expensive.

Another very valuable characteristic of high-level languages is that they provide an unambiguous, easily understood method of communication between one programmer and another. A program is always first written in documentary form before being punched into cards or rendered into some other form suitable for input to the computer. And a programmer writing in machine or assembly language has almost unlimited freedom to use the computer in any way he chooses, since his intentions are expressed in a series of single instructions.

Thus a programmer with an ingenious, perverse, or confused mind may succeed in drafting his instructions in a form that, while causing the computer to implement his intentions, is not easily comprehensible to any other programmer. His syntax is, in effect, unclear, his 'argument' turgid.

This can be disastrous when the need arises—as it almost invariably does sooner or later—for amendments to be made to a program. (These amendments may be made because a better method has been found for doing part of the job or simply because of changed circumstances.) Sometimes even the original writer of the program finds it difficult to unravel what he has done. When he has left the organization, others are left with this task, which has been known to take weeks. The amendment process itself also becomes needlessly complex.

The structure and terms of high-level languages obviate these problems. The terms used have no direct reference to machine language and the high-level languages may therefore be used in any system of suitable capacity made by any manufacturer, provided a compiler is available. Programs written for one computer system may therefore, with a minimum of modification, be transferred to another.

A compiler, on the other hand, can be used only on the make or model of computer for which it is designed. Its function is to translate instructions written in a high-level programming language into equivalent instructions in machine language, the latter being indigenous to the computer. This job is performed by software—a collection of programs designed solely for this purpose.

Compiler design is a very complicated and specialized job far beyond the capacity of the ordinary programmer, and computer users must therefore generally rely upon manufacturers to provide compilers. As might be expected in the circumstances, their offerings vary in efficiency—i.e., in the accuracy with which they translate, their vocabulary size, and the way in which they employ the central processor to do the job. Increasing use of high-level languages makes good compilers one of the most critical software requirements for many computer users.

You will have noticed, perhaps, that I have used the word 'compiler' in the plural. No-one has yet found a method of providing a computer with the versatility possessed by a human interpreter who speaks a number of languages. It is therefore necessary to design a different compiler for use with each high-level language the manufacturer wishes to make available to the computer user.

Since a compiler will be required each time an application program in a high-level language is processed by the computer, compilers are often stored permanently in a fast access external memory, such as a disc file. This allows the central processor to call them automatically into the internal memory where they reside during use. Later, they are returned to the external store.

Compilers contain far more instructions than are found in many user programs, so they demand a good deal of internal storage capacity which, during this time, is not of course available either for the storage of the application program or working data. Purely practical considerations therefore make it impossible for a computer with less than 32K internal memory to use a compiler. This limitation is sometimes overcome to some degree by offering a less comprehensive compiler which permits the user to employ a restricted version of a high-level language. This truncated form of the language may be quite adequate for the expression of fairly simple requirements.

Almost all the high-level languages in current use are purpose-designed. Thus, for programming business systems there is COBOL (Common Business Orientated Language)—a stylized form of plain English plus one or two elementary mathematical signs. FORTRAN —of which the fourth, FORTRAN IV, and fifth, FORTRAN V, versions are now current—is principally orientated towards technical and scientific applications. ALGOL is a high-level language designed for mathematicians. These are the best-known and most-used of the high-level languages.

To date, only one multi-purpose high-level language is available and this, PL/1 (Problem Orientated Language No. 1), designed by IBM, is a subject of considerable controversy. Part of this is, no doubt, due to the fact that IBM as a corporation tends to inspire strong feelings of loyalty or dislike among computer people, though there is also genuine ground for argument.

The many opponents of PL/1 maintain that its purpose is redundant since existing languages are perfectly adequate for their purposes and are already very widely used. It would be more practical, say these people, to invent other, highly specialized languages if and when the need for these arises; and these, being purpose-designed, would be less voluminous and therefore could be learned more quickly.

PL/1, say those who dislike it, is more difficult and slower to learn than other high-level languages and its use demands too much internal storage capacity. And its present usefulness is severely impeded by the fact that no manufacturer other than IBM has yet produced a compiler.

Counter-arguments put forward by IBM and supported by enthusiastic users of PL/1 are strong. An all-purpose language is immensely useful because it saves effort in the long run. Having learned the syntax once for all and acquired a basic vocabulary, the user can enlarge the latter as needs dictate. PL/1 already covers some requirements that are not yet catered for by other languages and has a design framework that allows its extension in any direction in future. This compares favourably with the built-in limitations of other high-level languages. (A case in point in this context is the control of remote terminals for which no high-level language yet caters. By the time this book is in print, provision for this will probably have been incorporated in PL/1.)

These characteristics, argue the proponents of PL/1, make longer learning time worth while—if, in fact, a longer time is required, which not everyone will concede. The language also confers the important extra advantage of permitting any programmer to write any type of program. (A programmer who knows only FORTRAN could not write in COBOL without a course of instruction but would need the latter if he were to program a business data-processing job in a high-level language.)

Core-store requirements today are smaller than when PL/1 was first launched and, say IBM, a 16K memory is now sufficient for some applications. Other technical difficulties met initially have now been successfully disposed of, it is claimed.

One of the advantages claimed for PL/1 is that it increases programmer productivity. At least one large user, whose work includes a wide range of business and technical applications, has said that use of PL/1 has substantially increased the productivity of programmers. In fact, users of PL/1 include some of the largest and most sophisticated (in terms of computer applications) organizations in Britain. This suggests less that the language is suitable only for larger users than that it is usually these who are prepared to experiment.

Competition in the computer world being as it is, one cannot be surprised that to date no compiler for PL/1 is offered by manufacturers other than IBM, its inventor. Apart from this, the language has not yet been perfected. If, however, the arguments in its favour are as convincing as they sound, its usage will undoubtedly increase. In this case, other manufacturers will undoubtedly write compilers as it is in their long-term interests to provide facilities for any widely accepted high-level language.

As a closing footnote to this discussion, it is worth remarking that IBM (in conjunction with others) also invented FORTRAN which is now used all over the world on computers of every make.

OPERATING SYSTEMS. The scene has now been set for a discussion of that vital piece of software, the computer operating system. It is this that is responsible for automatically minding an assorted collection of tasks concerned with the internal management of the system that is sometimes described as *housekeeping*. This housekeeping function has no direct connection with the specific applications you may put on a computer, any more than the engine of your car has any direct relationship to the direction in which you decide to drive it. But, like the engine of your car, the operating system of the computer has a very substantial influence on what you can do with it.

Stringent demands are often made upon a modern computer system of any size. It is expected to process a number of assorted batch programs simultaneously and possibly to assign priorities to some of these, yet often it must interrupt these without notice to comply with a request for real-time processing from any one of scores of remote terminals. It must often have at least one compiler on tap for immediate use; it must service a very large data bank. Often all its immediate peripherals must be working at the same time —usually on different jobs.

To do these and other jobs efficiently, the computer must be very well organized and it is the job of the operating system to carry out this organization on an *ad hoc* basis according to the demands of the moment. As you may imagine, the programming involved in designing an operating system is far too complex (and therefore time-consuming and expensive) to be undertaken by a user. This work is therefore normally done by a manufacturer who—reasonably enough —holds out an effective operating system as an attractive bait to the prospective customer. Most manufacturers give evocative names, such as Executive, to their operating systems so as to emphasize their importance. But whatever the name and whatever the individual refinements, all these systems are similar in broad outline.

The importance of a good operating system to a computer user cannot be over-stressed. For it performs functions whose lack—or whose inadequacy—can drastically reduce the efficiency of an otherwise good system and may well burden the user's programmers with a load of work they have a right to expect will be taken off their shoulders.

In fact, one of the basic objectives of a computer operating system is just this—to relieve the user's programming staff of work. They are then able to concentrate principally upon their specific applications—a task which is likely to keep them fully occupied for some time.

Another important aim of the operating system is to ensure that the central processor and peripherals are utilized as efficiently as possible. This implies, among other things, that as little of the system's overall capacity as possible is taken up in these supervisory and household duties. Failure to achieve this would result in a ridiculous situation where the computer spent a high proportion of its resources simply in organizing itself!

What, more specifically, does this organizing job entail? Let us take a look at a medium-size computer system whose peripherals include a card or paper-tape input reader, one or more forms of external memory housed in several handling units each of which the computer recognizes as an individual entity, at least one line printer, and a tape or card punch. This configuration is expected to be able to handle several batch programs concurrently.

The operating system must therefore accept the programs that are given to it and store them ready for immediate use. It must review all these jobs and put them into a queue to await use of the processor and peripherals and must assign priority to any job if this is requested by the operator at the control console. The actual processing of the work demands that the operating system handles the job like a sort of dynamic jigsaw whose shape is constantly changing. As soon as capacity is available in the core store, for example, it must seek out something awaiting its turn to use this facility. If work is ready for a printer which is engaged upon another job it must be filed until the printer is free.

But even this is almost childishly simple compared with the additional demands made by a system that includes real-time processing. Here the operating system must add to its tasks the handling of a large number of requests for information of processing emanating at random from remote terminals. It must deal with all these within the predetermined response time and, as each could well require the use of a different program, pull each program out of store and put it back when no longer needed. Many of these applications will require reference to the data bank and action at several terminals at once—terminals other than the one on which the demand for action originated.

Meantime, the operating system must cause the computer momentarily to interrupt work on one or more batch-processing operations and make sure these will resume, at exactly the point where they were broken off, as soon as capacity becomes available.

All these demands between them involve the constant movement of data from one location to another within the system, the dismissal of part-processed programs and data from the internal to an external store to make room for a new priority, and so on. It is small wonder that the preparation of software to control all these functions automatically is a very tough task or that a newly designed operating system seldom works smoothly.

No way has yet been devised whereby an operating system can be exhaustively tested. This is simply because of the astronomical number of possible combinations of demands that may be made upon it. All that manufacturers can do, therefore, is to make as many tests as they find practicable and then tinker with the operating system when a user runs into a situation which causes it to falter.

Manufacturers who offer compatible series of computers construct their operating systems on a modular basis. The user may select any combination of component parts (in much the same way that he selects the hardware) to accord with his particular requirements. In this way he assembles an operating system that provides him with the amount and scope of capacity that he needs.

I would like very much, in concluding this section on software, to give you some tips straight from the horse's mouth on how to assess the effectiveness of manufacturers' software. Unhappily, there is only one piece of advice I can give you and that is to investigate, as fully as you can, whether other users find the software operates satisfactorily.

More than one expert I have consulted on this subject has told me without hesitation that it is impossible, even for an experienced computer user, to assess software from the technical viewpoint. This leaves only one criterion: Does it work? As I have already suggested, most users of an operating system will probably have encountered at least some difficulty. But if the manufacturers have been co-operative and the problems have been solved reasonably expeditiously, you need not feel too apprehensive.

Summary

The following points have been made in this chapter.

(a) Soon after the first computers were used by business and industry it became clear that there would be a requirement to handle more than one job at a time. This is a facility possessed by all modern computers except the very smallest.

(b) The traditional way of using a computer is in the batch-processing mode, that is, processing a large number of like transactions in a single run through the system. Later, real-time computing was introduced. A real-time system is capable of handling single transactions fed into it through a large number of terminals situated at points remote from the computer room.

(c) Newer though it is, the real-time mode has not ousted the batch-processing mode except in applications where the former is clearly more desirable. A real-time computer will normally handle batch-processing in addition to real-time work, though the latter will always automatically get priority.

(d) The availability of hardware and software which permits direct communication between a computer and remote terminals or one computer and another raises new points, some 'human', others technical, when considering the centralization of computer facilities.

(e) Few facilities are at present readily available in this country for high-speed data transmission on the kind of networks outlined in (b). Some authorities believe this scarcity is disastrous; on the other hand, the need may not be as great as is at present imagined.

(f) The software provided by manufacturers is today at least as important as the hardware. The most essential form of software (and the most complex) comprises those programs which enable the user to employ high-level programming languages and which relieve him from the necessity of organizing the house-keeping within the computer system.

(g) The only practical way for a computer user to assess the effectiveness of manufacturers' software is to find out from other users whether or not it works satisfactorily.

(h) The following computer terms have been used in this chapter:

Multi-programming—a facility which permits a computer system to process several programs concurrently

Time-sharing—the same as multi-programming, except that this term generally presupposes use of on-line remote terminals

Batch-processing mode—a method of using a computer which demands the aggregation of a sizable collection of like transactions for processing in a single run through the system

Real-time mode—a method of computing which permits the processing of isolated transactions which come into the system on a random basis from terminals situated at points remote from the computer

Data bank—a very large direct-access file. Data banks are usually associated with real-time computing

Response time—the maximum interval which is permitted to elapse between conclusion of entering a request or transaction at a terminal and receiving an answer or initiating other action by the computer; this term is used in connection with real-time systems

Light-pen—a device used in conjunction with a CRT (TV-type) computer terminal. This, held in the user's hand, permits him to 'draw' on the surface of the CRT and in this way to establish direct communication with the computer

Conversational mode—instant, two-way communication between man and computer on a question-and-answer or other basis, through a remote terminal

Satellite—a computer directly linked to a larger computer system but capable also of handling its own work when off-line to the large system

Suite—a group of computer programs

Application (user) programs—programs written by the computer user to process his own routines as distinct from the functional programs generally referred to as software

Program—a detailed schedule of instructions for a computer

Machine language—the 'native tongue' of an individual make or model of computer (now almost never used)

Assembly language—a relatively simple programming code which is directly related to machine language but easier to learn and use

High-level language—a programming language which approximates to the terms used in ordinary communication—e.g., standard English or recognized mathematical signs

Compiler—software (programs written by the manufacturer) which interprets a high-level language automatically into machine language

Operating system—software, provided by the manufacturer, which automatically supervises and controls the internal organization of a computer system.

4. The impact of computers on commercial and industrial management

Ever since businessmen and computers were first introduced to one another, the prophets have predicted that computers would make a profound impact on business-management methods. It is only today, more than two decades later, that these ideas have begun to crystallize into a shape we can recognize and whose validity is apparent. Even now, the impact of computers upon management in general appears, on the whole, to have been so superficial as to suggest that the prophets' predictions were grossly exaggerated.

I do not think this is so. A look at history in any age reveals that changes instigated by the invention of a new technology are almost always slow of realization. Innovators, who by their very nature are more visionary than the rest of us, think in terms of revolutions. In fact, the time-scale is long and 'evolution' would be a more correct description.

New ideas take time to assimilate—and for most of us even more time fully to accept. And there is a long, weary, and uncharted road to travel before new concepts can be converted into working realities. Aside from this, new technologies are generally so crude and imperfect in their early manifestations that few can appreciate their ultimate implications. It is, for example, just possible that the unknown inventor of the wheel had a cloudy vision of the motor car; but wildly unlikely that anyone else, except perhaps his closest friends or a few other dreamers, believed he was talking anything but arrant nonsense.

Looked at in a wider perspective, the development in computers themselves and in their usage has been astonishingly fast. Only a quarter-century or so after the first electronic computer made its debut, severely practical people are beginning to appreciate that the forecasts were accurate. The advent and application of real-time computing in particular makes it completely realistic to expect that fundamental changes in our whole approach to management, particularly of large and widespread enterprises, will occur during the next decade.

In the beginning, everything conspired to reinforce the belief that, as far as businessmen were concerned, computers were in essence nothing more than souped-up accounting machines. They were invented by scientists to handle scientific calculations. They were used by scientists and mathematicians who alone could understand them.

Businessmen who heard about computers naturally turned their thoughts towards the area where most arithmetical calculations were done—accountancy, and sometimes also the laboratory. Manufacturers of the punched-card machines that business and industry had used for years to process accounting work and statistics saw computers as adding an extra dimension to these systems and were thus, naturally enough, the first to exploit them in this way.

True, quite a lot of people started to talk about 'management information'. But when one got down to it, this usually meant something similar in basic character to that produced by traditional accounting machinery. The only change—a highly superficial one, though this was not appreciated at the time—was that better analysed and more accurate information could be produced much more quickly than before. This provided management with a much more detailed and up-to-date picture of past events than had hitherto been available. Because this clearer picture could be created with the employment of far less clerical labour than was needed for older routines, it was naturally assumed that savings in this area would alone justify employment of a computer.

Early users of business computers were obliged to devote most of their resources simply to getting accounting work onto the machines and it was a cause for genuine congratulation when the system could be made to operate satisfactorily. But as computers became more efficient and more reliable and experience in their use accumulated, there was time for thought. And with this thought came slow changes in basic philosophies.

Two very important concepts have been formulated. First, that day-to-day accounting and statistical work, essential though it is and

E

well-fitted for computerization, is merely a means to an end. Secondly, that the true value of a computer lies in the ability it offers its users, not merely to review but to some extent to create an organization's history.

Let me amplify these statements.

Inevitably, conditioned as we were by history, we designed our first computer procedures primarily to produce the kind of documents that had always been found necessary in business— invoices, ledger sheets, payrolls, for example. Because these documents are so essential, their creation was seen as a worthy end in itself. General acceptance of the fact that the value of a computer resided principally in its capacity to do arithmetic fast and accurately and to print out documents at very high speeds contributed to this belief.

Abstraction and analysis of data from these documents to provide management with statistical and other information was therefore seen as a valuable but essentially subsidiary function. Often much detail was produced quite indiscriminately because it was vaguely felt that it must be useful to someone. As a result, managers were frequently deluged with paper the value of which was obscure.

This approach, as we see now, puts the cart before the horse. What management needs to run a business properly is the right kind of information. Day-to-day documents, while an indispensable vehicle for communication between a business and the outside world, should be regarded as by-products of a system geared primarily to the gathering and processing of the kind of information management needs.

This puts an entirely new slant on systems design. It implies that the first thing to think about is what information management needs. Later, day-to-day documents and routines can be designed which will efficiently perform their original function while yielding the basic management data.

Recognition and acceptance of the significance of this fundamental shift in emphasis is painfully slow. Even as I write, organizations who ought to be glad to benefit by the experience of earlier users are setting up computer projects which involve little more than speeding up obsolescent existing routines. Some may believe that savings in clerical labour will offset the cost of the computer—and will later be disillusioned (more of this in chapter 9). Many will have paid lip service to the widely accepted truth that the major payoff will come from 'intangible' benefits whose value cannot accurately be assessed beforehand and have therefore (quite correctly) regarded installation of the computer partly as an act of faith. But faith must be informed by intelligence and knowledge. Without this, they will be disappointed that the rewards are far smaller than they expected— if, indeed, they reap any at all. Chances are they will not attribute their poor results to their real cause but will blame some extraneous factor.

Some organizations have had the immensely disruptive experience of changing their systems approach in mid-stream. Not long ago I was talking to the data-processing manager of a large manufacturing company who was up to his neck in a prolonged, expensive, and heartbreaking exercise that entailed virtually complete redesign of computerized invoicing and other procedures. His predecessor, he told me, had designed the systems in current use. Only when these were well under way had it dawned on management that none of these documents yielded any really significant information. The only possible hope of justifying the substantial investment made in computer hardware lay in starting again. The first task was to find out as exactly as possible what information would be needed by management currently and in the foreseeable future. Only when this was known and agreed could new invoicing and other routines be designed.

How can a computer be used to help create an organization's history? In a nutshell: when it is employed by management as an authentic tool in conjunction with techniques that provide insight into present activities and an informed look at the future.

Side by side with the increasing exploitation of computer power, a new and much more sophisticated conception of the function of accounting has been developed. Traditionally, accounting is concerned simply with the collection of historical data and the periodic presentation of this in the form of a profit-and-loss statement. This method yields a minimum amount of useful information about what is actually going on within a company or how it is likely to fare in the future.

Management accounting, as the newer approach is called, works on the assumption that, properly collected, analysed, and manipulated, accounting figures not only reveal exactly what is happening at any given time within an organization but can be used to control its destiny in large measure. Knowledge is power, it has been said, and, even without accepting this statement unconditionally, one must concede that a business whose managers are aware of what is happening (and, of course, prepared to use the information) is in a far stronger position than one whose managers fly by the seat of their pants.

Because the computer is a fast, versatile, and accurate tool for the implementation of accounting theories and the manipulation of accounting data, it can effectively be used by management to help run an organization in a constructive way. Properly designed costing systems, for example, yield strictly realistic rather than the often fictional information these often provide for naïve organizations. Historical sales data is used not only to make an impressive story on the balance sheet but can be analysed meaningfully and extrapolated; the projection being used as a basis for planning realistic future strategy.

A management that has the means to determine the precise relationship, in terms of profitability and resource utilization, between all the products the company manufactures will be aware of what is involved if it proposes to change the balance of these factors. Management accounting—the constructive and creative use of accounting techniques and information—employed with other modern techniques permits management actively to influence the way in which a business develops instead of regarding it as a pawn of an imponderable fate.

The point I am trying to emphasize is not that modern techniques or computers are in themselves any sort of panacea; but simply that their intelligent use provides management with the most powerful tools yet invented. Any business which decides it can get along without these tools does so at its peril; and in my opinion you, as a manager, have little hope of seeing any benefit from your computer installation unless you regard it primarily as an instrument for more effective management.

What this boils down to is a recognition that a computer often demands a new way of life. The crying shame is that today there are still a good many managements who, having decided to install perhaps £200,000-worth of computer hardware, use this to implement philosophies which have long since been discarded by those who have learned the hard way. It is these who form the hard core of computer failures—the organizations who are bitterly disappointed and a great deal poorer because their computers have failed to pay off adequately. I hope that I may do something in this book to help you avoid joining their ranks.

Integrated data-processing systems

Some of you will recollect that, soon after business and industry began to experiment with computers, the air in more rarefied circles buzzed with talk about 'integrated data-processing systems'. This was obviously a very prestigious term and therefore much bandied about. Its meaning, however, like that of so many other phrases in this category, was often far from clear to those who used it and completely incomprehensible to the average business-man.

On questioning the more articulate and lucid computer specialists, however, one learned that this term described a system based upon recognition of the fact that anything done in one part of an organi-zation affects some of its other parts directly, others indirectly. Once this pattern of reaction had been perceived, a computer could be used to implement the necessary action in all the affected parts. This action would include the updating of files containing records of, say, stocks and costings, and ledger accounts, and the production of any necessary documents; and all these associated tasks would be per-formed by the computer as a result of feeding in one set of basic data. This contrasted with any known system where the same facts were repeatedly transcribed in a series of different formats to implement each of these requirements separately.

Control of factory production was seen as a very promising area in which to exploit this concept. For the connection between the various aspects of mechanized production is clearer than the relation-ship between the parts of a less stylized operation. Anyone can, in fact, appreciate that every factor from design and purchase of raw materials onwards must materially influence the number of products produced, the quality of these, the time-span within which they can be delivered to the customer, and so on.

It seemed clear that computers, with their ability quickly and efficiently to manipulate very large bodies of information, to maintain voluminous files, and to print out quantities of documents, could be employed to implement an integrated data-processing system. This would co-ordinate functions that until then had, of necessity, been handled as separate and self-contained procedures. Watertight inter-departmental barriers, erected as a matter of expediency because of lack of means to operate in any other way, could at last be demolished. Management would be able to run a factory as the single, organic entity it in fact is, and the many problems that had arisen as a direct result of inadequate communication and lack of overall vision would disappear.

This was a very exciting prospect. Unhappily, however, the idea proved far more difficult to translate into reality than to conceive. Baffling problems arose, partly as a result of the limitations inherent in first-generation and early second-generation computers, but even more from human factors. One of the most fundamental difficulties, for example, was to discover what actually went on in a factory as distinct from what its managers believed was happening. Even the fact that reality usually differs widely from theory was not always appreciated at this stage. Then there was the formidable task of designing and operating a workable system.

Many attempts were made. Many schemes quietly faded into oblivion. Even today, few companies in Britain (and not many in the USA) have successfully designed and operated fully integrated production-control systems—or other integrated systems for that matter.

This does not mean that the concept of systems integration has been discarded. It is far too exciting and valuable to be thrown on the dust heap and in fact is today being pursued with new ardour since the advent of real-time computing, because this offers far better hope of realization.

Meanwhile, many existing projects have got as far as the sub-assembly stage. That is, one or more groups of closely related routines have been integrated even though the final assembly stage—total integration—has not been achieved. There have also been a few outright successes—systems where factory production control, inventory control, and associated functions have been successfully integrated and an efficient working system implemented. One of these is described in some detail in chapter 6 'The computer on the factory floor'.

Management by exception

One of the most spectacular characteristics of any computer designed primarily for business data-processing is its ability to produce vast quantities of printed output at high speed. At first, this quality was seen as an unmixed blessing and exploited to the utmost. Literally miles of paper poured from the printers and executives soon found their desks stacked high with huge piles of reports.

Enthusiasm over-reached itself. Managers, enchanted by the knowledge that more data could be made available than ever before, called for more and more statistics, more and more reports. Some of these were of only marginal value; many were so voluminous as to daunt the bravest and it was not long before offices became choked with vast wads of unread print-out.

Naturally and inevitably, this led to the development of a new technique known as *management by exception* or *exception reporting*. This, broadly, substitutes chosen and meaningful information for a mass of 'raw' data which must be scanned before significant fact can be winkled out.

Thinking about what management really needs, people realized that often the only relevant facts are those that relate to certain changes in status. A warehouse manager, for example, is no better off if he is presented at frequent intervals with a report of how many of each item he holds in stock. What he does want to know is when he is running short of anything—preferably when the stock of each item has sunk to a predetermined level. He can then decide how many to re-order and when.

When routine reports are confined to these items, their very presence on his desk signals that review and perhaps action is required. Everything on the list is meaningful; no selective reading is required; computer time is saved. It is easy to cater in the computer program for a different re-order level for every item, if necessary. Thus, while a realistic level for one item may be 200, for another it may be 4. In either case, the computer will produce a report only when this point has been reached.

This is one very simple example of how exception reporting is used. There are many more. Although the usefulness of the technique is apparent, acceptance has been slow. Even today, many people distrust the accuracy and reliability of computers and therefore feel it is very risky to hand to them the job of watchdog over such vital items as stores supplies. Apart from this, we all tend to resist change, and exception reporting is a new technique, the antithesis of older methods.

All the techniques outlined above are applied to management in general. Others, such as network analysis, are used for the solution of specific management problems and are examined in the following chapter.

This seems a convenient moment, then, to pause and consider how managers and their attitudes have so far been affected by the use of computers and how they are likely to be affected. (As I am assuming that you are already a manager or a potential manager I have segregated this section from a later chapter, 'Computers and people', in which I discuss this subject in relation to the men and women you employ.)

Are men less important?

The introduction of a new technology always arouses fear that the human being will become redundant, or at least devalued. In the Industrial Revolution, for example, this fear was manifested by the Luddite Riots during which workers whose livelihood depended upon weaving cloth in their cottages smashed the machines in the new manufactories because they believed these would take the bread out of their mouths.

Subsequent events proved that, although great sociological changes resulted from the concentration of industry, there was plenty of work for all. It can, however, be argued that devaluation of a kind did occur, that painstaking individual craftsmanship was replaced by soulless labour in the dark, satanic mills.

Looked at realistically, is this not too sentimental a view? We like to think that every weaver, working in his simple cottage, was a meticulous craftsman who loved his work and wove part of himself into its fabric. Even a superficial knowledge of human nature suggests that it was far more likely there were as many sloppy or incompetent workers in that environment as there are in factories today. At least as much drudgery was involved in working at home as in a factory. And rural squalor, while better hidden perhaps and therefore less spectacular than the industrial variety that replaced it, was still depressing and distressing.

Certainly many of the old skills became redundant. But these were replaced by new ones that were demanded by development of the emerging industrial technology. There is no reason to doubt that some individuals whose previous work pattern offered little or no opportunity to exploit some innate abilities later found fulfilment as technical or personnel managers and supervisors or as mechanics in the new factories.

As might be expected—since the basic pattern of human development does not change—a parallel situation is emerging as the result of the application of computer technology. How this can be exploited by you for the benefit of your workers is discussed at some length in chapter 8 'Computers and people'. Meantime, let us take a look at the managers themselves and see what is happening to them.

Even at the risk of boring you, I must emphasize once again that a computer is neither a thinking machine nor a surrogate for human intelligence. It is no better than the systems and programs that are designed for it by men and which alone (apart, of course, from the engineering design) constitute the ingredient of intelligence. Its relationship to the human brain is identical to the relationship of a mechanical device to human brawn—that is, it provides a means of considerably amplifying the natural supply of power.

What are the qualities we esteem in a manager today? In human terms of the most basic kind, these add up to intelligence—a capacity quickly to absorb and interpret information and to react constructively to any given situation—and an ability to handle people. At middle management level, we often also value a capacity to keep track of a mass of detail. At the top, we recognize in the most successful a quality we call flair or intuition.

Intelligence and the ability to handle people are inborn qualities. They cannot be induced where none exists and are therefore indispensable and uniquely human. Their effectiveness, however, can be extended by education and training. Thus, though no computer can ever replace them, a good computer system can extend their range.

An intelligent man or woman, provided with better information, is better equipped to interpret, better able to react effectively. One might, in fact, argue that an intelligent man in conjunction with a computer forms a closed-loop system (as discussed in chapter 6 'The computer on the factory floor') which is by nature self-correcting. Intelligence dictates what will be incorporated into the computer system; information provided by the system provides a base for intelligent action; the results of this action fed back into the computer initiate the production of further information—and so on.

Successful man-management is, to a considerable degree, also aided by the availability of information. If this sounds unlikely, consider for a moment what qualities shop-floor workers esteem in a supervisor. One of the first to be named is fairness—impartiality. Clearly, it is easier to be fair when you are equipped with accurate background information. If, for example, the supervisor has immediate access to complete records of plant and equipment, he will not blame a man for low productivity when there is evidence that his machine is inadequate or unreliable.

Good relationships between managers at all levels and those they manage can be formed only when there is personal contact—a contact close enough to afford real knowledge of these men and women, their capabilities, their limitations and their circumstances. Many supervisors have little opportunity to form relationships like this because they are overburdened with paper-work of the least rewarding kind. By removing this load, a computer system offers the supervisor an opportunity to be human. It can also, by providing the forecasts yielded by comprehensive planning and control, give the supervisor a chance to warn his workers in advance when special demands will be made on them. Warned, they will generally rise to the occasion; unwarned, they will be resentful when, say, overtime is demanded suddenly.

Perhaps these points sound trivial. But it is neglect of the trivia that so often causes friction between human beings, who are usually vastly more irritated by pinpricks than by major difficulties.

Many so-called middle managers today have little time to exercise any real management function. Their days are spent in ensuring that a mass of detailed paperwork is properly processed. When a computer takes over this job, the middle manager may well be out of a job. In chapter 8, I offer some suggestions for redeploying people like this during the interim period. Meantime, I urge you, as a senior manager, to begin thinking seriously about the kind of functions that middle management will be expected to perform in the computer age. It is a fair inference, I think, that this new manager will be required to think much more constructively than he does now about the meaning of his job, the ultimate aims of his department; that he will have to make more decisions; that a higher proportion of his time will be occupied in creating and smoothing human relationships. This suggests that fuller, more comprehensive training and education will be needed than are normally provided today.

What of the quality of flair or intuition that is a distinguishing mark of the best managers? If this is indeed the sort of sixth sense many people believe it is, the computer can obviously do nothing to help. My own feeling is that intuition is often based upon nothing more mysterious than high intelligence and an unusually retentive memory allied to exceptional powers of observation.

Few of us use our eyes or ears properly. An 'intuitive' man or woman does, I believe. Though many of the things he records are not consciously registered, they are stored in the back of his memory. When he tells you he had a hunch that something would happen or that a certain individual was the right one for a particular job, he has probably based his decision upon a large number of these subconscious observations which, though individually insignificant and unnoticed, have added up in his mind.

If this is true, the computer has something to contribute. Simply by providing fuller, more accurate background information it can be used to form a sounder basis for good judgement and correct decision. And, by obviating at least some of the memory function, it may provide some less gifted individuals with a faculty akin to intuition.

These are some of the ways in which a well conceived and designed computerized system can amplify the power available to a manager through his brain. As we have seen, these facilities in no way obviate the necessity for constructive thought and considered judgement. They therefore, far from devaluing a man's human qualities, help him to develop and exploit these more effectively.

The impact of real-time computing

So far, experience with real-time computing, even in the USA, has been very limited compared with that gained from batch-processing systems. In spite of this, we have learned sufficient during the past five years or so of operation by a few large organizations to see what real-time computing is like in action, to gain a shrewd idea of where it is going to lead us, and to make a reasonably realistic appraisal of the kind of demands it already makes on management and will make in the foreseeable future. It is already clear that these demands will be a good deal more stringent than those exerted in the past, just as the demands made on a car driver are more exacting than those on the man who controls a horse and cart.

As I have explained in an earlier chapter, real-time computing brings the computer to the job through remote terminals connected directly to it. A large number of individuals in an organization, from the managing director down to the despatch clerk, will be provided with terminals, though each will use his in an entirely different way. Through this means, it is possible not only to effect direct communication between man and computer but for the computer to provide information based on a complete and comprehensive review of all available data which is always completely up-to-date.

What does this mean in practice? At first, real-time computing was regarded principally as a very sophisticated method of record-keeping. Today, horizons have widened.

To an airline like BEA, the use of a real-time computer system means that a reservations clerk can tell an intending passenger immediately if seats are available on any flight due to depart at any time from a few hours to two years or so ahead. Should the wanted flight be fully booked, the clerk can use the computer to investigate alternatives. Later, using the same remote terminal, the clerk can reserve seats, register the personal details and the computer automatically updates its inventory of available seats. Subsequent alterations of plan can be handled in the same way.

A somewhat similar procedure, though on a much smaller scale, is used by Southern Television for booking advertising time on the air. Agencies wanting to reserve time for their clients can be told immediately what spots are available and can book or provisionally reserve these.

The airlines, who pioneered the use of the then unexploited technique of real-time computing, were spurred on by the possibility of solving a single, very pressing and specific problem: how to cope with passenger seat reservations. The manual operations used until then had entailed the creation and handling of a great deal of paperwork and, of course, the employment of a large number of men and women on menial clerical tasks. The most serious drawback was that information could never be brought up-to-date on an hourly, let alone a moment-by-moment, basis. Apart from the sheer communications problem that arises when reservations emanate from a large number of points and the inevitable delay in handling large masses of paper, customers are at liberty to change their minds as often as they wish and up to the last moment. This meant that existing arrangements had to be cancelled and fresh ones made. In consequence, it was seldom possible fully to load an aircraft owing to the non-availability of accurate information on how many seats were actually available.

Simply in solving this problem, real-time computing offered a big benefit. Later, however, it became apparent that the possibilities of such a system were much bigger than this. Passenger seat reservation is, in fact, only one facet of a total operation which includes the preparation of tickets, the checking in of passengers, the scheduling of aircraft and of flight crews, the siting and maintenance of spare parts depots, the provision of in-flight meals and beverages, and even the distribution of baggage within the hold. These functions are not merely related but are aspects of the same overall function whose broad objective is to carry as many passengers as possible safely,

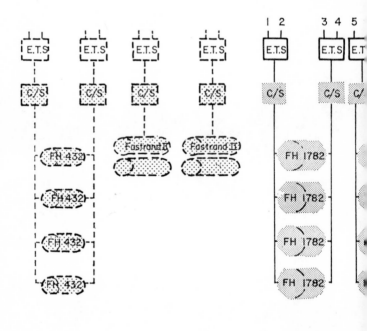

Phases I & II   1974   I

Standby   ///////.   ⁾

On-line   ▓▓▓▓   ▓

(note - core store expansion is s
would not be required for phas
1978)

E.T.S. - electronic transfer swit
C/S - control and synchronise

1   2   3   4   5

E.T.S   E.T.S   E.T.S   E.T.S   E.T.S   E.T.S   E.T

C/S   C/S   C/S   C/S   C/S   C/S   C/

Fastrand II   Fastrand II   FH 1782

FH 432   FH 1782

FH 432   FH 1782

FH 432   FH 1782

FH 432

1,310,720 A/N   129,761,280A/N 129,761,280 A/N   10,485,760 A/N
characters   characters   characters   characters
each drum   each drum   each drum   each drum

Fig. 4.1. This very large Univac 494 real-time configuration (specified for a customer I may not identify) is typical of systems already being installed for organizations requiring management information systems.

The items shown as being used for stand-by obviate interruption of service through computer failure. Normally, stand-by equipment is used for batch-processing work which is immediately discontinued when failure of the other processor triggers automatic switch-over to the stand-by unit.

The huge random-access storage facility is typical of the requirement for a large data bank.

Each of the three types of drum has a different access time (interval between a request for data by the central processor and receiving it). Thus data needed urgently can be stored on the fastest drums while information for which there is less fast demand can be maintained on the others.

The high-speed communications terminals could be of various types and all will be remote – perhaps many miles away – from the computer centre.

comfortably, quickly—and profitably—to their desired destinations.

It will not have escaped your notice that airline operations are particularly well suited to be the subject of the kind of total systems integration I outlined earlier in this chapter. The immense power, speed, and flexibility of a large real-time computer system offered a far better hope of success than before. In addition, the system, through its many terminals, can be made infinitely sensitive to change and can therefore react far more quickly than was dreamed of when batch processing was the only possible mode.

Manufacturers must be congratulated on the outstanding achievements they have made in providing software for real-time systems. This, coupled with the brilliant work of users' system designers and programmers, has already resulted in considerable progress along the road that will ultimately lead to what is now generally called a *total management system*. This brings us back to the concept of a corporate body which is regarded, not as a collection of discrete operations but as an organic entity with interactive parts, each with a unique function as the lungs, eyes, and limbs perform unique functions in the human body.

Talk of a 'real-time revolution' is, as you will agree, justified in these circumstances. For a total management system offers the same degree of flexibility and comprehensive co-ordinated control, the same bird's-eye vision that for many years has been denied to the managers of any large organization. Perhaps the easiest way to understand the significance of this statement is to pause briefly for a review of the structure and methods of a typical organization as it exists at present. Although we know how this functions, it is sometimes illuminating to step back and take a dispassionate look at something we have always taken for granted.

In many ways, the one-man business is the ideal commercial or industrial enterprise. When a single individual acts, in effect, as the company's purchasing, production, and marketing manager, as chief accountant, and as managing director, no communication problems arise. The operation is totally integrated because the information relating to all these activities is stored in one brain, one set of files. Intelligence and thought are sufficient to establish the relationship between, say, purchasing and production and sales policy.

As soon as the business begins to grow, complications begin. Other managers must be employed, many of the responsibilities and activities delegated. A board of directors is formed. Communication becomes more difficult, since even in face-to-face conversation there is seldom unimpaired understanding between all the individuals in a group. Physical separation in several offices or workshops, and the growth of individual filing systems further inhibit the free exchange of information. Functions become more and more specialized and often the production manager does not fully understand what the marketing manager is talking about, let alone appreciate his aims. And vice versa, of course.

As the years slip by, the business grows and prospers and the problems multiply. The idea of integration implicit in the one-man operation has long been lost. The size and complexity of the organization and the lack of any machinery capable of handling its operations in any but a fragmented way have led to the formation of many separate and specialized departments.

Time and human nature between them have combined to erect high walls round these departments and each has become a jealously guarded preserve. The inter-relationship between them becomes more and more obscure; the manager of each is so absorbed in his day-to-day problems that he begins genuinely to believe that its function is an end in itself.

Today, after years of this slow evolution, we have come to accept this kind of structure as perfectly natural and even desirable. It is only with a shock that we realize that the barriers behind which we live were originally erected as a matter of organizational expediency and should therefore be demolished at the earliest possible opportunity—i.e., as soon as re-integration becomes feasible.

Meantime, this artificial structure has had a profound impact on how we manage. Since the only reason for being a manager is to see that things get done (though even this fundamental truth is sometimes lost sight of); and the only way to get things done is through other people; and other people will play ball only if you treat them in the way they expect to be treated; we have developed a slow and elaborate ritual for implementing even the most basic action. This ritual is characterized by frequent meetings and, of course, wholesale creation of paperwork.

The net result of all this is that many managers spend a lot of their time simply in keeping their part of the organization functioning. There is no time, and less opportunity, for creative thought and constructive action. (Think what a ridiculous state of affairs this is—as though one ate solely for the purpose of providing enough energy to cook the next meal, for example!)

Then there is the inertia factor—the time lag between decision and effective action or between stimulus and reaction. This can so sharply reduce the manoeuvrability of a large organization as to threaten it with the fate that overcame the huge prehistoric animals whose extinction was due, at least in part, to the superior mobility of much smaller enemies.

Even more dangerous is the tendency of inertia to breed distortions —a situation that will be recognized by anyone who has been concerned with the design of control systems based on the closed-loop or feedback principle. Mr K. L. Smith, manager of IBM United Kingdom Service Engineering Centre, explained this effect* in terms of the control system of a steam engine. This operates on the basis of measuring the actual speed, comparing this with a desired speed, and using the error to correct the steam pressure supplied to the engine. This system works well when there is no delay in action and reaction. But in practice, there is sluggish response of the governor to speed change, slow opening or closing of the control valve, and delay in the engine's reaction to change of steam pressure. Given sufficient delay, the system can never catch up with itself and the system, so to speak, gets hysterics (not Mr Smith's term) and continually 'hunts' for an equilibrium position it never finds. Thus, the control system actually worsens the position.

To illustrate this point, Mr Smith cited Professor Forrester's famous study which shows how instability can build up in an inventory control system with four basic levels: retailer, distributor, factory warehouse, and factory. A change of 10 per cent in retail demand builds up to a fluctuating demand on the factory and produces apparent seasonal variations of plus 35 per cent in June and minus 52 per cent in November. The real cause of this apparent fluctuation is delays in order processing and inventory decisions but this is interpreted as a seasonal variation in demand. Management, noting this, redesign their policies in relation to employment, inventory control and advertising and in this way actually create a seasonal demand that did not exist before.

Summing up, then, the efficiency of management in a typical contemporary environment is seriously impaired in three broad ways. First, the machinery of administration has grown so clumsy that its operation occupies far too large a proportion of a manager's time, leaving little or none for the primary functions of man-management and decision-making. Secondly, there has been until now no efficient

* In a speech at a symposium on real-time computing, Computing and Management Institute, April 1968.

tool for the central collection of data, its effective correlation, and its presentation in a form that provides an overall view of the organization's activities and the interaction between these. Decisions are therefore often based on incomplete information that may well be dangerously misleading.

Thirdly, the sheer inertia of a sizable organization gravely reduces its manoeuvrability and, by building up in an unrecognized way, create a distorted picture of the truth which may unwittingly become further distorted by the application of management controls.

The best we can do with a computer system operating in the batch-processing mode is to superimpose new techniques on a traditional structure which may have grave and inherent defects. Now let us take a look at how a real-time total management system can change this.

I must, at the outset, play fair and tell you that no organization has yet succeeded in creating and implementing a total management system. As usual, a good deal of high-flown waffle has gone on about the subject. On the other hand, a number of organizations, among them the newly-formed computer company, ICL, are drawing up concrete plans.

Among the most detailed of these systems outlines is one devised by Univac for hospital management. Since this is based on the assumption that the hospital needs to apply many of the same criteria as are used in commerce and industry, I have chosen it as an example of the scope of a system of this kind.

The scheme is based upon the belief that the primary requirement of any hospital computer system is to aid medical and nursing staff in the care of patients. (These provisions can easily be transposed into commercial or industrial terms.) One major aspect of this aid is to eliminate the communications problems that, in a large hospital, incur errors and delays. Mistakes are inevitable when information is conveyed from one person to another in written or spoken form. And the large area covered by a modern hospital means that time is taken in transmitting documents between points. Records stored in conventional files can all too easily be lost or misplaced.

Since the patients are the only reason for the hospital's existence, it is logical that the key file for the whole system should contain patients' personal records. These, stored in a direct-access data bank, are available through terminals located at strategic points in each of several hospitals in a group. The patient record includes all the obvious detail such as name, address, and birth date, other vital information such as blood group and known allergies, and a summarized account of past diseases and treatments.

A large volume of data stored and accessed in the same way will cover financial, administrative, and planning requirements.

Every conceivable aspect of the hospital's functions—emergency and routine admissions, wards, operating theatres, X-ray, pharmacy, laboratories, stores, for example—is integrated by the computer system. A doctor on duty in Emergency Admissions will interrogate the system via a CRT terminal with a typewriter to retrieve within seconds any past record. If none exists, he will begin to create a new one, using the terminal. Through this same medium he will, as necessary, order lab tests, X-rays, drugs or surgery, confident that his instructions will immediately be conveyed to all relevant departments through similar terminals and that all records will immediately be updated within the data banks.

If the doctor orders drugs, the prescription and a label for the pill box or bottle will be printed out at the pharmacy. If this prescription causes supplies of drugs to fall below re-order level, a print-out to this effect will appear in the purchasing office.

Working in a ward, the doctor could order a course of treatment by the same method. This treatment is, perhaps, experimental. But he has noted this as he fed the details into the terminal and the computer will therefore, after a period determined by the doctor, automatically print out a warning that the time has come for a review. Meantime, the therapist has recorded through his terminal the details and results of the treatments, all of which will be available to the doctor on request through a terminal.

Before a patient arrives for routine admission, a warning will appear at a terminal in the appropriate ward. The admissions department, the information desk, and other areas and departments affected will similarly be notified. If emergency surgery is required, the computer may rearrange and print out revised theatre schedules and notify all the surgeons concerned, through the terminals, of these changes.

The computer can also be used to aid the doctor in his daily routine. A terminal placed at the doctors' entrance to a hospital can be interrogated for any messages recorded since the previous visit; it can print out a complete status report or census of each doctor's patients, giving locations, results of tests, new admissions, and a warning of critical status in any of his cases. Even a reminder of a doctor's schedule and appointments within the hospital for the day could be provided.

Patient monitoring—i.e., using instruments to record heart rate, pulse, respiration, temperature, and so on in areas like recovery rooms and automatically recording the data—is still a newish application. But in computer terms there is no reason why a real-time system should not also be used in this connection. The system could also be fed with electro-encephalograms (data on brain activity) and electrocardiograms (data on heart activity), could compare these, and could display the results on CRTs. Diagnoses based on these and other records could become available within minutes in physicians' own consulting rooms.

Even all these examples by no means exhaust the potential scope of the purely medical and administrative side of hospital work.

Financial control can be exercised by working from four basic master files—patient detail, stores and supplies, man-power, and capital equipment. The two vertical lines of blocks in Fig. 4.2 indicate the processing procedures that can be derived from these files, while the remainder outline the many other functions, ranging through cost analysis, budgeting, cash flow analysis, project planning, and many others, that can be exercised through use of this data.

One organization that is, at the time of writing, developing a scheme that will probably follow the lines of the Univac plan outlined above is the Jönköping County of Sweden. A pilot scheme is being set up in the ultra-modern Danderyd Hospital about 10 km north of Stockholm. By 1972, if all goes according to plan, the 1,750-bed Huddinge Hospital at present under construction to the south of the city will be brought into the system. Eventually, 12 or more hospitals in Stockholm County, which by then will have some 13,500 beds and 2,000,000 out-patients between them, will also be included.

The project is beginning with the installation of one Univac 494 real-time computer with 268 million characters of high-speed random-access drum-storage and a large number of CRT display terminals. This configuration will be expanded as required when new applications are added.

It is not difficult to envisage how a system like this could completely transform existing ideas about hospital management. Nor, by implication, how a system like this applied within a commercial or industrial organization could revolutionize its method of working.

Before discussing this in more detail, I must emphasize that none of the procedures outlined above in any way devalues the hospital

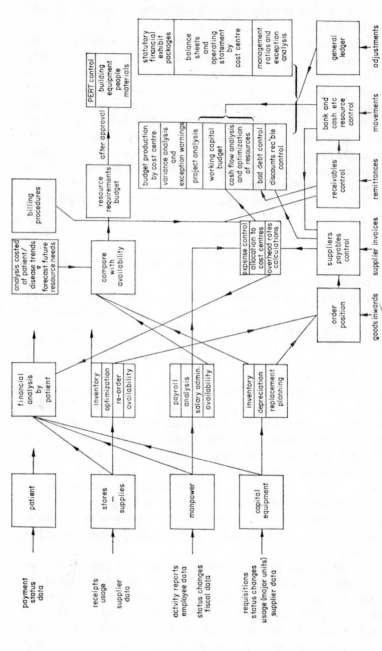

Fig. 4.2. Summarized information flow of Univac hospital financial information system.

staff or eliminates human responsibility and judgement. Even the purchase department, informed that the supply of a drug has dropped below re-order level, must ultimately decide if further purchase is required. Before doing this, they might well interrogate the section of the data bank on which are stored details of new drugs and, perhaps, a comparison of therapeutic efficiency, cost, and so on between these and existing preparations. This kind of information will help them judge whether or not to make a change.

Similarly, the fact that a doctor may use the computer to provide one or more tentative diagnoses based on correlation of certain facts he has provided plus information stored in the data bank, simply saves a search through reference books. It in no way absolves the doctor from exercising his intelligence, experience, and judgement, though this may, in turn, be supplemented by feeding extra inquiries or detail to the computer. The doctor therefore employs the computer, not to usurp his function, but to help him make sounder decisions. The manager of a business would use his computer in precisely the same way.

I think it is not stretching the analogy too far to equate the function of the hospital sister and the ward nurses with those of two levels of middle management within a business. For these nurses, one of the major benefits of the computer is its handling a load of clerical work and presenting automatically the information on which future action may be based. They thus have more time to devote to the care and comfort of the patient—and his relatives. Sympathetic human contact of this kind plays a major part in helping recovery.

In business, the patient is replaced by the customer and he, as we know, invariably responds well to personal attention. It is this element which is, in fact, often directly responsible for a customer's loyalty to a supplier of goods or services. Any difficulties he meets are straightened out at a personal level and this creates a bond of a kind that does not develop in dealing with a faceless organization which, the customer suspects, neither knows nor cares about his problems.

Whether one is willing to admit it or not, successful business always boils down in the end to successful contact with people. When, for example, I ask data-processing managers why they chose a particular make of computer, many tell me that, offered, say, three systems of approximately equal price and performance, they have decided finally on the basis of their satisfactory relationship with and esteem for the representative of one particular company. This company's men, they often add, took the trouble thoroughly to understand the problems and became personally involved, while the others did not seem nearly as closely interested. (In case I unwittingly mislead you, I should add that the favoured company is sometimes one computer manufacturer, sometimes another—not a single company.)

What kind of manager?

It has already become plain that the use of a real-time computer-based total-management system will result in fundamental changes in structure within the user organization. Traditional boundaries between departments will, of necessity, disappear or at the very least become far less rigid. The pattern of responsibility will also change.

Until now—though admittedly, not with the best results—it has been possible to install a reasonably efficient if not adventurous computer system in organizations where top management has been only marginally involved. Encouraging noises, the granting of sufficient funds, and a sympathetic attitude to the data-processing people and their problems has enabled top management to get by. The data-processing manager has been looked upon principally as a superior technician (and not infrequently is just this). Though he is respected for his special knowledge and ability, he is regarded as a subordinate and therefore plays no significant role in management of the organization as a whole.

A situation like this will not be tenable in the environment of a total-management system. Top management will no longer be able to duck responsibility for systems design. The data-processing manager will have to be given a much higher status because he will have to be fully accepted by the top management team with whom he will liaise very closely. Indeed, some people believe he must become a member of that team. He will therefore require far broader training in general management, a far deeper knowledge of the subject than he often possesses today.

Fundamental changes are already beginning to take place in some organizations. Among these is Tube Investments who, long users of batch-processing computers, are now working on a new system based on the use of a large IBM System/360 real-time system with remote terminals which will be used in the conversational mode.

The major objective of this system is to permit the use of considerably more sophisticated techniques for the planning and control of the production of straight steel tube. This demands a system that produces results immediately, says Mr R. G. Hitchcock, director of the Group's Computer Unit. Writing in *The Director* of August 1968, he goes on to say:

Fundamental to this new plan is the reallocation of senior management responsibility. From the beginning, Tube Investments has insisted that all except very small computers should be put in a service facility. That is, the large computers acquired by the group are available to the entire group and are controlled by a separate specialist unit who are responsible for preparing, scheduling and implementing job applications received from the senior management of companies within the group.

Until now in the Steel Tube Division, the computer unit has also been responsible for systems specification and design. That is, they were charged with the task of eliciting from management what its requirements were likely to be and translating these into a system whose refinements they decided upon for themselves, though in consultation, of course, with the users.

With the design of the new system, this pattern has been reversed and the management of the Steel Tube Division has accepted full responsibility for every detail of system specification. [My italics] The computer unit provides educational facilities in the form of general appreciation and more specialized courses; will advise on the technical aspects of the job and estimate costs. But it takes no responsibility for the type of management information produced or for any aspect other than implementation in computer terms itself. The implications of this are very important. In fact, the computer unit assumes its rightful place within the organization as a true service unit. . .

Mr Hitchcock goes on to explain that there are five somewhat similar companies in the Steel Tube Division participating in the exercise and it would therefore obviously be foolish to waste effort in catering for five different sets of requirements. Production programs are therefore being designed on a package basis. That is, they will provide a broad general structure within which variations can be introduced to suit the requirements of the individual companies.

To achieve this end, careful co-ordination and a degree of standardization of systems design requirements has been necessary. In 1966, three committees, finance, commercial and manufacturing, were set up to formulate policy on how the computer system was to be utilized. Top priority was given to the work of these committees of company directors, which were each chaired and co-ordinated by the appropriate divisional functional director. *No member was allowed to send a deputy to meetings, for example* [my italics].

One year later, three functionally similar steering committees, each chaired by a company director, were appointed. The job of these was to hammer out, in consultation with members of the computer unit, full details of the system. Plans were being made also, says Mr Hitchcock, to provide educational courses for middle management. These, a follow-up of earlier ones, would explain the shape and purpose of the new system.

One of the classic problems in almost any manufacturing concern is a clash of interest between production and sales. Typically, each believes that its function is an end in itself and of sufficient importance to demand the subordination of all other interests. Mr Hitchcock does not suggest that things in Tube Investments have ever reached this pass. But his article in *The Director* does outline a very important change whose implementation should do much, not only to get rid of long-standing barriers but to improve communications and general understanding in both areas.

After mentioning the importance of a computer system that produces results immediately, he names two principal areas where delay is a serious drawback: in answering inquiries about prices and delivery dates for orders; and in implementing alterations to existing production schedules. 'Much of the benefit of any control system must be lost without this kind of flexibility', he remarks.

We also believed it was highly desirable to have a system which would give to the sales department direct commercial responsibility for operation of the business. As things are now, the sales department operates in the traditional way. That is, it limits its responsibility to getting the orders and does not concern itself much either with the repercussions of its activities on the production department or the broad effects of changes such as the shifting of delivery requirements on profitability.

In the traditional set-up at present extant, it was impossible for the sales department to operate in any other way, Mr Hitchcock points out. Production and accounting functions exist in virtually watertight compartments and, even if it were considered desirable to break down the barriers, the data required for wider judgement could not be made available quickly enough in assimilable form.

With the new system, however, all the data that is needed by the sales department to make rational decisions within this wider context will become available on demand through on-line terminals. Through these, *it will be possible to get accurate estimates of feasible delivery dates in the light both of profit and production considerations* [my italics]. It will be possible, using the conversational mode, to extract from the computer data to show the effect of, say, altering existing production schedules to accommodate a new order; and to select from alternative process plans the one that will optimize profits while accommodating customer requirements. New orders will be fed in through the same source to trigger off a series of events that includes production of order acknowledgement documents and the updating of computer-held order files and so on. *For the first time it will therefore be feasible to give to the sales department direct responsibility for profitability in this area—and to pinpoint the effects of individual decisions* [my italics].

This shift is very fundamental in character. For, by making explicit the interaction between sales and production, it changes the nature of responsibility in both sectors. A production manager in this environment remains responsible for the efficient running of his department. He cannot, however, be blamed if, in doing this according to schedule, he fails to meet some impossible target set by sales; for sales, properly run, must have seen that such an objective was not viable. Equally, he cannot attribute inefficiency in his department to the extra planning required by the interpolation by the sales department of some new demand, for the computer will do the re-scheduling for him.

Sales, on the other hand, cannot plead that they could have achieved a given target if only production had been more co-operative. For they have at their disposal, on demand, data which indicates whether or not the production department can handle any given assignment; and exactly what this will entail in terms of delay on existing jobs and ultimate profitability. Both managers will undoubtedly benefit from having a facility which permits accurate anticipation of the results of making various kinds of change to an existing schedule.

(To avoid any question of ambiguity, I ought perhaps to point out that the comments in the last two paragraphs are my own, not those of Mr Hitchcock.)

For the following very specific ideas on systems philosophy, I am indebted to Mr J. V. Wilkinson* who formulated them after an extensive trip round computer installations in the USA. In addition to being one of the youngest 'old hands' in the computer industry, Mr Wilkinson has been responsible for the overall planning, design, and successful implementation (on a batch-processing computer) of one of the very few large-scale integrated production-control systems at present operating in this country (and which I describe in chapter 5 'The computer as a management tool).

Crystallizing the 'systems philosophy' of those organizations he visited, Mr Wilkinson begins by stating that computer systems will become increasingly representative of the entire business enterprise and that the data files, processing, and reporting must therefore match the needs and objectives of the user company. Increasing emphasis will be laid on computer planning, forecasting, and trend-analysis capabilities. 'Exception reporting' and the use of large data banks will reduce paperwork and lessen the need for people to make so-called 'decisions' which are really predeterminable responses to a variable but limited range of situations. This will require a computer management system which is able continuously to vary its response to highly variable demands made within a clearly defined environment.

In simulating a business, the computer management system must recognize the essential differences in the needs of different levels of management, says the report.

> For top executive management it must provide the information required for long range planning and annual forecasting such as market trends, volume capacities, resource requirements and cash flows.

> For middle managers it must provide budgetary and operational controls.

> Supervisors must be freed to supervise and time-wasting operations and paperwork reduced to a minimum.

Next comes an interesting and pertinent comment on how the computer system must be adapted to cater for the people who use it (not the reverse, you will note).

> Particularly in the supplies and production functions, the highly nervous and immediate reaction properties of on-line monitoring

* At that time, a director of C.A.V. Ltd.

equipment and real-time inquiry and processing computers must be damped down to meet the much slower responses of the people they serve. There is an analogy in an over-sensitive ammeter. It would frighten the average motorist out of his wits and has to be dampened to indicate only significant trends in the charge. Similarly, an inadequately cushioned computer monitoring or management system would simply set up supervisory stress and management tension instead of achieving its true objectives. These are (a) To provide an up-to-date commentary on those affairs of significance and (b) to indicate major fluctuation from a pre-determined and acceptable norm.

What, more specifically, are the requirements for such a system? Mr Wilkinson suggests that the following are basic if an 'adaptive' real-time management control system is to succeed:

(a) Management must understand, and be capable of stating in concrete and significant detail, the long- and medium-term plans of the organization. This applies specially to those responsible for designing the computer system, which will generally take at least three years to install and cannot be modified *ad lib* because top management cannot agree upon what its policy is or how this shall be implemented.

(b) Job planning, user requirements and modifications must be fully documented. Procedure manuals, key job breakdowns, and on-the-job instructions must be drawn up with equal care.

(c) Input, output, transmission, display, counting, and processing techniques and equipment must be increasingly automated in order to reduce the degree of system failure attributable to manual error.

(d) There must be clear, quantitative criteria provided for every job on which an evaluation is to be made, a control is to be exercised, or a decision either to change direction or enter a new routine is required.

(e) User departments must adhere to an agreed system.

I have selected these five points from Mr Wilkinson's list of twelve. The remainder are devoted to the more technical aspects, such as hardware design and capabilities and software requirements, of a real-time management control system. The outline he gives is, of course, aimed to cover the needs of one particular organization. But I think it is broad enough to sum up very neatly the kind of require-ments all managements are likely to have to meet.

What kind of man will be needed to meet successfully the challenges posed by designing and operating comprehensive systems like those I have outlined in the last few pages? It is almost certainly too early to draw his portrait in detail but a few broad features can be sketched in. It is clear, for example, that the top manager will have to be an incisive thinker; that he will need to have had a very thorough education in the techniques of management—and be prepared to continue this education throughout his working life. He will have to develop to the utmost an ability to plan on a long-term basis and I think he may well have to apply more self-discipline than is generally necessary today.

Well designed, a real-time management control system will provide top management with a more powerful and flexible instrument than has ever been at their disposal before. At the same time, this system could constitute a rope that will hang them very effectively if their ideas have been too circumscribed or their policy insufficiently formulated. Thus they will be faced with the paradox that although the system will, in many respects, uniquely equip them to 'play things off the cuff', it can also disastrously restrict them if they have made bad policy decisions at the systems-design stage.

This dual need for stricter discipline and wider perspective will apply right through management, down even to supervisor level. The kind of manager who delights in inventing and exploiting his own little quirks to circumvent the system simply will not be acceptable. The job to be done will require more imagination because the inter-relationship of the various functions will be more explicit. Action will therefore be seen in a new perspective: not as a local modification but as a tug on a net whose whole pattern can be thrown out of kilter by a new stress.

The essential dynamic nature of the organization—of any organization—will, I believe, become far more apparent. In practical terms this means that the manager who is today doing exactly what he did five or even two years ago will become a thing of the past. The system will permit of constant minor modification and managers will have to be alert to see when these changes are required. The analogy to the constant adaptation, the constant rejuvenation through physiological processes, the delicately-balanced inter-relationships that exist within the human body will not have escaped you.

This, then, is the kind of environment in which management will have to operate as the application of real-time computer systems enters into a new phase. Meantime, the moment has arrived to summarize what has been said in this chapter.

Summary

(a) Prophets have for long predicted that the use of computers would have a profound influence on the way organizations were managed. The fact that the evolution of really new ideas has been slow in no way invalidates this forecast.

(b) Change began with the realization that computers were potentially far more than speeded up accounting machines; and that their capacity to produce huge quantities of paperwork constituted a trap for unwary managements.

(c) With experience and the evolution of new techniques, such as management by exception, concepts of the computer's function changed. Managers began to see that its true value lay in its ability to produce precise, up-to-date and comprehensive information on what was actually going on in an organization, and to appreciate its use as a tool for further manipulation of this information to give insight into domestic and environmental trends.

(d) Early on, integrated data processing, a concept whose essential characteristic is the handling of an organization as a single entity rather than as a group of discrete operations, was seen to be highly desirable. But limitations in the computer and in human capacity made the implementation of this concept very difficult.

(e) Real-time computing—which offers far more powerful and versatile facilities than batch processing—has opened up further new horizons. Implementation of integrated data-processing systems, so comprehensive as to be described as 'total management systems', is now possible.

(f) Application of all these new ideas has been hampered to some extent by fear that the computer will devalue human beings. Experience, however, has revealed that the computer, properly used, enhances man's mental abilities in the same way that a machine extends the power of his muscles. Intelligence and judgement supplemented by the information that only a computer can provide are more effective than when used without this information.

(g) Fundamental changes in organizational structure and in the pattern of management responsibility are already coming into being as a direct result of real-time computing. Indications are that new types of manager will be required if total management systems are to be successfully formulated and exploited.

5. The computer as a management tool

In the preceding chapter, I have tried to paint you a very broad picture of the impact that computers have had—and will have—on our ideas about how organizations operate, how they can and should be managed, and what kind of managers will be required to operate computer-based systems in the future. Because my aim was to give you a vision (albeit, a realistic one, I believe) of what the managerial revolution is likely to mean, I ended on a high note by showing you the kind of results we are justified in expecting when real-time computing power is more fully exploited.

In this chapter, I shall go far more specifically into the ways in which you, as a manager, can use computers to increase the profitability of your organization. But as this is intended to be a very practical exposition, I must begin by bringing you down to earth with a bump.

One point I stressed rather strongly in chapter 4 is that the successful use of computers in business demands some very fundamental re-thinking. I emphasized this because I believe that one of the most dangerous traps that awaits the intending computer user is the belief that the principal value of a computer lies in its ability merely to speed up existing routines.

At the same time, I should be less than fair to you if I pretended that it is impossible to make a computer profitable by using it simply as a rather sophisticated accounting machine. I think cases of success in this area are fairly rare and likely to become rarer; and that they happen only when the managers concerned are fully aware of what they are doing and why they are doing it. One possibility of success in this limited way is for the organization whose principal task is in processing a very large volume of clerical work. Another is where a management that is inexperienced with computers uses a small system in this limited way to get its feet wet and intends to enlarge its horizons, in terms both of hardware and systems design, when it has gained more understanding of how computers work.

Let us then begin by considering how computers can profitably be used in this very restricted way. One of the major pitfalls to guard against is using the computer simply to perpetuate a system that should have been scrapped. There have been some glaring examples of this. In the June 1965 issue of *The Manager* (now defunct), Pearce Wright, now scientific correspondent of *The Times*, and I said in a jointly written article:

> Real failure [of a computer project] can surely only be attributed to those systems which show no signs of ever being able to earn their keep or which are used primarily to speed up procedures themselves redundant or anachronistic. In some trades, particularly hardware, for example, it is customary to assess current prices arising from changing discounts, etc., by adding or subtracting a series of percentages applied to a long-extinct basic price—and a computer is used to process and print out this whole series of redundant calculations. Payrolls in this country often involve equally wasteful practices. In the Liverpool Docks no less than 1,000 different ways are used to calculate wages because of the methods negotiated with the unions concerned and a computer is used to do all these calculations.
>
> While it would be unfair and unrealistic to underestimate the difficulties involved in rationalizing these applications, the fact remains that in these instances the computer is merely being used to perpetuate a basically inefficient system and can therefore in no circumstances be regarded as an instrument for progress.

You may wonder why I have chosen to quote an article written in 1965. My reason is simply that one of the sadder features of the computer scene is the inability of many organizations to take advantage of others' experience. Though the users mentioned in this article may well have changed their systems by now, the chances are that many others are preparing to make the same kind of mistakes. I therefore make no apology for trying to make sure you are not included among these unhappy organizations.

You should, however, beware of assuming that your existing systems are *necessarily* poor. There is no earthly point in turning a good system upside down just for the sake of change.

Sometimes all that is wrong with an existing accounting system, for example, is that it is too slow or the work volume is too large to allow the organization to operate efficiently. Though some change and some rationalization will probably be needed to utilize a computer efficiently, the machine will be valuable principally because of its speed, which facilitates the faster flow of money into the company. This can sometimes make the difference between profit and break-even or loss, as is illustrated by a talk I had recently with the chief accountant of a large, successful and diversified group.

This group is made up of a number of small companies whose activities are widely assorted and most of which were more or less going concerns at the time of acquisition by the group. In deciding to use a computer for the first time, the group felt it wisest to concentrate initially on areas which, though elementary as applications go, would yield a good return. The first job, which has involved the purchase of a basic Univac 9200 system at a total capital cost of around £32,000, is hire-purchase accounting. Here is what the group accountant told me about this operation:

> When we bought this hire purchase company we knew it had an unhealthily large number of bad debts. But when we had an opportunity to probe more deeply into the accounts, we found the situation was not nearly so bad as it had seemed. In fact, we were later able to obtain payment on a sizable proportion of the debts that the previous management had more or less written off.

> All that had happened was that the accounting procedures were inadequate to handle the work. They never got around to sending reminders to debtors. In my experience, the vast majority of people do pay their debts if only you remind them often enough.

At the time he told me this, the first trial computer run was in progress. The system, he told me, would handle day-to-day accounting on traditional lines, but once a week there would be a run during which the computer punched out cards (there were no magnetic tapes) containing details of all overdue payments. After being put through an electro-mechanical sorter, they would be fed back to the computer which would automatically print appropriate details into pre-printed reminder letters.

A week's delay in payment would trigger off a mild letter; a fortnight's delay, a somewhat sharper one. A delay of three weeks would cause the computer to produce a list which, handed to managers, would provide a basis for personal decision on exactly what further action should be taken in each case. (Note this point well. The company did not intend to endanger customer relations by sending off final notices via the computer without a prior assessment by managers of the pros and cons of individual cases.)

It is highly significant that, with applications confined initially at least to these very basic routines, the computer was expected to repay its capital cost completely within a year or so of installation—an extremely short period by any standards.

Similarly, it was a heavy load of clerical work which resulted in slowing down the flow of incoming cash that originally prompted Masius Wynne-Williams, one of Britain's largest advertising agencies, to install an in-house computer. (It was, in fact, the first UK agency to do this.) At that time, work was growing in volume so fast that the punched card installation used for accounting could not keep up. One of the most serious delays was in the production of monthly statements to clients. Many of the media in which clients' advertisements are placed demand payment by the fifteenth day of the month after which the advertisement appears. The agency's delays in invoicing resulted, in effect, in its lending money interest-free while paying for overdraft facilities at its own bank.

After the computer system had begun, statements were in clients' hands by the second day of the month. Indications were that savings in bank interest and clerical staff salaries alone would pay the computer's rental. This meant that any other benefits realized as a result of computerizing other jobs would rank as bonuses.

Two years after the computer had first come into action, the agency added magnetic tapes to the initial configuration. In spite of having acquired five major new accounts during this interim period, no extra clerical staff were needed and in some departments it had been possible actually to reduce numbers.

In the case of Masius Wynne-Williams, money was being spent in paying for over-drafts which became unnecessary when machinery was put into motion to recover cash more quickly from clients. In the previous example, money may also have been spent needlessly in this way. Even worse, a high proportion of the company's cash was tied up in goods supplied to customers who, by defaulting on hire-purchase payments, yielded no return on investment.

In neither of these cases did successful computerization depend upon fundamental re-thinking of the company's mode of operation. The original problems that the computers solved arose, not from

G

using systems that were basically ill-designed or obsolescent, but as a result of the work load's having grown too heavy.

One important characteristic both applications have in common is that the transfer of routines onto the computer with a minimum of modification had the direct effect of speeding the flow of cash into the organization. To find out whether or not the computer was likely to pay when used in this rather elementary way (initially, at least) therefore involved no very complicated calculation on the part of management. Had either company decided to transfer more or less *in toto* to a computer clerical tasks that did not impinge so directly on its finances, both stories might have been very different.

Having cited these cases against my main argument, I must re-terate that they are comparatively rare. Usually it is necessary to make a very fundamental reappraisal of management aims and methods before it is possible to decide whether or not it is feasible to install a computer. I shall not describe here the kind of work that is involved in this appraisal, as I have covered this thoroughly in chapter 7 'Choosing and installing a computer'. My present task is to outline some of the specific areas in which a computer, used in-telligently, may help to increase the profitability of a business. This may be done either by allowing the application of improved con-ventional methods or permitting the use of new techniques that have been evolved since computers became available.

Stock control

A computer, as we have seen, can do much to help the organization that has too much money owing to it because of its inability to keep track of outstanding accounts and chase these up. It can also aid the management of businesses who suffer from a rather similar problem that exists when too much cash is tied up in stocks—of raw materials, say. Many companies get into difficulties because no real control is kept over stocks and, in consequence, the stores are bulging with materials which, in extreme cases, are sufficient in quantity to last for half a century or more at the current rate of usage.

These stores take up space which might otherwise be used to better advantage. The money invested in them is irretrievably tied up and is earning nothing. Invested in new plant, for example, it could be working far more profitably. Even if the stores in question can theoretically be used in the foreseeable future, they may well deterio-rate and lose part of their value or have to be written off completely.

Wastage is encouraged anyhow when unnecessarily large quantities of stores are held in stock, as their value is not so apparent to those who use them and they are therefore handled carelessly.

Where the stock-keeping system is slack, pilferage is usually rife. (Though you may believe petty theft occurs only where stores are obviously attractive, you should remember that almost anything is saleable and therefore attractive to somebody.) All these things apply equally whether the stocks in question are of raw materials or finished goods.

Good control systems are therefore essential for profitability. At the elementary level, this control boils down to a well designed accounting system that keeps careful track of all movements of stock in and out of your stores and sees that the record is always up-to-date. Such a system not only guards against waste and pilferage, but enables managers to know precisely what supplies are actually (as distinct from theoretically) available at any given time. This may be very important to the sales side of the business as well as to the production manager. It permits the rationalization of purchasing, too.

One of the valuable by-products of a good stock-accounting system is that it allows the use of continual checks. These, done on a rota basis, ensure that physical stocks correspond to the figures on the record sheets. Known as 'perpetual inventory', this method replaces the laborious old-fashioned system of stopping everything from time to time while inventory is taken. Though this may sound a minor point, it is often of considerable importance. One hardware wholesaler who instituted a tight stock-control system based on the use of a computer was able to abolish the inventory check that had previously closed the warehouse for a fortnight each year. This closure had considerably harmed the business (hardware is highly competitive, and often an edge over rivals is maintained only by providing a superior service). Aside from this, it infuriated the company's salesmen who resented being dragged into what they, not unreasonably, considered the unsuitable task of helping out the warehouse staff at inventory-taking time.

Even at this elementary level, stock control is a good application for computerization when the items are many in number and/or turn over quickly. Where the company concerned is a manufacturer, stock control is generally considered as part of a production-control system which itself is applied through an in-house computer. In other kinds of enterprise, for example a wholesale warehouse, stock control is often integrated with sales and may be done by the company's own computer or farmed out to a service bureau (see chapter 6).

I have called this type of stock control 'elementary' to distinguish it from the type that uses special techniques to determine economic stock levels and to which I will return later. In fact, when allied with the use of a computer, stock control can be quite a sophisticated operation. You will recollect that I mentioned in an earlier chapter how the computer can be used to warn management when a predetermined re-order level has been reached. The system can also, of course, be designed to present reports to management on any other subject that may be critical—excess stocks or details of overdue orders on suppliers, for example.

In large and scattered enterprises, stock-control systems may be operated through on-line terminals situated at a number of warehouses and linked to a central computer installation. Westinghouse in the USA, for example, maintain, on random-access files, complete records of all stocks in warehouses scattered all over the country. Customer orders are entered through remote terminals; the computer interrogates its records to find out whether the required items are at the warehouse geographically nearest to this customer. If not, it extends the search in a widening radius until it finds what it has been asked for. It then automatically prints out at the appropriate warehouse the documents that authorize dispatch to the customer. As it does this, it also updates its stock files.

Aside from actually maintaining checks on stocks, either in the more modest way I have described earlier or by the more ambitious type of system used by Westinghouse, the computer can be used to present many reports that are of value to buyers and warehouse managers. Typical information produced in this way includes movements of the various items compared with figures in a corresponding period the previous year or with those of the previous month. This, of course, reveals trends. When these movements relate to sales of the items concerned, the computer, by indicating profit margins, can also show management how desirable these trends may be. The computer may also, perhaps, be programmed to produce exception reports on items that are very slow- or fast-moving. These are only a few of the ways in which it can be employed to monitor, on behalf of management, situations which that same management has decided merit their attention.

Analysis of the pattern of demand, as shown by records of stock movements, can be highly informative—and frequently surprising—and may well be the basis of fundamental changes in policy.

One supermarket, for example, who used a computer system to control and analyse issues to branches, discovered that its 'loss leaders' (items sold at break-even prices or even at a small loss to attract customers into the shop where they would purchase other, more profitable, lines) were better losers than leaders. Canny housewives in some of the poorer areas bought large quantities of loss leaders and left the shops with nothing else in their baskets! Thus, while sales of loss leaders were spectacular in these areas, overall sales, on which the profits of the business depended, remained static. It was only the speed and capacity of a computer system that revealed facts like these.

Information gained from exhaustive analysis of sales of fashion items can also be very enlightening—provided, of course, enough of the right kind of data is put into the system. Dissections like this have revealed, for instance, that large-size shoes sell faster than the smaller sizes in some parts of the country; or that the lacy black slips that London typists buy in hundreds are left on the shelves in more conservative districts.

Positive facts like this can be used by management as a basis for a more profitable manufacturing and distribution policy. This may have a double effect on profits as manufacture or purchase can be rationalized, thus reducing wastage; and shops can be supplied only with goods that sell well and with as much as they can sell.

Although the pros and cons of computer usage in general are discussed fully in chapter 7 'Choosing and installing a computer', this seems an apposite point to insert a caution about computerization of stock control.

Just as it is foolish to computerize a basically inefficient accounting system, it is asking for trouble to mechanize stockkeeping when the inventory is in a mess. It is essential, therefore, before embarking on computerization, to purge the inventory of duplication, redundancy, and obsolescence. These factors are often staggeringly high, particularly in an old-established business or one that operates in a fast-changing environment. In fact, it sometimes happens that the result of such a purging exercise reveals that a computer is not required!

So far we have talked about stock control through the keeping and analysis of records. This, however, is only half the story. If stocks are to be managed in a really profitable way, it is desirable to be able to establish a realistic minimum quantity so that no surplus of any item need be held on inventory. The object is to invest no more than is strictly necessary either in the stock itself or in the space it occupies; and, at the same time, virtually to ensure an ability to meet any normal demand within an acceptable time. These considerations apply equally to raw materials for use in manufacturing, to mobile plant for hire, or to finished goods for sale to customers.

What these quantities are will, of course, vary widely from one item to another in the same business as well as between one business and another. Factors to be considered in assessing economic level versus service requirement include availability from suppliers, price fluctuations, speed of turnover, pattern of demand, shelf life, discounts available on bulk purchase, and so on. The definition of 'acceptable time' is also, of course, subject to wide variation. For a wholesaler of pharmaceutical products, it may be measured in hours; for a manufacturer of steel products, in months.

I hope that even this very sketchy outline of the problem will indicate that the calculations required to provide a realistic assessment of economic inventory level, even for one item, are complex. When these calculations have to be applied to hundreds or even thousands of items, the volume of work is so great as to demand the use of a computer.

The following description of how a computer can be used to tackle this problem for a distributor is derived from a manual on the IBM package program known as Wholesale IMPACT. This has already been in use for some years and, say IBM, has abundantly proved its value. (I should, perhaps, remind you that a package program is designed for general use and, though largely ready-made, also demands some programming effort on the part of the user.)

To forecast demand—a basic requirement—IMPACT uses a simple yet effective mathematical technique known as exponential smoothing. What this does is to apply a series of calculations to historical information about demand, placing more weight on recent history than on older data. These calculations, by recognizing such factors as seasonal demand and compensating for minor fluctuations, reduce the data to a coherent pattern. This pattern is then projected to predict future demand. You may recognize here a refinement of the manual method your wife applies in deciding how much tea to buy for next week.

No forecast is, of course, entirely error-free, so no system is of practical value unless it provides for the inclusion of reserve stocks to meet emergencies that arise as the result of inaccuracy. The

IMPACT program determines what size these stocks should be by calculating—also by exponential smoothing—the size of the forecast error and allocating buffer stocks in proportion to this. To protect against such factors as clerical error and sudden large changes in demand pattern, it incorporates tests which detect large deviations from forecast demand. The program also detects forecast figures that are consistently too high or too low.

An aggressive sales manager would, of course, like to satisfy every customer order on demand. But to do this he might well have to put the company out of business because it would have to hold an un-economically large inventory. He must therefore resign himself to reconciling two conflicting factors—100 per cent service to customers and low inventory cost—using these to derive a figure that will allow him to provide what he considers an acceptable level of service, say 90 per cent, and the accountant to keep costs under control.

The IMPACT program includes routines that help the manager make a right decision in advance by producing a graph of service versus inventory.

Two types of order strategy, and several variants of each of these, are catered for. Independent strategy is based on the assumption that you order goods regardless of whether or not you purchase other items from the same supplier; joint strategy applies where economical considerations dictate the pattern of ordering from the supplier so as to take advantage of, for example, special terms for bulk purchase or faster delivery by making up a complete van-load.

When stocks drop to a point where it will not be possible to maintain the predetermined level of service without replenishment, the IMPACT program generates a report. In compiling this, it takes into account factors such as forecast demand and forecast error, lead time, and variability in lead time. The order quantity is dependent upon the order strategy and represents the basic economic minimum in the circumstances.

The program permits changes in rules and objectives (an increase in the level of service required, for example); and the information it produces helps management evaluate the effectiveness of the inventory management system.

What benefits can you hope to reap from a system like this in addition to reduced inventory cost? Chances are that you will be able to improve the level of service and offer a more stable service to your customers. Buyers are relieved from making routine decisions about purchasing matters. Management control is improved because the system consistently applies stated rules and objectives. The system also creates a foundation for other profitable applications such as speeding the flow of goods from suppliers by automatically generating orders.

Costing

How can you sell your products profitably if you have no accurate gauge of what it costs you to make or provide them? You can, of course, name prices slightly below those of your nearest competitor and hope you will make up the difference by stepping up your sales. But what will it cost you to increase your sales? And your competitor may run his operation in a way entirely different from yours. While he is making a reasonable profit, you may break even, or sell at a loss.

You may, on the other hand, prefer to play safe and price your goods a little higher than those of your competitors. This will probably put you at a disadvantage in a competitive market unless your products are so clearly superior to theirs or so much more effectively marketed that the public does not object. Even this, however, does not guarantee that your price is sufficient to give you a realistic return on your capital investment in men, machines, and materials.

It is a fallacy also to believe that, when you make or sell a spectrum of products, the one that sells best is necessarily the most profitable. Investigations by management consultants in this field have unearthed some bizarre facts. Quite often a product that a client regards as his most valuable because its sales are biggest is in fact the company's least profitable line. This being so, the higher the sales, the smaller the profits. Any profit the company makes comes from sources which the management probably regards as quite subsidiary and which therefore attracts but small notice from the sales manager.

It is possible, of course, that you have by accident selected a realistic price range. But this can hardly be called good management. While conditions are favourable you make an acceptable profit. But what will your strategy be when the tide turns against you? The best you can do is guess, as you have little solid information on costs. An all-round price reduction seems a good idea. But is it? Your sales have already dropped and you do not know the size of your profit margin so you cannot accurately forecast how this move will affect you.

Success in business today seldom comes for long to the amateur.

It is no coincidence that many professional businessmen who install a computer name costing as one of the earliest applications.

To fulfil its function properly—that is, to be realistic, comprehensive, and fully informative—a costing system must be designed by a professional cost accountant. For the system must not only take into account every last item concerned in the manufacture, marketing, and distribution of the products made and/or sold by the organization but must provide machinery, first for collecting this detail and then manipulating it in a way that produces meaningful management information.

This is no job for an amateur—or even for an accountant who has not specialized in costing. A poor costing system is as dangerous as none at all, because it may give management a false sense of security.

A realistic costing system must provide for continual comparison of actual with estimated costs. It is not enough to have discovered what the expected cost of making a certain product is. While these figures may be as accurate as it is possible to make them, they must of necessity be based on averages and cannot, therefore, take account of such day-to-day events as fluctuations in the cost of raw materials, machine faults or breakdowns, or an unusual amount of absenteeism. It is therefore vitally important to collect information on actual costs and to compare these with standard or estimated costs. Only this kind of system will yield significant information to management.

Continued discrepancy between standard or estimated and actual costs, for example, is a warning to management that the former are unrealistic. Occasional discrepancy may or may not be significant; but at least management, given the figures, are in a position to exercise judgement. Cost information, presented regularly and punctually to management, enables them to keep close tabs on this aspect of all the organization's operations and places them in a position to apply corrective measures as soon as undesirable results become manifest.

Costs are grouped together under 'cost centres' which relate directly either to the pattern of the company's operations or of management responsibility. This grouping is essential, for it permits meaningful analysis of certain defined aspects of the company's activities. Manufacturing cost centres, for example, might relate to groups of machine tools or some stage of manufacture.

Labour costs will often have to be split under a number of cost centres. A maintenance engineer, for example, may work during the course of one day in several locations each of which is a different cost centre and each of which should pay for the amount of time he spends there.

Normally, budgeting is mentioned by managers in the same breath as costing because the two functions are so closely related. In its simplest form, budgeting involves predetermination of the sums of money to be allocated to various departments. These totals are then sub-divided, sometimes by periods of time, sometimes by type of operation. A marketing manager's budget, for example, might be split between sales promotion, exhibitions, advertising, public relations, and so on, while that of a plant manager might cover raw materials, fabrication, scrap, inspection, and maintenance.

If a budget is to be used as an effective management tool it must be watched as closely as the costs. It is therefore customary to include budgeted versus actual figures in reports, on both a month by month and a cumulative basis. Many managements also find it useful to compare current figures with those relating to the same period the previous year. Thus they can keep a constant eye on how forecast figures tally with results and how much real progress is being made.

Since this is not a textbook on management, I shall not go any deeper into the subject of budgeting or costing. I think that what I have said will make it clear to you that costing and budgeting, except in their most rudimentary forms, involve the collection and analysis of a great deal of detailed information.

The collection alone of costing data is fairly costly. Thus, though a fairly simple costing system for a small organization may satisfactorily be applied by using keyboard accounting machines or a punched-card installation, these methods are seldom adequate for an operation that is widespread and complex. It is here that the computer comes into its own, for it can handle a wide range of exhaustive analyses and thus helps to justify the cost of data collection—provided, of course, that management usefully employs the information produced by these dissections!

One of the useful functions of a computer is to permit the employment of exception-reporting techniques. You as a manager are not particularly interested in any plan that moves along predestined lines; but you are concerned in any major deviations from the plan. Thus reports may be rendered that show only those costs that deviated by a predetermined percentage from the budgeted figures. In this way you eliminate a lot of reading and get a report whose existence immediately emphasizes the need for attention.

Where the basic data used in costing and budgeting is voluminous and detailed, it can involve shop floor workers in a great deal of clerical labour. Often the workers concerned are basically unsuited, either by education or by inclination, for tasks like these with the result either that the figures are incomplete or inaccurate or both, or that a considerable body of extra people have to be employed to do nothing else.

In cases like this, it may be well worth while to install a data-collection system which provides a method of handling most of this work automatically. Typically, as much of the basic data as possible is pre-punched into cards, leaving the shop floor workers only to enter a few variables via a keyboard or some other device. I have described data-collection systems in some detail in chapter 6 'The computer on the factory floor'. Meanwhile, I shall content myself with telling you that they may be used independently (off-line) or connected directly to a central computer (on-line) as needs dictate.

Budget planning

Although the application of a budget plan is relatively simple, at least in broad outline, the evolution of the plan itself is a complex exercise. For, if the budget is to be realistic, it must be based upon careful examination of information revealed by the analysis of historical data and the consideration of external factors such as the position of the company vis-à-vis the known plans of competitors, the possibility of government action, the economic environment in general, and so on.

A computer can be a very valuable aid to management in budget planning since it can be used, not only for fairly simple jobs like the extrapolation of existing figures to reveal trends but for the far more complex task of manipulating a variety of factors to determine the effect on the others when one or more of these is changed. I have dealt with this kind of planning in more detail under the heading 'Business planning' later in this chapter.

Marketing and sales management

Few businessmen believe today that the world will come knocking at their doors, even if they have built the best mousetrap ever. If a company is rich or clever, or both, it will begin by finding out whether its intended customers raise any objections to the design, proposed price, or any other feature of the prototype mousetrap. If

objections are voiced and seem valid, the company will try to eliminate their cause before going into production. If it cannot resolve the
difficulties or if the reaction of prospective customers to the prototype is too discouraging, it will probably abandon the idea altogether,
thus saving itself a great deal of loss in money—and perhaps also in
reputation. (It is said that three out of four new products are stillborn
today as a result of this kind of preliminary research.)

Reassured that the product has a good chance of acceptance, the
manufacturer goes into production and marketing. He takes his
mousetrap into the market place, where he shouts about its merits
until he is hoarse, waving it invitingly under the noses of those whom
his research has suggested are mouse-infested.

Market research today is such a scientific job that it is generally
handled by specialist organizations. It is therefore sufficient for me
to remark here that it is doubtful whether it could be carried out on
the scale it is, with such sophistication or at realistic cost and speed,
if computers were not used to process the data collected by the
researchers.

Computers are also beginning to be used by advertising agencies
to help them judge where (to return to my original product) to find
the greatest body of mouse-infested customers. Data relating to such
points as the readership of various publications—number of readers,
type, interests, etc.—is fed to a computer along with characteristics
of the product which can use this as a basis for suggesting where press
advertisements are likely to pull best. Similar but more complex
applications involving, among other things, the use of information
on the reactions of TV audiences (information itself processed by a
computer) can be used to help assess the likelihood of profit through
television advertising; and to decide how a TV advertising budget
can most usefully be deployed. Though human judgement must, as
always, govern the ultimate decisions, the computer's capacity for
exhaustive review and analysis of a mass of background data provides
information which helps to remove at least some of the hazards from
marketing.

I have already described in some detail how a computer can be
used to provide much valuable information on sales and thereby
help you formulate a marketing strategy. I now want to mention
some other ways in which you can employ electronic data processing
to aid you in the marketing area.

One of the things it would be very useful to know, for example, is
why some customers do not buy your goods. (Perhaps you have your

suspicions: but these are no substitute for information based on systematic analysis.) You also, as an alert sales manager, want to keep tabs on individual salesmen's performance. You want to know which products are going well and which are lagging, and eventually you must decide whether these results are due to one product's being more acceptable than others or simply requiring less selling effort and ability. You want to know, too, whether your salesmen are abusing their freedom to negotiate prices.

All this information, and more, can be derived from salesmen's report forms, provided they are carefully designed. As no salesman is ever willing to do more than an absolute minimum of paperwork, you must be cunning in this design work. Your objects are: first, to get all the data you want; second, to devise a system which will allow salesmen to provide it more or less painlessly; third, to render the data in a form which can easily be punched into cards or some other input medium.

How about customers' objections to your product? If your sales force has been properly trained, its members are already aware of the kind of objections likely to be raised (and, of course, told how to counter these). It should therefore be quite easy for you to list these on salesmen's report forms and require that each man, on failing to close a sale, should tick one or the other; if failure has occurred for some other reason, he should name this concisely in a space provided for the purpose.

I do not want to go too deeply into the question of form design. It is worth mentioning, however, that the use of the yes/no approach (i.e., tick where appropriate rather than write words) saves writing and encourages busy people to provide all the detail you need. And the use of codes (for example, customer reasons for rejection could be numbered, as could the salesman, his territory, type of customer, etc.) speeds and facilitates input-data punching. I can foresee your asking yourself how on earth one could pre-code a customer objection not listed on the form but supplied through the salesman. Perhaps the simplest way to deal with this would be to allocate a code meaning 'other objections' which could be used for punching and computer analysis purposes. Any forms marked in this way could then be returned to you for scrutiny after data preparation had been completed.

Information of great value to the factory can be gained by analysis of documents completed during after-sales service. Breakdowns like these can reveal, for example, that certain parts have too short a life;

that the design of a machine encourages mis-use (and subsequent damage) by customers; that the controls are confusing, the instruction booklet inadequate or misleading, or the machine unnecessarily dangerous in use. All such information, when heeded and acted upon, helps the manufacturer to improve the design of the product and therefore to give greater customer satisfaction. It can also, of course, substantially reduce your after-sales service costs and rationalize the spares inventory.

I hope that even this incomplete review of the subject may stimulate you to think of the many ways in which your organization could profitably employ a computer as a sales and marketing aid. Generally speaking, the limitations lie not in the capacity of the computers in use today but in the ideas of those who install them. I shall therefore shamelessly seize the opportunity to say, once again, that to employ a computer simply to carry out the most elementary type of document-processing and data-analysis is shamefully to under-use a potentially valuable management tool.

Production planning and control

You will remember that in chapter 4 I mentioned how the control of factory production has, almost since the beginning, been seen as a particularly promising application for computerization. I also pointed out that experience has proved that the design and implementation of such systems is a far harder task than had originally been anticipated. Some of these difficulties were a direct result of the inherent limitations of early computers. Far more, however, arose from problems that are human in origin, to which I shall return shortly.

Nevertheless, interest remains keen. 'A recent survey suggests that in the future the use of computers in the production and inventory control area will rival their present usage in accountancy', wrote Mr Peter F. Frost in a foreword to a one-day symposium on Production Control held in mid-1967 by The British Computer Society (and which nearly 1,000 people attended). Speaking on the same occasion, Mr J. D. Humphries of the National Computing Centre stated that approximately half the computers now being sold have production control quoted as one of the primary applications.

More and more of these are for companies who cannot justify a computer on the traditional bases of saving staff and increasing speed. They are staking their future on the intangible benefits of better control offered by the computer. This change of emphasis towards the smaller companies is reflected in a change of pace of development. The compact environment and the economic pressures produce an atmosphere of 'get on or go bust'.

Early prophecies, then, have proved correct and production control and planning will eventually be one of the most rewarding of computer applications. Meantime, 'the degree of success achieved has varied dramatically', Mr Humphries stated.

One of the major problems has always been—and continues to be —the difficulty of obtaining a true picture of what actually (as opposed to theoretically) happens in a factory that is a going concern. Some organizations have fallen by the wayside because they were naive enough to believe that factory personnel actually slavishly followed the procedure manuals—which might well be hopelessly obsolescent or unrealistic to begin with. Some under-estimated the importance of thorough systems analysis or failed to do the job thoroughly. As a result of either of these situations, the resultant computer systems bore little or no resemblance to the true functions or requirements of the factory whose production they attempted to control. Others failed because they lacked the considerable skill required to think out a complex control system fully and translate the organization's requirements into workable computer systems. In consequence, results were usually worse than those achieved with far less sophisticated methods.

How can these gaping pitfalls be avoided? Mr Humphries of the National Computing Centre (which is particularly geared to helping the small and medium-sized business) said, 'It has been possible to suggest now a sequence of development most likely to bring success'. The stages, he said, were as follows:

(a) An educational programme to create the right environment. Too many organizations, he believes, go into this field knowing nothing of what they are in for.

(b) The establishment of a data-processing system to get the facts and figures sorted. When this is running smoothly, it can be developed into a management information system from which the data can be obtained necessary to design self-optimizing systems. Consideration of the variations in resources and time scales involved in many case-studies suggests that the efficiency of the utilization of resources is very poor. (Here is our old enemy, lack of ambition and enterprise in the application of a computer rearing its ugly head!)

Listing the more common problems encountered in setting up a production control system, Mr Humphries named:

(a) the limits of comprehension of personnel not adequately educated in the detail of the problem;
(b) basic lack of understanding of the theoretical problems of production control;
(c) limits on accuracy of communication within an organization;
(d) creating and maintaining the basic master data for the system.

The National Computing Centre, he added, is carrying out work in all of these problem areas.

It is not my intention, in citing all these problems, to depress you or discourage you from attempting to institute your own production-control and planning system. I feel, however, that in view of the increasing popularity of this application I must at least give you some indication that the way is hard.

The rewards are commensurately great. Often there is a big reduction in stock holdings. Reduction of work in progress is often up to 50 per cent, Mr Humphries asserted. Output may rise by 10 to 50 per cent using the same resources as were formerly available. Often there is an improvement in general morale, because people are aware of what is going on and where they are going.

What, exactly, are the objectives of a production planning and control system? The objective of a manufacturing organization as a whole is to manage materials, machines, manpower, and money in such a way as to maximize profit. This, in turn, involves providing ordered goods at promised dates, providing them at a realistic price, and manufacturing at a cost which is smaller by an acceptable margin than that at which the goods are sold.

These objectives cannot be achieved without planning. This is required at two levels. In the long term, planning involves the formulation of strategies, a subject about which I have something to say in a later section of this chapter 'Business planning'. In the shorter term (the area with which we are concerned just now), planning demands the formulation of a method of working that will enable the factory to fulfil all the requirements made of it, as dictated by orders on hand, the quantities of finished products to be held in stock or other factors decided upon by the management.

A system designed fully to control a factory in such a way that it can carry out this plan must provide for all or most of the following:

(*a*) Recording and acknowledgement of customer orders
(*b*) Production of estimates of cost and/or delivery date if these are normally expected or provided
(*c*) Scheduling of orders on hand so that requirements as to delivery dates, quantities, and so on can be met. This implies the maintenance of full records of the present and future availability and commitment of resources—men, materials, machines, and money. Re-scheduling must also be possible so that new priorities, cancellations, and other *ad hoc* requirements can be coped with.
(*d*) Control over the purchase and usage of raw materials and bought-out components
(*e*) Control over every stage of manufacture from the issue of drawings and allocation of raw materials or components right through to final inspection. This implies also control of the design and specification of components used in manufacture.
(*f*) The issue of works orders, details of individual operations, and other documents required during manufacture, both as originals, or as amendments to originals if required.
(*g*) Complete control over costing
(*h*) Control over stocks of finished goods, and spares where applicable
(*i*) The issue of delivery notes and possibly also of invoices or other accounting documents
(*j*) Procedures for the collection and processing of all relevant information (e.g., on costs, times, job progress) generated during any stage of manufacture so that records may be immediately updated and frequent management reports produced.

You will notice that the last of these requirements adds a final feature to the system—a method that will accurately indicate to the management how well the short-term (and possibly also the longer-term) plan is being implemented. This is a very important proviso, for without it there would be no method of reconciling theory with practice and no reliable information on which to base any corrective action that may become necessary.

Obviously the precise requirements of any production-planning and -control system will also vary considerably from one organization to another, as dictated by such factors as whether the factory is a jobbing shop or operates on batch- or continuous-production lines. Nevertheless, the broad principles do not change.

H

It will, I think, be apparent from the foregoing list of requirements why it is not easy to design a good system; and why integration is so natural and so desirable. All the requirements are interrelated, so that obviously it makes sense to use the same basic data to do as much work—i.e., produce as many documents, update as many files —as possible.

How intimate these interrelationships are is best demonstrated by citing a real-life example of an integrated production-planning and -control system. This was designed for C.A.V. Ltd of London, manufacturers of a wide range of diesel and electrical equipment for commercial vehicles, by its own staff and had, at the time I investigated it, been operating with considerable success for over three years. The following material is drawn from an article I wrote for the journal *Data Systems* and which was published in September 1967.

Expressed in its broadest and most simplified form, the C.A.V. manufacturing cycle, which occupies three months, can be outlined as follows:

First, the sales plan is drawn up. This is a collection of orders which the planning department schedules according to delivery or other requirements. This plan is then 'exploded', using a computer master record, into its basic elements—all the sub-assemblies, components, bought-out parts and materials required to complete the products listed in the sales plan. (More of this master record later.)

Orders for these components are then allocated to the company's several factories and to the purchasing and sub-contracting departments, as demanded by current practice and/or shop-floor capacity and loading. As components are manufactured or received from outside sources, they are sent to a transit store to await calls from assembly departments in any of the factories. After final assembly, products are delivered to a warehouse for despatch to customers or to internal departments, as determined by the sales plan.

Requirements for the integrated control system were, in brief, to accomplish the following:

(*a*) Exercise complete control over components so that: standardization was enforced—i.e., where possible the same part was used on a number of products; no confusion could arise when modifications were made or new components introduced; and that no obsolescent components continued in use. This control covered items made by C.A.V., sub-contracted, and bought-out.

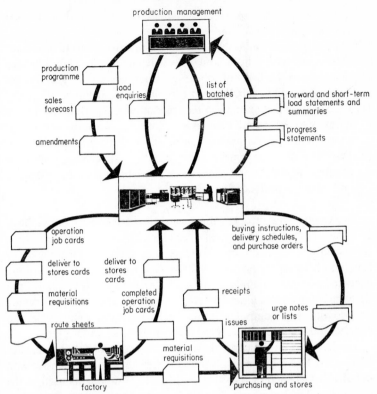

production management

production
programme

load
enquiries

list of
batches

forward and short-term
load statements and
summaries

sales
forecast

progress
statements

amendments

operation
job cards

buying instructions,
delivery schedules,
and purchase orders

deliver to
stores cards

deliver to
stores
cards

material
requisitions

completed
operation
job cards

receipts

route sheets

issues

urge notes
or lists

material
requisitions

factory

purchasing and stores

Fig. 5.1. Flow of information and documentation in a production-control system. This diagram was prepared by International Computers Ltd. to illustrate a manual on their package production control program, PROMPT I reproduce it (with the company's permission) because it gives a very good picture of the scope of a computerized system. The PROMPT package contains four stages: breakdown (for a complex product requiring multi-stage manufacturing and assembly); stock control; factory planning and control (forward loading, short-term loading, works documentation and progress control); and purchase control. It is designed to allow the whole or individual parts to be utilized.

(b) Create a system that would monitor and control the entire manufacturing process and associated functions such as stores and purchasing, from the moment the sales plan was produced to the time finished products were delivered.

(c) Institute a comprehensive costing system that would include materials, machines, direct and indirect labour, and all overheads. This would cover every item manufactured. Separate systems

were needed for experimental items and for work done for the
R & D department.

(*d*) Devise systems that would produce frequent, accurate feed-back
from the factory floor and other departments. This feedback
would form the basis of job progressing, costing, wages, day-to-
day management reports, and top management information.

(*e*) Process data fast enough to reduce planning lead time from three
months to one; and turn-round time on customer orders for
spares to a fraction of the existing six-week time lag.

(*f*) Present top management every month with detailed, accurate
accounts and statistics, these to be available a few days after the
end of the manufacturing cycle.

The system now in operation meets all these basic requirements.
In addition, it includes control over plant inventory, service returns
(statistical information on products sent back by customers for
repair); processes a payroll of 9,000 (1,000 workers at Liverpool are
excluded because of distance) of whom around 1,000 are paid on a
daily basis; produces a mass of statistics on costing, sales, personnel,
and so on. The computer is also used for sales forecasting and
exponential smoothing (see page 90) for the sales order plan.

The key item in the control system is the component. The master
file in C.A.V.'s integrated system is therefore a comprehensive and
detailed list of each of the 100,000 different components used in the
company's 4,000 products. The components are listed on a 'used on'
basis so that when, say, a modification is contemplated it is possible
to find out immediately which products will be affected.

Data for this file can be supplied only by the design department
via the modification control department who alone are permitted to
amend it. As the detail includes the drawing number, this file also
acts as a master list for all design drawings.

This file is the source of all other data used in the system. Elaborate
check systems have been designed, therefore, to safeguard its
accuracy. For example, when a modification is made, full details
both of the old and new specification are printed out; a date is set
for manufacture of the modified component to start; and from then
on, the computer will ignore the old specification in the planning
routines. Obsolescence cannot occur unobserved, as an automatic
count is kept by the computer of the calls made on each component.
Each month, a print-out is made of all components that have not
been used for two years. Should the design department decide to

retain these, a positive instruction to this effect must be given to the computer. Should they decide to discard the components, no positive action is taken, but the computer will automatically remove the component from the file and print out a report to this effect.

In addition, samples of the record are taken at regular intervals to ensure correctness. The file data is used as a basis for making the components selected and these are checked physically against those made in the normal course of events on the factory floor.

Basis of cost control is the cost record file. This, *using only component data derived from the master file*, contains complete details of cost in terms of materials, labour, and overheads for production of every component, expressed in shillings per hundred. Other detail includes: a list of every manufacturing operation required; the departments in which these are done; the machines used, plus any attachments needed; and the grade of labour employed. This file therefore embodies what is virtually an operational layout for manufacture of every component—a process that averages ten separate operations.

There is a number of other basic files, each of which can derive component data only from the master file. The stock-plan record-file stores details of all completed work that reaches the warehouse (i.e., is ready for delivery) giving total manufacturing cost and number of units. This file also contains details of warehouse allocation to customers and so provides sales statistics.

The plant inventory record has a detailed 'personal' history of every piece of plant installed in each of C.A.V.'s factories. The service returns file keeps detailed account of all items returned to the factory by customers for servicing. Two personnel detail files, one for salaried workers, the other for weekly-paid employees, contain all the personal data required for pay and other administrative purposes. Customer sales and service stock also have files of their own.

An outline of the control procedure used for shop-floor production will indicate the comprehensive scope of the total system.

The production cycle begins with the feeding of the sales (i.e., production) plan into the computer. Referring to the specification and 'used on' detail in the master file, the computer explodes this list of products into components; and then, by grouping like with like, produces a consolidated list showing total requirement for each component. The computer also prints out raw material requirements; sub-contract requirements; and a stores issue list. This, given to the men in charge of the transit stores in the factories, informs them what components they will receive from the factory floor and other sources and to whom these should be issued as assembly proceeds.

Referring to data on the consolidated components list and the cost file, the computer allocates a work-load to each factory (it will be remembered that all manufacturing detail is held on the cost file). This print-out details the number of hours by machine type and labour grade required by the coming month's schedule and thus provides shop-floor management with information on which to calculate whether overtime will be required, and if so, what type and how much. Inability to fulfil the demand means that the work may be sub-contracted.

The computer also prints works-order masters which give a complete breakdown of all the factory operations needed for the month's production. Printed on forms backed with hectographic carbon, these works orders are placed in spirit duplicators located in the factory offices and are used to produce all the ancillary documents required to progress the jobs through the shop floor.

Feedback from the factory floor begins when the first shift of the first day is completed. Production data comes from two main sources—operators' work sheets and clock cards. The former, filled in by bonus clerks by hand, give minute details on standard and actual performance. Completed, they give sufficient information both for detailed cost analysis and for calculations required for the highly complex wage payment system. Data for indirect labour is completed in a similar way, so that, *by the end of the shift, detail on every relevant event on the factory floor has been minutely documented.*

Every day, each factory foreman gets a detailed report on the work done the previous day by his shift. This takes the form of a departmental earnings record which details performance and earnings of each worker. One copy is perforated so that a slip may be given to each man, giving him a check on earnings; the whole record is retained by the foreman.

Each factory foreman also gets detailed weekly statistics relating to his department. The report includes a detailed analysis of time worked, wages earned, hours lost, cost of losses for direct operators; statistics on the number of indirect operators used, hours worked, wages, cost of consumable tools and materials, cost of tool maintenance broken down into material and labour; cost of scrap in terms of money and as a percentage of direct wages; and a very detailed analysis of labour losses and of types of indirect operators used.

Each week, foremen also get a running summary on somewhat

similar lines, accumulated over a 13-week period. These returns, between them provide factory supervisors and managers with valuable daily and longer-term information to help them run their operations efficiently.

I have cited the C.A.V. system at some length because it provides an excellent example of what integration of systems means in practice. As a footnote, I should add that the system is all the more remarkable for using a small, second-generation computer without random-access facilities. By the time these words are in print, however, the company will have replaced this by an ICL System 4 with disc files which will obviate much of the time at present used handling tapes, and allow considerable extension of the control system.

A few statistics will give you an indication of the size of the operation. At any given point in time, 40,000 drawings are in current use and some 500,000 operations (excluding assembly and sub-assembly) in progress on factory floors. The company makes 4,000 different products which between them use 100,000 different components. Its world-wide service operation handles some 2,000 order lines each day from a list of spares including some 30,000 different items. Employees number about 10,000.

What benefits has the company realized from operating this integrated production planning and control system? To begin with, there is comprehensive control on the lines listed at the beginning of this history. Standardization of components alone and avoidance of obsolescence is no small advantage. Dramatic improvements have been made in customer service on spares. Previously, turn-round time on orders averaged six weeks, though there were 60 clerks, many of whom did extensive overtime, on the job. Today, with only 30 clerks, this time-lag has been reduced to 12 to 36 hours. Stock records and customers' orders are held on magnetic files and the computer schedules orders each day by producing packing and advice notes for the warehouse. After delivery, it produces the invoice set. The stock record file, printed direct onto offset litho plates by the computer, provides a price catalogue which is more accurate and up-to-date than when printed outside the organization and is produced at half the cost.

Stock planning, hitherto done manually, is now carried out by the computer, using exponential smoothing techniques. Stock holdings have been reduced by 10 per cent, and 96 per cent of orders for spares can be fulfilled from stock. Previously, stock outs were fairly frequent.

Though the computer compiles most of the data used in the very detailed accounts presented to top management each month, lack of capacity made it necessary to produce the final consolidated reports manually. These will, of course, be produced by the computer when the new system is installed. Altogether there are 19 highly detailed reports which provide a full and accurate picture of every aspect of the operations, both of individual factories and of the company as a whole.

Savings have included nearly 200 staff. These were not made redundant, but were absorbed elsewhere in the factory to fill vacancies left by natural wastage.

Distribution

During the past decade, big changes have occurred in the pattern of distribution—changes which make the availability of full, up-to-date, and accurate information of increasing importance to those responsible for profitability.

What these changes are was outlined by Dr J. B. Jeffreys, secretary-general of the International Association of Department Stores, in a conference* held early in 1968.

First, there has been a tremendous increase in the actual volume of consumer goods distributed. Sales of goods at constant prices has increased by around 33 per cent in the past 10 years and *per capita* consumption has increased by about 25 per cent.

Second, merchandise itself has changed and is changing as a result of the development of new materials and new products. In some trades as much as 75 per cent of the merchandise now on display was not seen 10 years ago.

Third, distributive organizations have grown greatly in size. At the same time, there is an absolute decline in the number of outlets and more goods are distributed by fewer shops; and retail establishments have increased in size.

Fourth, there have been significant changes in methods of selling. Chief of these are the use of self-service, disappearance of traditional lines of demarcation between trades (e.g., grocers sell nylons, chemists paperback books), and a sharp rise in the capital investment per square foot of space. Many large new warehouses have been constructed and many of these are highly mechanized and this, of course, implies increased capital expenditure. Finally, there have been

* Distribution Computers Conference, organized by the Distributive Trades EDC and held in London on 19 March 1968.

changes in the location of selling establishments—a tendency to build shopping centres around the periphery of cities rather than in the middle.

For the distributor, this has two main effects, said Dr Jeffreys. First, he needs information of a type, in a form and at a frequency that is quite new. Secondly, he has to start thinking in the same way as industry—in terms of the return on investment.

The tremendous increase in the number of products, the continual appearance of new lines and new products and the trend towards the widening of the range of merchandise carried in the larger shops—for example, non-food merchandise in food shops—means that the distributor, if he is going to avoid over-stocking or serious gaps in his assortment, needs a constant flow of information to help his decision making. He needs information regarding what is moving and what is not; by supplier, by product group, by merchandise classification. He needs information regarding brands and the substitutability of products from the point of view of the customer. He needs information on the influence of price changes on sales, and in particular he needs information on his semi-net profit per square foot and per product line.

The supermarkets, in particular, have brought the kind of calculations outlined in the last sentence to a fine art. For example, the way the goods are arranged on the shelves is frequently dictated by the profitability of certain lines as against others which have a smaller profit margin or are bought by only a small proportion of customers.

In the past with smaller warehouses, smaller shops and a more limited assortment, with a slower rate of product innovation and with counter service, sharp eyes and ears together with some shrewd questioning and calculations on the back of an envelope provided a good deal of the answers to these questions. Today, these methods are no longer adequate. Even the staff right on the selling floor day after day in a large supermarket only has a very vague idea of what is happening by product line because of the width of the assortment being carried and because of the selling methods used.

Equally, in the non-food trades, the buyers, faced with an increasing number of selling units and with the disappearance of the traditional departmental grouping of merchandise in favour of customer-orientated boutiques, can no longer rely on a quick visit to a department or a telephone call to collect the information which is necessary. *The inadequate flow of this new type of infor-mation has already resulted in a slowing down of the rate of stock turn which brings, of course, a decrease in the return on investment* [my italics].

In fact, said Dr Jefferys, he would guarantee that the rate of stock turn for distributive trades in 1966 (the figures were not at that time available) would be lower than it was in 1961.

Growth in the size of distributive organizations means that more and more decisions have to be taken automatically rather than on the basis of a series of individual judgements by executives, he pointed out. For example, the economic delivery load from ware-house to branch, the route to be followed and the frequency of delivery can be determined mathematically, as can also the economic re-order point of merchandise, and so on. And top management in these bigger firms had neither time nor energy to follow the detailed operation of every unit.

Performance measurement becomes of increasing importance.

The increase in capital expenditure, both at the wholesale and retail level, means more and more that retailers need to measure their performance in all its aspects, in terms of the return on investment made; investment in retailing, being the capital invested in land, buildings, equipment, fixtures, fittings, vehicles, in stocks and, in those cases where they exist, in accounts receivable.

This concept, which is known as ROI, particularly in the United States, is increasingly being studied and introduced as the touch-stone of performance in the distributive trades.

Department, branch, product lines, warehouse, are measured in terms of return on investment (ROI). The traditional method of saying 'this will increase sales' is no longer a valuable judgement between alternatives, nor is profit in relation to sales any longer a touchstone for use in the distributive trades. Only the ROI factor will govern present and future use of resources. There must be a calculated return on investment.

This demands new types of information regarding the operation of the company and of the unit, on capital invested, on the space being used, on changes in space and in stock. It calls for flexibility in determining different ratios that are calculated from these figures.

Before examining some of the more recondite factors mentioned by Dr Jefferys, I should like to give you an indication of how the intelligent use of a computer helps to solve the day-to-day problems that arise in distribution. Because I prefer, when I can, to cite a case I have investigated personally, I have drawn the following material from an article (5.1) I wrote early in 1968. In addition to showing how a computer can be used to aid the mechanics of distribution, it shows how intimately this operation is linked to inventory control.

The company concerned is William Timpson Ltd of Wythenshawe near Manchester who manufacture footwear but also distribute lines produced by other makers to a large number of retail branches. Their story is interesting, not only because they had an opportunity to reorganize the distribution machinery almost from scratch but because they utilized this opportunity so well.

Timpsons decided to replace a dozen small warehouses scattered all over central Manchester with one large central warehouse just outside the city. Manual systems used in the old warehouses had long been unsatisfactory as they demanded too much clerical effort and could not keep pace with stock movements so that orders from retail branches could often not be met immediately. Computerized control systems were developed as part of the new project and planning of these and warehouse systems was integrated from the start. Every detail of the interior of the warehouse, even down to the best size of storage rack, was considered before it was constructed. In fact, the walls were built to clothe a carefully planned layout.

The computer concerned was initially a Univac SS-80. This had, at the time I wrote the story, just been replaced by a third-generation Univac system, a 9300 with magnetic tapes.

The broad objective of Timpson's scheme was to re-stock each of its 400 retail shops regularly: the largest twice a week, the remainder once a week. This involved the following:

(*a*) Tight control over warehouse inventory so as to ensure orders could be fulfilled completely and punctually. The number of lines, originally 16,000, was reduced to between 6,000 and 7,000 styles of footwear from about 1,500 different suppliers. The warehouse throughput was estimated as around 250,000 pairs of shoes a week.

(*b*) Control stocks at branch level so that each shop was supplied with the goods that would sell best in its area. Under the old system, branch managers had to discern sales trends as best they could—no easy job with an average range of 1,500 different styles in stock. Orders on the warehouse had been based principally on replenishment of items sold. This meant, in practice, that some of these orders were for goods in small demand which might later have to be disposed of at reduced prices.

(c) Utilize labour as efficiently as possible by reducing clerical work; placing goods within comfortable reach; cutting down the amount of walking done by each storeman in replenishing warehouse stocks and picking orders by testing availability of stock prior to printing dispatch list and invoice. These measures would increase productivity and reduce errors.

(d) Integrate production of orders, invoices, dispatch notes, and other documents related to inventory control and order processing.

(e) Organize paperwork and warehouse procedures so that goods for delivery to branches (by the company's own vans) could more readily be assembled for loading in route order—first in, last out of the vans—and be accompanied by delivery documents.

(f) Organize warehouse procedures so that all packages were assembled with the main order for van delivery. (Some minor warehouse departments dealing with sundries such as hosiery were excluded from the main computer scheme.)

(g) Ensure that all orders were turned round within the appointed interval. This was very important because a predetermined number of orders was to be processed each day.

(h) Produce reports that would supply management with meaningful and up-to-date information on sales patterns, inventory status, and so on; and produce sales forecasts.

The working area of the warehouse was divided into smallish zones, numbered according to stocks contained in them. The stocks in turn were numbered by a code that indicates type and style. Each zone therefore contained a certain range of styles.

A Fisher & Ludlow Flowlink Duo-Track conveyor system was installed. Designed specially for Timpsons, the conveyors hung on this were fitted with large, free-running wheels to allow their use as hand trolleys. A lever at the top of each carrier operates pins on the conveyor and can be set in various positions which cause the carrier to take one of several predetermined routes.

Documents are moved from computer room to warehouse and within the warehouse by a Dialled Dispatches pneumatic tube system. Work-flow principles were applied throughout; goods inwards entering the warehouse at one end, dispatches going out at the other. A control room was situated near the dispatch point. There documents were completed and the physical movement of packed goods from packing lines to final order assembly points was controlled.

The order content for each branch is determined by the sales bills completed in that branch and a predetermined stock pattern based on analysis of past sales and of current trends. Sales bills from branches are sent to head office, the data is punched into cards, and the computer compares this with the predetermined stock pattern. The main document used in the integrated procedure is in three parts —dispatch list, invoice, and labels—separated by vertical perforations. A separate set of forms is printed for each warehouse zone concerned in fulfilling an order so that one complete branch order often uses a dozen or more sets of forms.

The reason for this apparently wasteful procedure is that the documents accompany the goods around the warehouse. When each zone has a set, all zones concerned can work simultaneously on the same order. (This, I would like to point out in parenthesis, is intelligent use of a computer's fast printing facilities.)

After completing all sets of forms for one branch, the computer prints a summary of the information contained in them. Each form in the set is given a serial number and the statement is always the last in the series. The statement number therefore shows how many forms have been used to complete the invoice. This is but one of many checks incorporated to ensure that error is minimized.

A permanent schedule lays down which branches' stocks are to be replenished each working day. As this leaves little leeway in terms of time, the first sets of forms are taken off the computer before the first run is completed and dispatched to the warehouse through the pneumatic tube system so that work can begin as soon as possible. The summaries go straight to the control room; the dispatch lists are used by the storemen as picking documents. The form provides for the entry by the storeman of details of any item he cannot supply and of the total number of pairs supplied. He also enters this detail on the invoice part of the form.

An order made up, the storeman detaches the dispatch list and puts it in the pneumatic tube for the control room. The remaining two parts of the order document—invoice and four pre-printed labels—he puts into a holder on the carrier which he directs via the conveyor system to the packing department. There the carrier is manually directed to any of several packing stations.

The packer re-checks the container contents against the invoice and makes up the goods into one or more cartons, using the pre-printed labels. He then pushes the boxes onto a gravity-fed roller after having tucked into the top of the first the invoice form.

Meantime, in the control room, clerical staff have partly prepared a three-part delivery note. Basic consignment details are entered from the summary and dispatch list; details of goods from small non-computerized departments are obtained from dockets supplied by these. Final details of the main consignment (e.g., number of cartons, number of pairs in each) are noted as the parcels are called off the packing lines by means of a push-button control panel. At the same time, the invoices are removed from the leading boxes. Finally, the checked packages move towards a wire-binding station and are afterwards placed on gravity-fed conveyors that carry them to the appropriate order assembly point.

The completed delivery note gives a very detailed analysis of the consignment. One copy goes to the computer department, the other two with the goods. On delivery, the retail branch manager checks the consignment and enters details of any returns that are to be made to the warehouse. The driver signs both copies, handing one back to the branch manager and returning one to the warehouse when he gets back.

Dispatch lists are meanwhile returned to the computer department where details of any out-of-stock items (as entered by the storemen) are punched into cards. This provides data for adjustments for inventory and branch-stock records. A similar procedure is used for returns noted on delivery notes coming back from the retail shops.

There is also a computerized goods-inwards procedure. Suppliers enter details of deliveries on special forms provided by Timpsons and laid out to facilitate subsequent card punching. After the goods have been physically checked, any necessary annotations are made on the forms which then go to the computer department. New stock is taken on inventory by the computer twice a day.

Timpson's have three main types of management report which differ from one another chiefly in the amount of detail contained in the analyses they provide. Among the statistics produced by the computer are analyses of stocks in the warehouse, in the shops, and on order for 13 weeks forward. This is done on a week-by-week basis and cumulatively over a 26-week period. Current figures in all these areas are compared with those for similar periods the previous year. The percentage increase/decrease in sales over the past quarter is also compared with the same quarter the year before.

When the Univac SS-80 was used, only a few of the retail shops were on automatic stock replenishment but the machine was being used for two full shifts. When two Univac 9300's were installed instead, they worked for only one shift although all 400 branches were on automatic stock replenishment. The larger of the two processors had a 32K store, card reader, line printer, and six magnetic tapes. The other, with 8K store, card reader and printer, is being used principally for printing direct from magnetic tape.

I have described Timpson's system at some length because it demonstrates remarkably well how a carefully designed integrated computer system can rationalize the physical process of distribution while obviating clerical work and maintaining control over branch and central inventories. Almost every order is now completed immediately, as opposed to the previous system where almost half could not be fulfilled at first picking. The factors that determine how retail-store stock is replenished are current sales and information about the local sales pattern (in turn derived by analysing historical data), not the unco-ordinated observations of branch managers who have plenty of other things to do. Wastage is cut and sales increase because the most-wanted goods are available and little or no dead wood is carried. (The system also, incidentally, incorporates manual procedures which permit branches to obtain extra-fast deliveries occasionally when some specific item is required in a hurry.) And the manager has more time to devote to pleasing his customers. At the same time, top management gets reports that enable it to watch trends, to assess progress in individual branches, and to make informed decisions on future policy.

You may remember that, at the beginning of this history, I mentioned that Timpson's warehouses had been arranged to put goods within easy reach of storemen. Computerization—or the prospect of it—often provides a heaven-sent opportunity to rationalize the arrangement of warehouses. It might seem obvious that storemen must be more productive if they are saved from unnecessary movement. In spite of this, the process of order picking too often requires literally miles of walking each day—a shocking waste of time and energy. A system designed to eliminate this can be very rewarding and may, in some instances, permit the employment of men or women unfit for strenuous exercise. If (as I very much hope) you are sincerely interested in exploiting the available powers of handicapped or elderly people, this is a factor worth consideration.

Timpson's system also enabled it to cut some of the physical work of vanmen during delivery by more efficiently organizing the loading of vans. This is but one small aspect of transport which is, of course, usually a very vital factor in distribution costs. There are several other ways in which computers are used to reduce expenditure in this aspect of operations.

Some of these applications are quite mundane, in the sense that they are simply efficient record-keeping systems. It makes sense, for example, when one runs a transport fleet and has access to a computer, to use the system for filing full details of vehicle histories and to help ensure that preventive maintenance schedules are punctually and thoroughly carried out. Programs like this, though not exciting in computer terms, can do much to aid management in keeping a fleet of vehicles in top condition and constantly on the road.

Far more sophisticated (and suitable only for computer processing) are the problems involved in delivering goods from a variety of points in the most economical way. This, as you may recognize, is the famous 'travelling salesman problem' in one of its many guises. You will see why only a computer can find the best answer when I tell you that for a journey including 10 delivery points there are over 3,000,000 possible routes, while with 12 points this total rises to nearly 500,000,000!

Many of these theoretically possible routes are, of course, disqualified because they are too long or because of limitations of vehicle capacity. But even when practical considerations whittle down the number to a few hundred, it is difficult to find the most economical ones, bearing in mind such constraints as total milage, traffic congestion on certain roads, type of load carried, and the effect of early closing days.

A problem like this can often be solved by a package program used in a service bureau. The following much abridged description is of a program of this type developed by English Electric Leo Marconi (now absorbed into International Computers Ltd).

Data supplied by the user includes all depot locations and call points. The program can allow different speeds for town, local area and country travel and a route can include up to 128 call points with up to 1,000 served from a single depot in one program run.

Towns have special references so that calls made within them can be routed using the special town delivery speed; and up to nine different town areas can be included in each run. The program also allows for up to 10 different capacities of vehicle within the fleet and up to 99 vehicles of each capacity are provided for. Though varying types of load can be catered for, the program does not provide for mixed loads. Collections as well as deliveries can be routed, though both cannot be handled in the same computer run.

Other factors taken into account include: standard or special call times (durations); route limitations by distance, number of calls, or time; the accommodation of individual customers' requirements such as early closing or certain times of day; and the existence of bridges or congested areas.

For the routes produced for each depot, the computer prints out the following:

the order in which to make the calls on each route with details of any calls to be made at a specified period of the day;
the capacity of vehicle most suitable for doing the route;
the total milage of each route;
the total time taken for each route;
the total milage travelled by all vehicles in the fleet from the depot;
details of any points not assigned to routes because they were too far from the depot to be reached in the time or because all vehicles were fully assigned.

The program designers recommend that the program be first applied to the problem of planning transport fleets. It is possible, for example, to try out the effect of several different fleet compositions quite quickly and to highlight the one most suited to the distribution pattern. Should results show that an existing fleet is not composed of the correct type of vehicles for the routes normally made, this can be borne in mind by management until it is possible to make changes.

With a fixed fleet, the program may improve upon regular routes. Used by one customer who called regularly on 90 shops, the program permitted calls to be condensed into four journeys instead of six.

One company that used a mixture of road and rail transport for distributing its products wanted to investigate whether using its own vehicle fleet would show a saving and used this computer program to find out. Various routes were planned and results analysed, and it was found that up to 50 per cent of distribution costs could be saved if all goods could be held up for a week so as to combine deliveries.

Company policy, however, insisted upon a 24-hour delivery; so this solution was not acceptable. But the program also showed that to keep to this standard using its own fleet rather than the previous means would have cost the organization nearly twice as much.

Siting of depots is another problem susceptible of solution by mathematical techniques and is, in a sense, a facet of the previous application. Here the object is to find, taking into account any constraints of a geographical or other nature (e.g., existence of a suitable railway station) the most advantageous spot to site a depot designed to supply customers or factories within a given area.

One particularly interesting experiment on this theme which I had a chance of seeing in action used CRT terminals and was being carried out in the Chemical Engineering Department at Cambridge University. The program was split into two parts: one provided a grid upon which the user could draw a rough map, indicating relevant geographic features such as rivers, and railways; the other allowed the user to indicate customer locations and to move the depot location from one position to another by means of a light-pen (see page 35). This movement caused the computer automatically to calculate ton/ miles for each depot location.

I found this experiment especially interesting because it permitted the exercise of ordinary human common sense in conjunction with the computer's unique calculating capacity. Faced with a visual, as distinct from a purely mathematical, statement of the problem, the user had an opportunity to try first what seemed the most obvious possibility; quickly to obtain results; and then to try another. Common sense precluded solutions that were manifestly absurd and chances were that an optimal answer could be found more quickly than by conventional methods.

This also illustrates well how the latest graphic techniques can help those who understand little of mathematics. Some mathematical formulae used in solving management problems are totally incomprehensible to the average businessman. Offered a CRT terminal to use in this way, a manager has an immensely powerful version of the pencil-and-paper method he would probably use himself to work out the solution to a problem like this.

This seems a good point at which to digress for a while from my discussion of specific management problems and try to describe what is meant by a 'mathematical model'—a thing that is increasingly ubiquitous in sophisticated computer applications of all kinds.

Mathematical models

Normally, when we talk about a model we mean a physical representation of something, usually in scaled-down form. And a working model has parts that can be moved (though not necessarily by the same kind of power) in the same way that those of the full-size object can be moved.

A mathematical model, on the other hand, is an abstract representation. By 'abstract' I do not mean that it fails to represent real facts but that it does not make use of anything one can see or touch.

In a sense, a detailed map is a mathematical model of the countryside because it charts and measures every feature, telling you how long the roads are, how they twist and turn, how high the hills or deep the valleys are, where there are rivers, and so on.

One can gain some idea of the function of a mathematical model, therefore, if one thinks of it as a kind of multi-dimensional map which represents, say, every aspect of the operations of a complete organization, or one part of it, such as a machine shop or the marketing division. The map is prepared by mathematicians, who must be as careful as any conventional cartographers to ensure that every detail is correct, not only in itself but in its relation to all the other elements. This implies a need for considerable skills in collecting, analysing, evaluating, and interpreting data as well as in constructing the model. For, as a driver could lose his way by following an inaccurate map, a company could be seriously misled by findings derived from an inaccurate model.

Given an ordinary working model, you can find out, by observation and measurement, what happens to every other part when, say, you turn a wheel. A mathematical model is constructed to allow the same kind of manipulation. The data describing it is fed into the computer which is programmed to manipulate the model so as to calculate the effects of action in one or more parts upon the whole.

Mathematical models have several very valuable properties. Because they are not bounded by physical limitations they can be used to represent objects too complex to be expressed in concrete form. Various specifications can also be changed without the difficulty that would occur if, for example, one wanted to change the dimensions of part of a material model. The time element can be telescoped and calculations representing years of real-life experience packed into a few minutes—or even seconds. This is what is done in business games whose purpose is to give the players vicarious management experience.

Various mathematical techniques are used to manipulate these models. One of those you will probably hear referred to often is *simulation*. This uses the mathematical model as the basis for exploring all kinds of situation that may occur, to try to find out the best feasible way of dealing with them. One might, for example, when planning a new supermarket, use simulation to find out how many cash desks were required to get every customer out with not more than, say, seven minutes' waiting time under normal conditions.

Another much-used technique is *linear programming* whose purpose is to examine the relationships between a group of variables with the object of pinpointing the most desirable situation. Suppose, for example, one wants to formulate a cattle feed as economically as possible from materials of varying nutritive value, consistency, taste, and price. The ideal formula will, of course, relate directly to the availability and costs of raw materials and the computer will be fed with data on these and information on the desired result in terms of moisture content, food value, and so on. Its task is to work out all (or, more commonly, selected) permutations of these variables and come up with an answer that fulfils all the specifications at lowest cost.

You can imagine that to attempt to do this task manually would take months of calculation during which much of the basic data would probably have changed! But a computer, using a well designed linear program, can produce an answer within minutes. This, I must emphasize, is not necessarily the optimum answer, by which I mean it is not guaranteed to be *the* best. The main reason for this is the astronomical number of permutations involved, which implies a volume of calculation far too high to be done in reasonable time by even a powerful computer. Nevertheless, a result achieved by this method is likely to be considerably better than any available through manual techniques. The art of designing a good linear program depends partly upon the ways that can be devised to limit the volume of calculation while allowing production of an answer as near optimum as possible.

I am not a mathematician myself, as you will have noticed, and I feel I would waste your time by attempting to explain (at second hand, inevitably) any more of the basis of the techniques like these that are used in operational research (whose general function I have outlined on pages 133–136). There are several good books on the subject written specifically for the layman. One that I can particularly recommend is *Management science* by Stafford Beer (5.2) which is lucid, entertaining, and lavishly illustrated.

Project planning and management

One of the most popular and widely used of all the new computer-based techniques that have been introduced during the past few years is Critical Path Analysis, or PERT (Project Evaluation and Review Technique) as it is often called. This is a method which rationalizes the planning of all types of project and enables those responsible for their management to keep close tabs on progress and take corrective action, if necessary, before schedules go awry.

PERT is used for projects varying from the installation of a computer through shut-down maintenance of a foundry to construction schemes stretching over several years. The reason for its popularity is not far to seek. It is very versatile. Properly applied, it is extremely effective. Its overall purpose and value is easily appreciated even by those who do not generally pay much attention to 'scientific' management techniques. Almost every computer service bureau offers a package PERT program that can satisfactorily be used in connection with projects varying widely in size, duration, and type. In fact, this application is exceptionally well suited to handling on a bureau basis. Finally, most government organizations and an increasing number of other organizations now insist that contractors and sub-contractors use PERT so that their activities can be properly timed and regulated.

The simplest form of PERT comprises an analysis of the times involved in completing the various activities that go to make up a project and to establish the relationships that exist between these. Its broad objectives (which I will describe in more detail later) are: first, to provide an accurate estimate of the total time it will take to complete the project; second, to produce a schedule indicating when each activity must begin and at what date it must finish if the schedule is not to be thrown out; finally, to use data gathered during the actual progress of the project to calculate how any deviations from the original schedule will affect future activities and the completion date.

The first task for the prospective user of a PERT program is to enumerate every single activity and event that must take place during the project. He must next make an estimate of the time that will be required to complete each. Finally, he must represent this information as a diagram which shows the relationships existing between these events and activities. This diagram is known as a 'network' and for this reason PERT is sometimes also referred to as *network analysis*.

Although there are small individual variations, the basic method of network drawing is always the same. The time continuum always flows from left to right, so that the start of a project always appears on the extreme left of the network, its completion on the right. The network itself is composed of events, which are represented by circles or boxes, each given a unique number; the activities as lines connecting these.

If you represented your morning journey from home to your place of work in the PERT convention, the diagram might look like this:

START ....1............2............ FINISH
            6   20–25   4

The start point is your departure from home; event No. 1 is your arrival at the station; event No. 2 your arrival at the station nearest your destination; the finish is your arrival at the office. The activities are the various stages of the journey. You will notice that these are not given serial numbers. The figures written against them represent the estimated number of minutes taken for each. The first and last activities are short walks whose time can be precisely estimated. The centre activity, however—the train journey—cannot be so accurately timed so you have given a minimum and what you hope is a maximum time for this.

A glance at the diagram tells you that if you are to arrive not later than 9 am you cannot afford to start from home later than 8.25 am (the train journey time includes the moments taken in getting in and out of the stations and the train). You can also deduce that, if you arrive at the second station after 8.56 am, you will not make it (we will assume you have a wooden leg and cannot reduce this walking time!).

Though this example is childishly simple it illustrates the basic principle. When there are hundreds or even thousands of events and activities, drawing a network is no easy task. (Nor can the calculations economically be performed by any means other than a computer.) Many first-time users of PERT have told me that, even if they had had no other benefit from it, they valued it for the discipline it imposed upon them. To list every event and activity, to arrange these in logical order, and to assign a time to each demands very careful thought.

Exactly what print-out you get from a computer after it has done the calculations associated with your network depends partly on

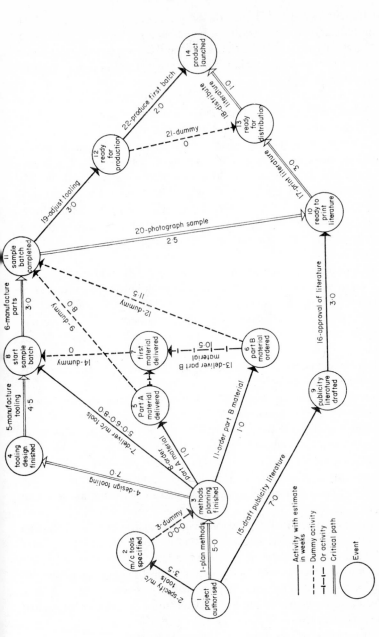

Fig. 5.2. PERT network: introduction of a new product

what facilities are afforded by the program, partly on what your own requirements are, as most offer a range of choice. But one report you will certainly want will list the earliest and latest possible start dates for each activity in order that it may be completed in time to adhere to the overall schedule.

For many activities, there will be quite a lot of leeway. You may find, for example, that a three-day job can logically begin 10 days before it is due for completion. I will give you a simple example. If I were writing an article for a journal and this was to be illustrated by existing photographs supplied by an outside source, I might know I could obtain these within 36 hours of my requesting them. We will assume that I know exactly what illustrations I need before I begin writing the article, a week before it is due to reach the editor. I may therefore request the photographs at any time between my beginning to write and 36 hours before I am due to post the article.

In a few of the activities, however, there will be no time leeway at all. A job takes seven days; it cannot be begun until seven days before it is due for completion. This is where the *critical path* comes in. It is, in fact, a line traced between the events on a network where there is no spare time at all. If the activities covered by this line are not completed on time, it is *impossible* for the overall schedule to be adhered to. There is no catching up. The term, critical path, is therefore a very apt one.

Once you know the course of this critical path you can, of course, be on your guard and ensure that no avoidable delays occur in these activities. But the network analysis technique is equally valuable in showing you areas where leeway exists. You will, I am sure, recollect situations within your own experience where you have gone all-out to get a job finished that is allegedly urgent, only to find that had the planning been better you could easily have been given another two days.

Typically, your PERT print-out will list earliest and latest starting dates for each activity, the completion time for each, and the amount of 'float' (leeway, in terms of time) available. These may be broken down in any way you wish—by department, for example, or according to areas of management responsibility. Each manager will be given a schedule which shows him what must be done in his department if the schedule is to go according to plan.

But things do not, of course, always go according to plan. For this reason, it is important to re-analyse your network, after the project has begun to get under way, so as to ascertain precisely what effects any deviations will have on the whole. What these effects will be is sometimes far from obvious.

Let us return for a moment to your 30-minute imaginary journey from home to office. We will suppose that one morning you over-sleep and do not leave the house until 8.50 am, 25 minutes after your safe start time, 20 minutes after your latest possible start time. Ah! you may say, I shall arrive 20–25 minutes late at the office. But is it as simple as this? Your original schedule was based on a journey earlier in the day. Now your walk to the station lengthens because traffic has built up and you have to wait at traffic lights before you can cross roads. Trains are less frequent. In fact, you may well be 40 minutes late in arrival.

In a more complex project, cumulative effects like this cannot be calculated until you have re-analysed the network in the light of events so far. This implies that you will have carefully collected data while the project is in process so that the computer will be able to provide you with an amended schedule.

I think I have said enough to indicate how immensely valuable time analysis will be. You know what activities are critical, which are non-critical. You know how much time is available for each. You can find out, by re-analysis, where you will have to speed up if you are not to lose more time (quite a few float times may have disappeared, for example)—and where extra effort is unnecessary. This enables you to control your project in a rational way.

So far, I have mentioned only one kind of time analysis. There is a second, very valuable application of PERT: resource analysis. This deals with the manpower (and possibly the machines and materials too) required to carry out a project.

In examining time analysis, we tacitly assumed that the finish date of the project was optional. When estimating the time taken for each activity, therefore, we based our calculations upon use of an existing labour force. If, for example, we allowed seven days for brickwork we were thinking in terms of, say, two bricklayers.

Sometimes, however, time of finish is all-important—the job must be completed by a predetermined date. In this case, we must find out how many men (probably in each of several trades or skills) are required to meet the target. To do this, we must analyse the network on a somewhat different basis. The finish date must be stipulated, the earliest start date for the entire project may also be unalterable. We must therefore get the computer to estimate the duration of each activity in the light of these fixed dates. Given these, we are in a position to estimate how many men are required for each.

However manpower requirements are estimated, it is useful to employ the computer to list for us how many men in each trade group are required each day or week for the duration of the project. Often, the first list that comes out reveals a very unsatisfactory picture which, drawn in profile, might well resemble a mountain range. One week, for example, you need 20 bricklayers, the next only 10, the following 15; and patterns for other trades are equally jagged.

In practical terms, this is quite unacceptable because labour simply cannot be produced on this basis. So the PERT program is used to smooth out the requirements to produce a more workable pattern. To do this it must, of course, have leeway—more time available for some activities, perhaps, or a chance to stipulate overtime. Though it will seldom be able to level the peaks and valleys of demand into a perfectly smooth line, it will at least reduce the mountains to mole-hills, the valleys to small depressions.

Similar procedures may be used for machine requirements. Smoothing of the first result can therefore succeed not only in a more even loading on in-house resources but also in a more realistic pattern for plant hire in applications where this is required for the project. Rented machines can thus be utilized as fully as possible.

Estimates by the manager on what materials will be needed to complete certain activities can be used by the computer program to produce materials schedules. These are helpful, not only in rationalizing the purchasing process but in organizing deliveries. On a construction project, this may be very important, as much wastage can occur through premature deliveries which incur unnecessary handling because they clutter up the site or lie around for long periods during which they deteriorate or are pilfered.

One building company I met had the materials question reduced to such a fine art that each man was issued each day only with the exact quantity required to complete the day's work. Though this involved extra handling and some packaging for the more fragile items, it was found worth while because of the enormous reduction of wastage.

PERT can also be used to keep track of costs during the progress of a project. ICL's package program, for example, permits the analysis of cost of individual activities, total and summary costs of various trades, cumulative costs of different materials, costs of sections of the project, comparison of actual and estimated expenditure, and comparison of value of work accomplished against estimated or actual expenditure.

The cost of resources can be adjusted to keep pace with changing circumstances and wage fluctuations during the life of a project. Information on the effect of these alterations on cost can thus be made available with a minimum of delay. The management may also impose cost restrictions so that the work is scheduled in such a way as to keep within a budgeted rate of expenditure.

The ability of the computer program to print out information in the form of histograms or bar charts (see chapter 2, page 23) is particularly useful for an application like resources allocation, as the data is presented in a form that is much more assimilable than a list of figures.

One building firm I met used histograms to show labour requirements for a total project and a bar-chart format to analyse labour needed for each of a number of houses built as one project. Across the top was a time-scale; down the left-hand side a list of the houses. The chart showed the start and stop times for each kind of labour, and the planning manager coloured these in with crayons, using a different colour for each labour category. Pinned on the wall, this made an inexpensive yet effective display which conveyed information at a glance.

PERT, critical path analysis or network analysis—whatever one cares to call it—is currently used for planning a very wide variety of projects. It can safely be said that, in any undertaking that involves a sizable number of people in a spectrum of activities of any kind, this technique can greatly contribute to the efficiency of overall planning and day-to-day management. Rationalization of planning alone often reduces the total length of a project considerably— sometimes as much as 50 per cent.

Basic training in network drawing and data preparation for PERT normally occupies only a few days. This, like most other skills, can be utilized effectively only when supplemented by on-the-job experience, during which one learns much by trial and error. Many regular users have invented refinements which, applied to their particular jobs, make the drawing and amendment of networks easier.

Business planning

Large organizations have long recognized that the days of 'flying by the seat of one's pants' are gone for ever. Though long-range planning cannot, of course, guarantee success, it can help to identify the ingredients required for continued prosperity and point to danger areas.

The computer has made a substantial contribution towards assisting managers planning operations for five years or more in advance. Until now, its principal value has been in handling all the arithmetic involved in such calculations. This it does so accurately and so fast that it is possible to work out the effects of a number of tentative decisions in various areas and evaluate one against the other within hours. In future, the computer will undoubtedly enhance its value by assessing, on an inter-active basis, the effects of changes in a number of key areas and displaying results on graphs which management can manipulate by using CRT terminals and light pens (see chapter 3). The experience of Westinghouse, which I shall relate later in this section, will clarify this statement.

I have already outlined how a computer can assist business planning by extrapolating historical data on, for example, sales. I shall now give you an example of how this projection technique can be used in a more comprehensive form of long-range management planning. I cannot, unfortunately, cite the name of the organization who used the method described below as, for reasons entirely unconnected with the success of the computer exercise, this has now been discontinued. The method itself has, however, in no way been invalidated; it merely cannot be used because certain basic changes in management structure have occurred.

The program concerned was devised with the object of taking the drudgery out of business planning and ensuring that the arithmetic was accurate. It was not, its writers emphasized, capable of making decisions for managers, nor could it reduce management involvement in the planning function.

Each divisional manager in this multi-divisional organization prepared basic data relating to five separate planning areas: sales, capital assets, manpower, manufacturing space, and capital expenditure. Data on sales, for example, included last year's results, current objectives, and existing contracts, plus targets to be aimed for during the ensuing five years.

All the data for one division could be contained in a pack of less than 100 punched cards. These were fed to the computer which produced, within 15 minutes, a draft plan. This plan, which was essentially an extrapolation or projection of each of the elements, was modified automatically by the computer program to take account of non-company factors such as inflation rate.

This computer-printed plan gave the manager a chance to find out whether courses of action that looked promising in theory were likely to work out well in practice. If, for example, his draft plan had involved increasing sales very greatly during the next five years, the computer would work out what this would entail in terms of demand for manpower, productive space, capital expenditure, and so on.

Some of the demands might be unacceptable on various grounds. The manager would then take a look at the unsatisfactory elements in the projected results, make amendments, and return the fresh data to the computer. Again, only 15 minutes would elapse before he was presented with a fresh set of results. This kind of experimentation could continue until he was able to produce what he believed was a feasible plan for the coming five years.

International Computers Ltd has recently launched a system to aid business planning in a similar way. Called PROSPER (PROfit Simulation, Planning and Evaluation of Risk) it enables the user to construct and run company models on a 1900 Series computer without programming effort on his part.

Computer models provided by PROSPER may represent the whole of an organization's activities, particular aspects of it, or individual projects. Input can be in the form of basic data—e.g., actual values achieved and/or forecasts for sales and production volumes, unit sales prices, unit or bulk raw material costs, overheads, or re-equipment schedules. The object of the system is to enable the manager rapidly to obtain answers to the 'what will happen if?' questions that must precede decision-taking.

PROSPER is used in much the same way as the program I have described in the preceding paragraphs. The program incorporates a range of profit-measuring techniques—payback, single- and dual-rate discounted-cash flow, using variable rates and cut-off periods if required, key ratios, and rates of growth. The system also incorporates a technique that enables the user to express the degree of uncertainty in his forecasts and compare the risk element of alternative decisions.

In this connection, I should also perhaps mention that package programs are available for computerizing accepted techniques for investment evaluation. One of the latest of these is developed by Honeywell and is designed specially for investments in plant, buildings, and other resources that qualify for investment grants and tax allowances. The program calculates return on investment by time necessary to recover the capital used (payback period) and average interest rate, together with rate of return, present value of the project, and profitability index. These results are based upon the application of recently developed discounted-cash-flow techniques that take into account the timing as well as the volume of a cash transaction, the true value of a transaction being dependent on the future date at which it occurs.

An advanced technique for management planning, based on the use of CRT (TV-type) remote terminals was described at the IFIP Congress held in Edinburgh in August 1968 (5.3). This system was first developed for the Laundry Equipment Division of Westinghouse Electric Corporation of Pittsburgh, USA.

The object of the system was to help managers determine marketing and production plans for their products. Data on actual sales history, previous production schedules, inventory status, and so on was provided by the data bank which is a feature of the computer system used by this division. The computer also provided, through use of a model, an approximation of future sales.

Other relevant data is provided by the marketing manager who estimates such factors as the impact of merchandising plans and provides an evaluation of competitors' performance and various other intangibles that he is best able to judge; and the production manager who knows the status of the factory, labour situation and other detail relating to the manufacturing side of the operation.

Between them, these managers, working with an on-line CRT terminal, develop a sales and production plan that is used as the specific goal for the coming period. To make this plan involves balancing four complex sets of variables:

expected demand;
merchandising plans;
available inventory;
available production resources.

These have to be weighed against one another to provide as good as possible a solution for the division. This solution takes the form of sales, production, and inventory plans for each model of machine manufactured and in each of a number of colours. The aggregate of these is, of course, the complete plan.

'Each of the models is considered at each level of aggregation,' the authors explain. 'What may seem "right" at the model level may seem "wrong" at the overall level. For example, the aggregate sales level may appear unreasonable, the total inventory too high, production levels too variable or production capacity under- or over-utilized.' Figures 5.3, 5.4, and 5.5 show in more detail how the system works.

Reporting on the impact of this system, the authors make the following observations:

> [It had a] very distinct and marked effect on the management decision-making process. The overriding effects evolved from the

			FROM		TO	
GRAPH-NON CUM	TOTAL PRODUCT	ALL COLORS				
GRAPH-CUM	PRODUCT LINE X	WHITE	JAN	1966	JAN	1966
TABULAR	MODEL 1	AVOCADO	FEB	1967	FEB	1967
RECONCILE	MODEL 2	COPPERTAN	MAR	1968	MAR	1968
	MODEL 3	GOLD	APR	1969	APR	1969
	MODEL 4	TURQUOISE	MAY		MAY	
	MODEL 5	YELLOW	JUN		JUN	
	MODEL 6		JUL		JUL	
	MODEL 7		AUG		AUG	
	MODEL 8		SEPT		SEPT	
	MODEL 9		OCT		OCT	
	MODEL 10		NOV		NOV	
	PRODUCT LINE Y		DEC		DEC	
	MODEL 1					
	MODEL 2					
	MODEL 3			SEASONAL AXIS		
	MODEL 4			NORMAL AXIS		
	MODEL 5					
	MODEL 6					
	MODEL 7					
	MODEL 8					
	MODEL 9					
	MODEL 10					

PROCEED -

Fig. 5.3. Graph specifications. This is a typical specifications display. The user selects one item in a column with the light-pen and then the action function PROCEED. If the user were to touch GRAPHCUM, PRODUCT LINE X, ALL COLOURS; JAN., 1967, DEC., 1967, and PROCEED, he would get the graph in Fig. 5.4.

> impact of the response time of the system. The time between the manager's posing a question or asking for some information from the system and the point at which the system came back with the answer was so short (one to ten seconds) that the managers were led to a different form of problem-solving than the one they had employed before. This was an inter-active problem-solving process where the managers tried many more solutions and employed more analysis than before.

> Other effects noted were stimulation of re-thinking of the methods and process of analysis and a demand for more data, and more

manipulation of this than had seemed necessary before. The managers were able to browse through the information, searching for problems and a means for investigating these from various angles. They were able to uncover more problem areas and, through discussion, to acquire a firmer understanding.

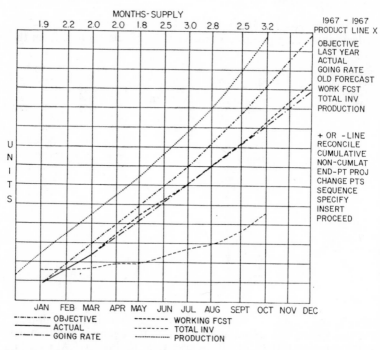

Fig. 5.4. End-point project. Suppose the user finds the year-end working forecast total units satisfactory. Instead, he would like to see what an increase to his year-end objective would do to his position, starting the increase in May. He touches the word MAY to indicate the starting month and WORKING FCST to indicate the data type; he types in the new forecast, touches the control point for END–PT PROJ, and then PROCEED. This results in the display in Fig. 5.5.

The premises on which managers based their strategies for solution were crystallized: use of visual displays made trends and deviations stand out clearly from the data. Solutions devised by the managers could be tried out and their impact seen clearly.

This led to a sharp reduction in discussion among the participants as to the likely impacts of certain alternative strategies and the time spent in the decision-making process itself was spent much more productively.

I have quoted this example at some length, not only because this exercise is an advanced one in terms of technology but because it justifies theories that, used in ways like this, computers extend the range of man's mind, challenge his powers rather than devalue them.

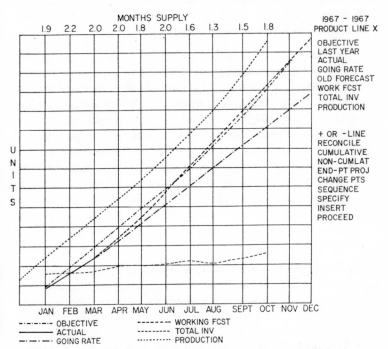

Fig. 5.5. New working forecast. The response to the previous request is a new working forecast line. As can be seen from the month's supply of inventory figures at the top of the graph, the inventory in October is now 1·8 months supply, down from the previous 3·2. The user might now want to alter the production schedule to bring his inventory to a higher level. This can be done using any relevant control points.

Operational research

Operational research is a subject that tends to unnerve many business managers because they feel that it leads them badly out of their depth and therefore deprives them of control of situations whose resolution should lie in their hands. This reaction, though perfectly understandable, is hardly rational for one might as well argue that lack of electronics training constitutes an excuse for not using a computer.

One of the characteristics of our age is increasing reliance upon experts in one field or another. We cannot escape this. But we can at least endeavour to understand broadly what they do, why they employ certain techniques, and why the hoped-for results are unlikely to be achieved by alternative methods.

In a new book (5.2) which I have already commended to your notice, Stafford Beer comments thus:

> Management science deploys a skill and methodology originally developed for the investigation of nature at large to do research into the manager's own job. It is only trivially concerned with the processes being managed. It operates in an area dominated by hunch and value judgement; it sets out to determine what factors actually do influence affairs, and to measure those. Management science must also seek to incorporate the resulting quantities in some account of the situation which included hypotheses about the reasons for its working as it does and the 'laws' by which the whole situation is sustained. All this is going to involve more than measuring things; it is going to involve operational research. And again we must note that research into costs and processes will not be enough.

Mr Beer goes on to point out that in a management situation, like a battle situation, all the basic data will never be available soon enough to help in formulating a successful strategy. Success, therefore, depends upon using such relevant information as can be obtained as a basis for certain logical inferences. Operational research, therefore, deals less in analysis and deduction, more in experiment and induction. Given only some of the facts we have to find new ways of inferring a conclusion. 'Although OR [operational research] begins with the measurement of variables, it ends by computing probabilities about future events.'

The term 'operational research' therefore describes a type of approach. A blanket term, it covers a group of techniques which are scientific in method, are mathematically orientated, and are applied to the solution of certain types of management problem. You will notice I write 'certain types'. Not all—though perhaps more than one might at first think—problems are susceptible to this approach. 'There is always danger,' says Patrick Rivett, professor of OR at the University of Lancaster, (5.4) 'in slapping a standard mathematical

poultice on what the inexperienced man hopes is a standard management boil. Sometimes the target is missed and the mis-directed
slapping can be painful to the patient.'

Three factors—the ability to define an objective, choice of alternative, and measurement of consequence—combine to form the elements of a decision-making problem, Professor Rivett points out.
And it is the consequences of decisions in complex situations which
OR seeks to study. This also presupposes that the key elements of
the problem can realistically be quantified.

In an excellent book (5.5) written by Rivett in collaboration with
Russell L. Ackoff, Professor of OR, Case Institute of Technology,
Cleveland, Ohio, OR problems that can be solved by OR methods
are classified under eight different headings:

Inventory—problems concerned with utilization of resources to
obtain something else of value, e.g., faster service to customers.

Allocation—the apportionment of given resources to obtain a predetermined result, e.g., the allocation of work among a group of
machines.

Queueing—arrangement of service facilities, e.g., of airline check-in
points to process passengers as fast as possible or of ships' berths to
give minimum turn-round time.

Sequencing—the arrangement of operations in an order that completes them in the most efficient way, e.g., scheduling of customer
orders for a steel rolling mill.

Routing problems—e.g., design of travel routes for a transport
fleet so as to fulfil given demands in the most economical manner.

Replacement—determination of a policy for replacement of, say,
machine parts that minimizes both the costs involved and the inci-
dence of breakdown.

Competition—problems whose solution is contingent not only upon
one's own resources but upon decisions made elsewhere.

Search—problems concerned with formulation of sampling
methods that give coverage of a given area and also discover any
pattern of deviation that exists. This, applied to, say, customs
inspection would catch a realistic proportion of smugglers and would
indicate if there were an increase in, for example, drug traffic.

A good many of the problems susceptible of solution by OR methods
contain a mixture of these elements.

If you have read the earlier chapters in this book you will know
that I have already outlined a number of these problems and the

methods used to solve them. The overwhelming advantage of using mathematical techniques for this purpose is that they provide a very good chance of obtaining a much better answer than can be arrived at by non-scientific approaches.

Operational research, then, is used not because it is more glamorous than traditional methods or because 'science' has a special virtue of its own, but because of its purely practical value. It is, like a computer system, a tool whose usefulness and effectiveness depend on the intelligence and appropriateness with which it is applied.

If your own background is not mathematical, you will find it impossible to grasp the finer aspects of the techniques used. But you should make a point of ascertaining *why* a particular method is considered the best, broadly *how* it works, and *what* answers it will provide. This allows you to consider in a rational manner whether or not a specific exercise is worth the cost and effort involved.

Summary

The following points have been mentioned in this chapter:

(*a*) The successful application of computers demands careful and fundamental thinking about the objectives of a business and the methods whereby these can be attained.

(*b*) Among the broad areas in which a good return can be expected when a computer system is properly used are:

day-to-day accounting, particularly when the systems speed the flow of money into an organization;

stock control, to reduce costs of inventory, improve purchasing practices, raise the standard of service to customers;

costing, whereby a true picture is obtained of the cost involved in maintaining an organization's activities, thus allowing it to rationalize its sales and other policies;

budgetary control, which permits management to allocate fixed sums for expenditure and to monitor these in detail;

marketing and sales management, to allow the formulation and implementation of realistic marketing and sales strategies and to monitor performance;

production planning and control in all kinds of manufacturing operation so as to utilize resources to the best advantage and monitor the progress of work;

distribution—the planning and implementation of realistic policies and methods;

project planning and management;

long-range business planning.

(c) The scientific and mathematically-orientated techniques grouped under the general heading of 'operational research' constitute an effective means of solving certain types of management problem. But their value lies not in their sophisticated nature, as such, but in the results they can achieve.

References

5.1 TATHAM, L. Warehousing problems brought to heel. *Data Systems.* May 1968.

5.2 BEER, S. *Management science: the business use of operations research.* Aldus Books, 1968.

5.3 MORTON, M. S. S., and STEPHENS, J. A. The impact of interactive visual display systems on the management planning process.
Material from this paper and Figs. 5.3, 5.4, and 5.5 from the same source are reproduced by kind permission of the authors and the International Federation for Information Processing in whom the copyright is vested.

5.4 RIVETT, P. New horizons for operational research. *Business* (now *Business Management*). August 1966.

5.5 RIVETT, P., and ACKOFF, R. L. *A manager's guide to operational research.* John Wiley & Sons Ltd, 1963.

6. The computer on the factory floor

Until now, I have looked at computers exclusively in their capacity as data-processing systems—that is, as a means of manipulating the facts and figures that emanate from an organization. Some of these applications relate to the day-to-day or periodical accounting and other management operations involved in the running of a business; some are concerned more specifically with manufacturing functions —e.g., the control of factory production or of inventory; yet others involve the solution of management problems by the scientific methods described as 'operational research'.

Diverse though these are, they can all logically be grouped under the general head of 'data processing'.

My principal subject in this chapter is not data processing in this sense but the use of computers as an aid to or controller of the actual physical production of goods or of processes. In data processing, the computer manipulates information to produce reports that guide management. In the applications discussed here, no human being is interposed between the computer and the machines or plant that carry out the manufacturing processes. Or, to put it in another way, man does not perform an interpretive function and there is direct communication between computer and productive equipment.

Before discussing the numerical control of machine tools and process control, the two groups under which these direct control functions are categorized, I want to pause to describe data-collection systems. These, in fact, are more related to data processing than to direct control systems. But because this chapter is devoted solely to various aspects of manufacture, it seemed more sensible to describe data-collection systems (which are used exclusively in factories) here than elsewhere in this book.

Data-collection systems

A data-collection system is a group of special machines which, situated at various strategic points on the factory floor, act as input stations for information related to factory operations. These input stations may take various forms, but usually combine an automatic reader with a keyboard for manual entries. They may be connected by communications lines directly to a central computer or to an intermediate machine, such as a card or paper-tape punch, situated in the computer room.

The object of a system like this is to speed up the collection of information, to ensure that all relevant data gets into the system, and largely to automate its recording so as to obviate the considerable body of clerical work normally associated with this job. Fed to the computer direct or at frequent intervals from the intermediate machine, this data can be manipulated to afford frequent and comprehensive reports to management on progress in the works. It can also, of course, be stored by the computer for future use in the production of payroll, the compilation of statistical and other reports, and in the formulation of future production plans.

Typically, the input stations used in a data-collection system will automatically read basic information from pre-punched cards, from special plastic badges issued to operatives, or from both of these; and will also record the time of entry from an automatic clock. This provides a means for the fast, accurate entry of all static information that can be pre-recorded—for example, operatives' clock numbers and details of the job in hand. It remains only to enter the variables, such as number of parts completed. This is done by a keyboard or by push-buttons.

A data-collection system used on-line to a central computer may also include output stations—typically printers, which will produce new instructions or other messages originated by the computer program. An off-line system may have a card-punching output station which will produce fresh operations cards on-site in the factory.

A less mechanized form of data collection which operates in a similar way uses Kimball tickets (which are miniature punched cards). In this case, sets of tickets are pre-punched and accompany the job round the factory, one part being detached as each operation is completed. Additional detail on completed operations may be entered (in numerical form only) by placing the ticket in a specially modified cash register which punches additional holes. On receipt at a central point, the tickets are put through a converter which reads the data from them and punches it into paper tape or cards or writes it onto magnetic tape.

One of the newest and most interesting data-collection systems is known as Hancock Telecontrol. Designed in electro-mechanical form by Hancock, an American company, it was considerably refined by a British company, C.A.V. Ltd, in conjunction with Hancock. Now electronic, Telecontrol has at the time of writing been used with considerable success for some $2\frac{1}{2}$ years in one of C.A.V.'s own factories and plans are afoot to offer the system in this country on a commercial basis.

Telecontrol is more sophisticated than any of the systems I have yet mentioned because it automatically monitors production on machine tools by counting components as they are made and logging the production data. It also contains provision for the immediate calling for help by an individual operative whose machine goes down or is in some other kind of trouble.

Modular in design, the system comprises the following basic components: at the machine tool, a control box; on the shop floor, a speech and lamp communications system for the summoning of assistance; in a central control room, a monitor cabinet, display cabinet, master console, memory unit, and teletype machine with paper-tape punch.

At the beginning of each shift, the load for each machine is pre-set on the display panel. This setting shows the number of parts to be made on each and the total automatically decreases each time a part is completed.

As a part is produced, a sensing device on the machine tool generates a pulse and this is fed automatically into the control room monitor cabinet and to the memory drum. The drum stores the number of pulses and automatically activates the mechanical balance counter for the machine concerned.

Piece count, productive time, and down-time are stored on the drum where the number of the machine, of the operator and of the job are also stored. A combination of three small lamps on the machine tool control box is duplicated on the control room panel. Steady green shows the machine is being monitored and is not on downtime; steady red shows down-time; combinations of yellow and red identify the type of help call that has been made.

In need of help, an operative throws a manual switch on his

control box, thus lighting a signal in the control room. The controller then pages the appropriate charge-hand or other supervisor over the public address system. On diagnosing a fault, the charge-hand plugs the jack of a telephone hand-set he always carries with him into the control box and reports to the controller who then, if necessary, summons further help.

Only a charge-hand can put a machine on down-time, using a special key. As he does this, the piece count stops and the down-time record starts. The reset button which returns the machine to productive status may, however, be used by the operative.

For full information on the status of any machine, the controller interrogates the memory drum from his console. The report may be shown on the console's illuminated display panel, or be printed or punched into paper tape, or both, at the teletype machine.

Among the benefits claimed by C.A.V., who are using the Tele-control system on nearly 200 machine tools, are significantly improved machine utilization, shop floor communication, organization and loading of works orders, works engineering maintenance, and management information services. It is liked by the operatives because it allows the immediate summoning of help when difficulty is met and very accurately records their production figures.

Numerical control of machine tools

Numerical control (or N/C as it is now almost universally called) is a means of automatically directing the movements of machine tools by using a set of instructions expressed in the form of digits. These instructions are punched into a paper tape or written on magnetic tape which, fed to a controlling device, causes the machine to move its various parts at speeds and in directions laid down by the instructions.

Numerical control is therefore fundamentally different from older automatic systems which control machine movement through mechanical devices such as templates or cams. The easiest way to emphasize this important difference is, perhaps, by simple analogy.

If I use the older form of control and ask you to draw a picture I have envisaged, I will put a pen in your hand, place the pen on paper, cover your hand with my own and guide its movements. If I want you to carry out the same process by numerical control I will go about it quite differently. I will first make my own drawing on a fine grid—graph paper, say—each of whose lines has an unique index number. I can draw only by following the lines of the grid, that is, I cannot make any diagonal move across any of the tiny squares. When I have done this, I will painstakingly make a list of every 'map reference' or co-ordinate I touch and in this way describe my drawing.

To cause you to duplicate this, I will place a pen in your hand and put an identical grid before you. I will then read out, one by one, the list of references I have made. If you follow my instructions precisely, you will make an exact reproduction of my original drawing, accurate to every detail.

This, in fact, is exactly what happens to a numerically controlled machine tool. In this case, though, the discrete steps are so tiny as to be almost undetectable by the human eye. As a result, the machine appears to move quite smoothly, the machined metal is smooth to the touch.

In its most elementary form, N/C is used to direct the movement of a machine tool in two directions only—in a way analogous to the movement of a pen on paper. These directions are known as the x- and y-axes. Useful though this form of control is for applications such as cutting shapes in sheet metal, it is obviously severely limited. Addition of a third dimension, the up-and-down or z-axis, considerably enhances the scope of numerical control, for it means that, in operations like drilling, depth as well as positioning of holes can be dictated.

Carried to this point, numerical control involves no very complex work in preparing instructions. These are not quite as childishly simple as they might appear from my description, since factors like machine speed have also to be taken into consideration. Just as you cannot direct a car to make a sharp turn without slacking speed, you cannot direct a machine tool. Your instructions must therefore (since the tool, like the computer, is inherently an idiot) direct the tool to slow its speed before major changes of direction, and must describe the steps in this speed change.

All the same, it is perfectly possible to prepare these instructions with the aid of a desk calculator, or even pen and paper. It is in the more sophisticated aspects of numerical control that a computer becomes literally indispensable.

The most sophisticated of modern N/C systems for machine tools are multi-dimensional—that is, the machine tool can be directed to perform any task within the limits of its own mechanical versatility and without any human intervention at all.

Governed by a numerical control system like this, a machine tool can cut non-geometrical curves, can fabricate parts with many surfaces themselves complex and with complicated relationships with other surfaces and can change its own tools. In consequence, the preparation of instructions is immensely difficult. If you try to imagine how you could work out numerical instructions that would enable me to carve, say, the naturalistic figure of a woman out of a block of wood, you will get some idea of the complexity of the mathematics associated with sophisticated machine tool control systems. There are hundreds of thousands of co-ordinates in several dimensions to define. Manual methods would be ludicrously inadequate because of the vast amount of time they would occupy and the inevitable inaccuracy of the results.

Before going on to outline how computers are used to handle N/C calculations, I ought I think to answer one question: 'What makes all this worth while when the system, even at its best, merely duplicates the work of a skilled machinist?' This man studies an engineering drawing and acts upon the information contained in it—in fact, he uses his intelligence and skill to translate the graphic description into physical action which produces the part concerned.

This question is answered, not only by the fact that the use of N/C is increasing rapidly in the USA (though rather more slowly here) but by the fact that the Ministry of Technology has recently set up an advisory service to encourage and advise smaller businesses to exploit numerical control (I will return to this topic later). A big research plan on N/C has also begun at the National Engineering Laboratory.

To summarize the ways in which N/C is used, I can hardly do better than quote an article by David A. Richemont (6.1).

Though generalization is dangerous, it might be fair to say that, on the whole, numerical control is likely to be most profitable when requirements are: (a) To make a large number of identical parts whose design incorporates complex curves, a large number of holes on several surfaces, or other features which make conventional methods difficult and therefore slow and expensive; (b) To perform a number of different machining operations on one piece; and (c) To produce in one piece a large and complex form which would otherwise have to be separated into several different components. Numerical control has to date [1965] been found most effective in milling and drilling operations.

Outlining the benefits of N/C, Mr Richemont, who is both a numerical control and a computer specialist, continues:

Among the advantages numerical control can bring when suitably applied, is a great reduction of lead time in the planning of complex parts. Designs which might take months to reach the machining stage can be realized in weeks. Tooling time, also, is reduced to almost nil. When there is a machining centre—a multipurpose machine tool—this can, by numerical control, carry out a large number of operations with the work-piece fixed only once on the machine. Time normally spent in moving parts from one machine to another and in intermediate setting-up is saved.

A numerically controlled machine tool, points out Mr Richemont, can work for longer periods at a stretch than a human operator who gets tired and bored. In consequence, the total time taken to produce large numbers of parts can be drastically shortened.

Finally, one of the most valuable advantages of numerical control is that the computer system can embody the skills, adjustments and judgements which must normally be supplied by a human operative. All these factors are stored in a compact form (paper-tape or cards) which can, if necessary, be filed for long intervals and re-used at any time to reproduce the operations in an identical way.

This last point has particularly important implications. For it means that it is possible, for instance, to reproduce with the utmost precision even the most complex piece of engineering in one factory in another—at the opposite side of the world, if needs be. It also means that human skills need not die with their possessor.

APT: A PURPOSE-DESIGNED SYSTEM. As numerical control increased in scope and sophistication after the Second World War, it became apparent there was a need to devise some method that would simplify and formalize the translation of engineering drawings into N/C instructions. In the USA, the Aerospace Industries Association, the Massachusetts Institute of Technology, the Illinois Institute of Technology Research, and several large computer manufacturers formed a group to tackle this formidable project.

The result of several years' intensive work by this body was APT (Automatically Programmed Tool), a very powerful and comprehensive computer program which employs its own, purpose-designed high-level language. The version of this program extant at present is the third, APT III. The facilities it offers are, in summary, as follows:

(*a*) A language that enables an engineer to describe concisely and precisely the content of a drawing of a component that is to be produced automatically by a numerically controlled machine tool. The APT III language is based upon plain English and standard engineering terms, and can therefore quickly and easily be learned by an engineer. Versatile and with a very large vocabulary, it can be used for programming not only tools like milling and drilling machines, lathes and machining centres, but also flame cutters, shot peeners, draughting, and inspection machines.

(*b*) A computer program which automatically:

translates the APT program language into the computer's own language (the compiling function described in chapter 3);

expands 'skeleton' descriptive data provided by the designer into detailed part geometry;

uses this geometry to calculate a cutting path for a machine tool;

checks the logic of the design as it goes along, providing print-outs to draw attention to any anomalies that may have occurred during interpretation and computation of the data;

calculates and inserts the data on acceleration and deceleration of the particular type of machine tool to be used;

produces a complete set of machine tool control instructions for any given make or type of machine tool and punches these out onto paper-tape or writes them on magnetic tape, as required by the control system.

Under the APT system, instructions for the machine tool are therefore prepared in three well-defined stages. First comes part geometry, the definition in mathematical terms of the part to be produced by the tool. Next comes part programming, where this definition is converted into generalized and complete machine tool instructions. The final phase, post processing, involves the conversion of the generalized instructions into instructions for a specific make and type of machine tool. Thus a single APT application might have a number of post processors so as to permit its use on a variety of machine tools.

APT III, like most modern programs, is modular in structure so that it allows for amendment of any section of a design without re-writing any part other than that directly affected by the changes. This valuable property was neatly demonstrated by the National

Engineering Laboratory and Univac at the 1968 IFIP (International Federation for Information Processing) Congress. Members of an audience for this demonstration were invited to alter one of the dimensions of a small part that had been fabricated by the APT system. A few fresh cards were punched on the spot, the data transmitted via a 1004 terminal to the distant computer at East Kilbride, and new cards punched on the 1004 from data prepared on the remote 1108. No other modifications were required and the entire operation was completed in a very few minutes.

So valuable is the basic concept of APT that various simplified versions have been written. These, though obviously not as comprehensive and versatile as the full program, are perfectly adequate for the simpler types of N/C application and allow the APT method to be used on medium-size computers as distinct from the very powerful systems that are required for the full-scale version. In Britain, the National Engineering Laboratory has recently produced a family of APT-derived languages which include 2C,L for milling, 2P,L for drilling, and 2C for turning. At the time of writing, this family is being extended to provide improved facilities for lathe work and machining centres and will be made freely available to any firm wishing to use it, says NEL.

The application of the APT program can go much further than the machining of parts. The full mathematical definition of the object to be produced can be fed to an automatic plotter, which will draw it out, thus presenting it to the designer in visual form. From this drawing, he can see what kinds of alteration may be required, feed these back into the system and, if he wishes, produce a second drawing. The APT program can just as well be used for the production of the tools designed to make the required object as the object itself; and also, of course, to prepare models, if these are needed. If final inspection of the finished object can be carried out by machine, the APT program can look after this function, too. Little imagination is needed to appreciate how the use of this system can save time in the production of complex designs.

Huge sums of money were invested in research and the development of APT. And, as might be expected in a program so large and complex and associated with an expanding technology, APT is subject to constant development and amendment. A special, US-based organization, IITRI (Illinois Institute of Technology Research Institute) has been set up for this work and for the exchange of information between APT users all over the western world. The APT

III program is therefore available only to subscribers who, in return, receive basic program documentation and associated information, an advisory service and quarterly amendments to APT III. The APT III system is, however, also available for use through some large computer service bureaux who subscribe to IITRI.

THE MINTECH N/C SERVICE. In 1967, the Ministry of Technology opened a Numerical Control Advisory and Demonstration Service to accelerate the introduction of N/C machine tools in British industry. This service aims to assist companies by assessing the benefits they can obtain from N/C equipment; advising on the selection of tools, programming, and machining components submitted by individual firms; and providing courses and symposia on the advantages and problems involved. Subjects of these symposia include technical and economic aspects, machine techniques, and programming and computer techniques. The service is provided through the Royal Aircraft Establishment at Farnborough, the Production Engineering Research Association at Melton Mowbray and commercial organizations.

MOLINS SYSTEM 24. Developed by a British company, Molins Machine Co. Ltd of London, the Molins System 24 is almost certainly the first completely integrated system of manufacture for small and medium-size components and as such, says the Ministry of Technology, 'points the way towards the fully automated machine shops of the future'.

As I have had an opportunity of seeing only a static model of this system (though it is in actual use in Molins' own factory), I have drawn the following description freely from an article written by the company.

System 24, by concentrating on light alloy and providing a complete range of equipment to extract the maximum value from the almost unlimited metal-removal rates possible with aluminium alloys, achieves the highest productivity levels ever obtained from numerically controlled equipment, Molins claims. At the same time, it blends these elements into a computer-controlled flow-production system giving complete flexibility and a minimum batch size of two components.

A series of complementary machine tools is arranged as a completely flexible transfer line. Each machine tool in the line has a different function. Taken as a whole, the line is capable, says

Molins, of 'the most complex milling, boring, drilling, reaming, and tapping operations and this capability will be extended in the future'.

Because the capability of each machine in the line has been limited, the designs are simple. Linking the machines is a conveyor system which carries pallets loaded with blanks from the loading station to the first machine and from one machine to another without loss of accuracy. The System 24 unit can incorporate a varying number of machines of varying types and can thus be set up in accordance with the individual user's requirements. It can also subsequently be changed or added to, if necessary.

The system is controlled by a small digital computer and can, for example, run throughout a 16-hour night shift, unattended apart from maintenance. During the day, people are required only to load and unload the system.

The computer controls the scheduling of parts to be manufactured and also controls, on a moment-by-moment basis, all the movements of parts from the time they leave the loading bays until their completion. The last action of the computer is to issue a ticket at the end of the return conveyor to show the destination of a batch of completed parts.

Actual machining operations are controlled by a separate unit that employs cassettes of magnetic tape prepared beforehand by the computer. Thus, when work is loaded and ready for a machining operation, the computer hands over control to the magnetic tape; and when the operation is finished, again takes over to move the work onto the next stage. The entire process is checked and counterchecked at all stages. Notification of any faults is printed out at the computer typewriter as a warning to maintenance staff.

The total number of staff required for a six-machine system is 48, says Molins. Most of these are girls and this total staff requirement includes materials preparation and part programming. Thirty of these people may be semi-skilled.

It is claimed that a six-machine System 24 has an output equivalent to about 300 conventional machine tools working single shift. Development of a pilot system, which is being installed at Molins' own Deptford plant for the manufacture of components for its cigarette-making machines, is being partly financed by a grant from the Ministry of Technology. The machine tools and control equipment are due for installation early in 1969 and are expected to be fully operational after a 12-month working-up period.

This concludes my section on numerical control of machine tools, a section in which I should, perhaps, remark, I have only barely scratched a fascinating subject. There can be little doubt that the use of N/C techniques will increase in every industrialized country. In the UK, government organizations such as the National Engineering Laboratory (who have a sizable research project using a Univac 1108) and various other branches of Mintech are making strenuous efforts to promote its wider adoption.

Process control by computer

The function of a process-control computer is fundamentally different from that of the data-processing computers which are the subject of the greater part of this book. Though both types of computer are digital (see page 5), a process-control system exercises *actual physical control* over plant and machinery. This contrasts with the data-processing system which is used purely for the manipulation of facts and figures.

Frequently—as in a factory production-control application—these facts and figures relate to the utilization of plant and machinery. But the computer controls this only at second hand. You could think of a production-control system as traffic lights which direct the movements of a car only by giving signals to its driver. A process-control system, on the other hand, replaces the driver by assuming control of the car.

Process control operates on the *closed loop* system; that is, it is self-adjusting. The computer collects from the machines or plant under its supervision, via recording instruments, information about their status; it compares this information with data it holds in store about how the machines should perform in a given situation; and it feeds back to equipment that controls the machines locally any necessary instructions that will adjust their performance. What these instructions are is dictated by the program used by the computer and the calculations it carries out on the data it receives.

This, as you will recognize, is an elaboration of the simple principle that underlies the operation of a thermostat.

There are two levels of sophistication in process control. At the lower level, the computer, while exercising direct control over the process, works to a pattern laid down by the control engineers. In effect, the computer is told: 'This is how the process should run; these are the tolerances within which the various parts of it must be maintained. Keep these controls in balance, and notify me only if some action is required that you cannot cope with'.

The second, and by far the more difficult and ambitious method of process control, employs the technique known as *optimization*. We have met this already in chapter 5. In process control, optimization involves giving the computer no predetermined pattern to work to. Instead, it is provided with a mathematical model of the process it is to control and informed merely of what products are to be manufactured today. Here, in effect, the computer is told: 'This is the type or mix of products we want to make now. Find out the most satisfactory way to do this ("satisfaction" being defined sometimes on a day-to-day basis by management) and control the process in accordance with your decision'. This puts upon the computer the onus not only for adjusting the machine controls but for setting the pattern to which they are to be adjusted.

In the first of the levels of control sophistication, you could compare the role of the computer with that of the factory operative who is given precise instructions on what he must do and utilizes his machine in accordance with these instructions. In the second, the computer's function more nearly resembles that of the factory manager whose orders are merely to produce certain quantities and types of product and is left to decide for himself what measures are needed to achieve his target.

I am aware that this analogy is rather dangerous because it suggests that the computer entirely usurps the function of a human manager. I feel therefore I should emphasize that the quality of the decisions taken by the process control computer depends absolutely upon the skill with which the mathematical model of the operation has been constructed and the control system designed. So once again, we are back to fundamental reliance upon human ingenuity, skills, and thought.

My presentation to you of optimized process-control systems suggests that these are absolutely superior to the less sophisticated type. This is not strictly correct, for it applies only when the process to be controlled can be considered as an integrated operation; that is, an event that happens in any part of the system directly affects many other parts of the system. In such instances, it is clearly of benefit to optimize, if possible, for only in this way can the control system be most fruitfully exploited. (This statement is easy to write: the problem of optimization is extremely tough.)

In some instances, though, the optimization concept may be totally irrelevant. A case in point is a system now partly installed at Henry Wiggin & Co. Ltd of Hereford (a subsidiary of International Nickel). This involves automatic control by an IBM 1800 computer of some hundreds of machines performing creep tests or strain tests or X-ray spectrographic analysis on samples of metal alloys manufactured by the company. Though the computer will eventually control all these functions concurrently, no machine has any connection with the others as each is engaged in a self-contained testing operation. In a set-up like this, there can be no requirement for optimization.

(At the risk of being thought chauvinistic, I will add that the Wiggin project is larger than any of its kind in Europe and is probably a world first. Developed at Hereford, it is being watched with considerable interest by the American parent company. By the time you read these words, the greater part of the system will probably be in full operation.)

Many industrial processes, however, whether they are continuous in character like the generation of electricity, or batch operations such as the manufacture of paper or the brewing of beer, are inherently integrated. But until the advent of the electronic computer, it was not possible to control them in an integrated way. Though some of the control equipment is sophisticated (and is sometimes marginally more accurate than digital computers) no medium was available for automatically linking groups of equipment together. The best, therefore, that could be done was to rely for integration upon a control engineer who, presented with displays from the various groups of instruments, gauged the effects of one group of operations upon another as best he could and adjusted the controls accordingly. Action taken in these circumstances is based upon knowledge and experience and can fairly be described as informed guesswork. Even were it theoretically feasible to carry out on desk machines the elaborate calculations required to discover exactly how to adjust the controls to best advantage, lack of time would preclude this as a practical proposition. Process control is, of necessity, real-time control.

Very few industrial operations are controlled even as closely as I have outlined in the preceding paragraph and in many even the concept of integration is alien to the managers. In view of this and the fact that very valuable physical assets are at stake, it is not surprising that computerized process control has gained ground only slowly in this country. An estimate of the total UK market given me by AEI Automation (now absorbed into General Electric) early in

1967 puts the figures for process control computers installed each year at 50 in 1967, 70 in 1968, 98 in 1969, and 135 in 1970.

Nor is it to be wondered at that the earliest industries to use digital computers for process control were those like electricity generating, petroleum distillation, and chemical processing. For these had already sophisticated their control systems to the limits of existing equipment and thoroughly understood the benefits to be obtained by integrated control.

PROCESS-CONTROL HARDWARE. Before the invention of the electronic digital computer, the only way automatically to control plant and machinery was by analogue devices. Though these analogue computers operate on the same closed-loop system I outlined earlier in this chapter, information fed into and instructions emitted by them take the form of a continuous but fluctuating flow of electric current. It was very natural that this method should be used, as all recording and local control devices operate in the analogue mode (think again of a thermostat).

Analogue computers are capable of exercising very delicate and sensitive control because adjustment is continuous. A great many are in use and it seems unlikely the principle will ever be discarded as completely obsolescent. There is, however, one serious limitation in an analogue system and that is its inability to perform the complex and voluminous calculations required for integrated control of a system with more than quite a small number of input and output devices.

This disadvantage has been overcome in the digital computer which, as we have seen, is capable of controlling hundreds of devices on an integrated basis. This function is known as *direct digital control* (DDC). Input information, by the time it reaches the computer, is expressed in the form of discrete electrical pulses (as opposed to a continuous flow). Pulses like this are, of course, meat and drink to a digital computer (the holes on a punched card are ultimately translated into this form, for example). Control instructions are put out in the same format because this is the only way in which a digital computer can work.

There is, therefore, what one could call a communications gap between the computer, which operates in the digital mode, and the input and output equipment which (of necessity) works in the analogue mode. This gap is bridged by a device known as an analogue-to-digital converter.

Quite simple in electrical terms, this device accepts continuous current at one end, amplifies what is usually a very weak signal into one of manageable size, and breaks this down into a series of discrete pulses whose value closely approximates to that of the original signal. You may have noticed there is an analogy here to the numerical control method I have described in the previous section of this chapter. The analogue-to-digital conversion is very similar to the process of transcribing the smooth outline of an artist's drawing onto graph paper and being permitted only to draw along the pre-printed lines of the grid. Your finished work will not be quite as sensitive and elegant as the original, but will certainly convey with reasonable accuracy the impression the artist intended to give.

The conversion process is, of course, carried out in reverse when the computer emits instructions to the local control equipment.

You will, I hope, appreciate from my description that the process-control computer is not fundamentally different from the data-processing computer. In fact, you could argue that the process-control machine (whose analogue-to-digital converter is usually built-in) succeeds only because it is capable of turning analogue signals into data and processing this.

The main point of contrast is that the process-control computer is designed specifically to handle a very large number (150 to 200 is probably the minimum) of loops, each of which has its own input and output device; and normally has insufficient capacity to operate more than a few 'conventional' high-speed peripherals such as line printers, magnetic-disc files, paper-tape readers, plotters, or CRT terminals. This is seldom a disadvantage as the requirement for these is usually small and the system can support a sizable number of low-speed peripherals. Typically, these are typewriters which inform human operators when action, such as re-loading of a machine, must be taken by them.

By the very nature of its job, a process-control computer must operate in real-time. It must regularly accept data at predetermined intervals from the measuring instruments attached to the machines or plant it controls; it must, without delay, perform any calculations that are necessary; and it must immediately issue fresh instructions to the local control devices.

When it comes to hardware configuration, there are two broad methods of approach. One is to employ a single central computer; the other to set up a hierarchy. In a hierarchical structure, several very small computers each exert immediate control over a little group of machines; and two or more of these small computers are on-line to a larger system which co-ordinates and further processes the partly digested data these supply to it. The hierarchy may end here with one or more medium-size systems; or these may, in turn, be satellites to a yet larger computer.

Which kind of approach is adopted will depend partly upon the type of operations to be controlled, partly on the preference of the user. Proponents of the hierarchical approach argue that this provides a system more flexible and easier to manage than a large central computer. On the other hand, the superior power of a large machine may be valuable in its own right because the system is capable of tackling complex scheduling and routine data-processing jobs in addition to its control function.

If the operations to be controlled are of any size, the central computer must operate on a time-sharing basis, as otherwise it would be necessary to have an uneconomically large system. Time-sharing, you will recollect, demands that the computer be capable of momentarily interrupting any activity at any time in favour of another—in fact, able to perform a perpetual juggling act to accommodate the demands of a number of programs under way at any given time and to accord overriding priorities to remote terminals.

In the light of what I have described in earlier chapters and the strict time-schedules implicit in a process-control application, you will not be surprised to learn that a good operating system is as essential in this type of computer as it is in a data-processing system. The process-control programmer has a good many intricate problems to face anyhow. Without a good operating system, it is doubtful whether he would succeed in getting a complex system to run within five years or more of starting his work.

During the past few years, computer manufacturers have built up a considerable body of software support for process-control applications, though application software is, perhaps, thinner on the ground. There is not, on the whole, as much freemasonry among users of process-control systems as among users of data-processing systems. A proportion of users of process-control systems are so secretive about their applications that they will tell even the computer manufacturer nothing, preferring to tackle their problems without help from this quarter. As a result, a good deal of software which is developed within companies does not become generally available.

BENEFITS OF COMPUTER CONTROL. As my opportunities for personal studies of process control by computer have been few, I have drawn heavily in this section and in the one following on a paper* by F. A. Snow, who at the time he wrote it was sales manager, computer automation, AEI Automation Ltd and is now with Honeywell Computer Control Division.

The potential benefits of integrated process-control automation are listed by Mr Snow as follows:

Cost of control system. In a chemical plant with more than a basic minimum (typically 200) control loops, a computer-based integrated control system can be genuinely cheaper than its non-integrated analogue counterpart. Even on absolute cost, the computer system may win; and there are, in addition, the advantages offered by a properly designed computer system. These include:

better control arising from a wider and more stable range of controller settings and the ability to apply more advanced formulae for control;
greater flexibility in control configuration;
automatic determination of controller settings;
a central facility for producing process logs, efficiency reports, and so on;
the ability cheaply to extend the system to include other processes, alarm scanning and optimizing functions, and off-line computation services like routine data-processing applications (off-line in this connection meaning apart from the process control application).

Plant costs. In new plants, an integrated control system can reduce capital cost. A good example of this may be drawn from the cement industry where an accurate on-line raw-meal-blending system can obviate the need for large batch-blending tanks.

Plant throughput. The throughput volume may be an important ingredient in profitability and may often be increased by the application of integrated control techniques. Among the means that achieve this increase are the following:

(*a*) Improved scheduling of production among batch units. This results in better plant utilization and an increase in production.

* Systems Assessment (Part I) by F. A. Snow. Read at the IEE Conference on Integrated Process Control Application in Industry, September 1966.

Machine shops and motor tyre factories provide examples of this kind of benefit.

(b) Improved prediction. Given a mathematical model of the plant, a computer-based integrated control system is better able to monitor process-state and predict the termination of a batch process with exactitude. A typical example is the oxygen steel-making process, where steel is produced by injecting oxygen into a rotating vessel containing a mixture of limestone, scrap steel, and iron ore, whose analyses and weights approximate to but cannot precisely meet a designed recipe. The objective of a computer system is to predict the exact process time and amount of oxygen to be added, as calculated from the actual weights and analyses of these components. Normally, this job is done by a human being whose margin of error gives rise to a need for more frequent correction cycles after elapse of the predicted time. In consequence, production is lost.

(c) Improved control. When a process becomes less stable and more difficult to control as throughput rises, the greater sensitivity of integrated control may offer the only means of achieving maximum production. In papermaking, the interaction of many variables must be taken into account when seeking to make a sheet within specifications at maximum speed. Penalties for poor control include low speed, high consumption of raw materials, and breakages on the machine.

Manpower requirement. A reduction in manpower is not a common benefit of integrated process-control systems, Mr Snow asserts. But if these bring centralized control of remote plant units which would otherwise have to be manned, savings may be made. To my own knowledge, savings of this kind are anticipated by the Eastern Gas Board which, at the time of writing, is about to begin installation of a complex communications system which includes control of some aspects of gas distribution. Human readings of instruments at certain points in the network will now become unnecessary, though the control process itself will not initially be automatic. Certain requirements will be set by engineers at a central control point to which all the automatically collected data will be fed through the communications system. The status of the distribution network will, when necessary, be changed by the manual re-setting of these central controls.

The saving of manpower becomes a significant factor in industries where labour is hard to get and where the process is vulnerable to absenteeism: coal-mining is a case in point. Here the primary object of control systems is to allow the collieries to keep on working with reduced manpower.

Often the jobs that are abolished are very tedious. For this reason, it is difficult to get people to do them and hard to obtain accurate recordings. A man, for example, whose job is merely to note down certain readings at intervals becomes hopelessly bored and tends (though not intentionally) to see what he expects rather than what is actually there.

Product quality. Here the gain to be looked for is less an absolute level of improvement in product quality than less variability about a specified mean. This is an important consideration for plants that make a product sold as a raw material for another process.

Paper manufacture again is a good case in point. During a personal conversation, Mr Laurence Clarke of Elliott Process Control cited the example of Wolvercote Paper Mill which now has automatic, computerized control. Savings were made in eliminating variations in the weight of the paper which were sometimes as much as six per cent. Paper sold by the sheet must have a guaranteed minimum base weight and if one does not keep as close to this as possible one is giving away a certain amount of paper. At Wolvercote, the original control was manually operated and was changed every 15 minutes. The computer could make changes every half minute and could thus strictly regulate the weight. 'This can represent considerable savings,' Mr Clarke commented.

Process efficiency. This, of course, means different things to different industries. Power-station heat-rate and output per man in coal mining are two examples named by Mr Snow. There are many others.

Cost of raw materials. Better control can lead to the acceptability of more variable and consequently cheaper feed-pulping plants in the paper industry and the continued use of pulverized fuel in combustion processes. An example cited by Mr Clarke was in the manufacture of a certain type of steel where phosphorus impurity must be kept to a very low level—sometimes as small as 0·008 per cent. A control device which monitors phosphorus content of ore as it passes along a conveyor and will direct to one side any that has too high a content will permit the latter to be used in conjunction with other material that has less than the permitted percentage so that a balance can be established.

Safety. In addition to close control, computer-based integrated-control systems offer rapid monitoring of alarm conditions, automatic fault diagnosis, and instantaneous emergency action. Among plants that rely upon these capabilities are nuclear power stations. At at least one factory in the USA, manual methods simply cannot be applied if the computer fails; the plant simply ceases production. As this happens only very seldom, it is more economically viable to accept close-down when necessary, as the computer control system is so accurate as to allow running very near the critical point. Plant throughput can, in this way, be substantially raised. (Incidentally, it is highly probable that this decision was reached by evaluating the two alternatives by computer, though I cannot vouch for this.)

Information transfer. The ability to monitor, digest and distribute information to the right place at the right time is a feature of most integrated control systems. Knowing what is going on at any given moment is a great deal more useful than the very best post-mortem.

The feasibility study for process control

In this section I have again drawn freely on the paper by Mr F. A. Snow mentioned on page 155. But as he is far more knowledgeable than I about process control applications and has expressed his points very succinctly, and as my job is to help you rather than try to bluff you, I make no apology for picking his brains in this way.

In emphasizing the expert knowledge required to make a useful feasibility study for a process control application, Mr Snow echoes the views of others skilled in this field. Specialist knowledge will probably have to be drawn from many spheres of science and engineering and in consequence the organization contemplating installation of such a system may well have to depend to some degree on the staff of the system supplier.

Commenting on the difficulties which have arisen in the past through reluctance of prospective users to disclose confidential information, Mr Snow says this has slowed down the application of integrated control systems. In this connection, it is perhaps worth noting that, in the opinion of some eminent authorities in the USA, a good deal of the steam has gone out of shop-floor computer development as a whole. Nelson Metcalf of Hughes Development Corporation is one of those who deplores the fact that very few gifted men have found the area a sufficiently glamorous base on which to build a reputation and therefore tend to avoid it.

But to return specifically to process control: no really useful feasibility study can be carried out without full and free transfer of both technical and commercial information between all members of the team. (The alternative is suggestive of the dilemma that confronted the old-style Japanese emperors, whose tailors were not permitted to lay hands on the 'divine' personage and whose clothes were, in consequence, always ill-fitting!)

A formal secrecy undertaking signed by the equipment suppliers which protects the user's trade secrets offers a realistic solution to this problem, suggests Mr Snow.

Typically, a feasibility study lasts from 4 to 12 weeks and may involve from two to six permanent members of the study team. The time scale must be named and the staff must be very carefully selected to include those skilled in the following subjects.

(a) Process theory. Most integrated control systems require some form of mathematical model for their inception, design, and application. There is no substitute for the insight which a scientifically founded understanding of process mechanisms provides.

(b) Process practice. Very few processes behave on an industrial scale in the same way as one would expect them to behave in theory. Accumulated operating experience is therefore almost indispensable—though this may have been gained elsewhere than on the plant under study.

(c) Instrumentation. While computer techniques can get around intractable instrument problems, there is no substitute for good measurement. Instrumentation has recently developed very fast, and a feasibility study team should include someone with up-to-date knowledge and experience of instrumentation solutions and developments from a wide range of industry.

(d) Control theory and practice. In this area, theory tends to be well ahead of practice and control designers (like their counterparts in data processing) tend to adopt traditional solutions and simply duplicate an existing control philosophy. While one must avoid going too 'far out', it is also important to recognize the significance of the latest practical developments.

(e) Operational research. Many OR techniques can be applied during a feasibility study, particularly in defining the objectives of an integrated control system.

(f) Computer hardware and software. A sound appreciation of these is essential for realistic judgement.

(g) Administration. Under this heading, Mr Snow groups all the human functions associated with any feasibility study—the canvassing and sifting of comment and opinion at all levels, for example. Among the points he suggests need careful looking into are: the comments of the man on the job who has often acquired knowledge and adopted strategies of which management is unaware; the actual on-the-job performance of instruments which often varies from one application to another; sources of process disturbances (as revealed by discussions, recorder charts, progress logs); performance fluctuations—which are not always revealed by logs because of the human factor I mentioned earlier.

A look should also be taken at the economic environment of the plant because this may affect overall performance. Factors like the extent of competition, availability of capital, potential life of the product and whether this is to be sold or to be used within the parent organization are all relevant considerations. System design may depend upon company policy—e.g., a desire for better customer service, an intention to expand, and so on.

Labour considerations are also important. Are suitable staff available? How much training will be needed for new and existing staffs? Will relocation of staff be necessary? Will there be any redundancy?

(h) Distribution of effort. Mr Snow suggests that time and effort on a feasibility study for process control might be allocated as follows:

Preliminary exchange of information and explanations (team members get acquainted, outline the programme for the study, allocate duties)	5 per cent
Interviews with staff	20 per cent
Examination of technical incentives for integrated process control	15 per cent
Examination of economic incentives for integrated process control	15 per cent
Hardware and software evaluation	15 per cent
Preparation of report	30 per cent
	100 per cent

Economic incentives

The benefits of integrated process control may be divided into three categories: simple, incremental, and inferential. Simple benefits are those directly associated with a total saving in production cost and have little or no interaction with other benefits. Incremental benefits are those that result in increased plant throughput. Inferential benefits are those with no precisely assessable hard-cash value (our old friend, intangible benefits!), e.g., customer satisfaction, prestige, and better quality products.

Benefits in any of these categories may be further specified as absolute—predicted with certainty; or statistical—where improvement can be established only in terms of probability.

What are the applications of process control? I have already mentioned some of the principal ones. They include the production and distribution of electric power, chemical processing and in particular petro-chemical processing, the manufacture of paper and of cement, the production and processing of steel, the electrolytic smelting of aluminium, the mining of coal, and many others. One of the most spectacular process-control exercises at present under way is the road traffic experiment in West London, which is proving highly successful.

In general, I think one can safely say that any industrial or other operation that creates a dynamic situation involving the balancing of a large number of interactive factors offers a possibility for integrated computer control.

Summary

The following points have been mentioned in this chapter:

(a) Data-collection systems perform a useful function by gathering at a central point production information from the factory floor. They can also be a means of saving much clerical labour.

(b) Numerical control applied to machine tools is fundamentally different from older methods of control. Its nature is different; and it is far more powerful and versatile.

(c) Except in the simplest forms of numerical control, use of a computer is essential. The APT III system, a very powerful program with its own high-level, problem-orientated language, has been designed specifically for this purpose. It can cover not only

162 THE USE OF COMPUTERS FOR PROFIT

the operation of machine tools but can be used at the design, drawing, model-making, tooling, and inspection stages of manufacture.

(d) Among the organizations set up to help British industry employ numerical control of machine tools profitably are the National Engineering Laboratory and Mintech Numerical Control Advisory and Demonstration Service.

(e) One of the most interesting recent developments in machine tool automation is Molins System 24 which completely integrates manufacture of small and medium-size components made in light alloys. A fully working system should be in operation by 1970.

(f) The integrated control of industrial processes by computer offers important possibilities in increasing plant efficiency, lowering costs, raising throughput, improving product quality, and sometimes saving labour. Development in this country has, however, been relatively slow, partly because the problems are complex, partly because very valuable physical assets are involved.

(g) Process control can be exercised at two levels of sophistication. The simpler form involves using the computer to work to a pattern prescribed by control engineers; the more ambitious type uses the computer itself to determine what the pattern of operation should be to achieve predetermined results.

(h) The feasibility study for a process-control application is an exacting task that can successfully be undertaken by a team whose members have a mixture of skills.

(i) Two broad approaches are possible in determining the configuration of computer hardware to be used in process control. One is to use a hierarchical system with a series of small computers on-line to larger ones; the other is to hand the whole operation to a single powerful computer. Either of these may be entirely satisfactory. But the prospective user must decide whether he prefers the greater flexibility of the hierarchical system or can benefit more by having a powerful single system at his disposal.

Reference

6.1 RICHEMONT, D. A. Notes on APT III. *Data & Control* (now *Data Systems*). November 1965.

7. Choosing and installing
a computer

While I was planning and writing chapters 1 to 6 of this book, I thought of you principally as people seeking theoretical knowledge. I therefore first described how computer hardware and software are designed and used, and later outlined some of the theories underlying the application of computers in business and industry and some of the techniques employed in utilizing the computer as a management tool.

The time has now come for me to shift my emphasis and to regard you as managers faced with the possibility of installing a computer within your own organizations. I have therefore devoted this chapter to discussing some of the purely practical and technical factors that you must consider when tackling this job. Lest the title of the chapter should suggest that it is a sort of computer user's *Which?*, let me hasten to disabuse you now. It is, quite candidly, outside my competence to compare in real depth the merits of rival computer systems. And even could I do this, I believe the exercise would be of very limited usefulness within this context as changes occur so frequently and so fast. I have therefore confined my discussion to the broad areas where fundamental change occurs relatively slowly and which, in many ways, are of greatest importance to executives and managers.

Is your computer really necessary?

In my Preface, I pointed out that there is only one valid reason for ever using—let alone installing—a computer at all: The possibility of increasing the profitability of the user organization. I should like to stress this again.

There is some controversy about how, precisely, one should

measure profitability. But this is hardly the place to start an argument about the merits of the different formulae that may be applied to assess this factor. I shall therefore merely caution you to make sure that whatever your theory may be, it is a strictly realistic one.

Many traps await those who decide to examine the possibility of computerization. To the outsider, the most obvious of these is summed up by the opening lines of a Noel Coward song, 'Everybody's doing it, doing it, doing it, Everybody's doing it now!' Though we like to believe that the days are over when businessmen bought computers chiefly for the pleasure of being able carelessly to refer to 'our computer', this view is almost certainly over-optimistic. Many well informed people have told me that a number of organizations, though they have succeeded in concealing the unpalatable truth from themselves, purchase a computer principally for prestige reasons.

This is an extremely expensive hobby. In a not altogether frivolous spirit, I would suggest that such companies would suffer less if they rigged up a dummy with a few nice flashing lights and continued with their existing systems if they were reasonably efficient.

Equally disastrous is the fallacy that a computer will put an end to the ills of an ailing business. In such cases, the management are like a couple who, through lack of insight or by self-deception, persuade themselves that a child will shore up a shaky marriage. In either kind of case, there is tragic evidence to prove how wrong the assumption was.

Certainly a computer can restore an organization to economic health. But only if its troubles have arisen from causes that a computer can cure. A computer can do nothing but burden a business that is fundamentally sick through poor management and an attempt to superimpose one in this situation simply compounds the malady.

It seems fair to suggest, therefore, that any company that considers at all the use of a computer without having first taken a careful look at itself is asking for trouble. Unresolved conflicts among top managers, for example, will be aggravated by installing a computer, since the quarrel will extend to who is to be in charge of it, who is to get first crack at using it.

In organizations that are labour-intensive, an O & M study will often reveal that the kind of staff reductions management believes (often erroneously) a computer might bring, can be effected by a revamping of conventional methods at far smaller cost. Wofac

Corporation, a firm of consultants that specializes in office re-organization and during the past seven years has worked with some 200 British companies, has found that most can save 30 per cent in staff simply through the application of realistic measuring techniques to the output of clerical staff. This procedure often reveals that poor organization manifested, for example, in a bad work distribution pattern, has led to severe under-employment in many areas.

Typically, a department may be split into sections each dealing with, say, contracts within a certain range of monetary value. This can lead to a situation where one section is worked off its feet while the others get on with their knitting. Absurdities may arise as a result of staffing to meet recurrent peak periods. Labour is taken on permanently to cover this situation, but inevitably some people are under-employed during slack periods. Management, eager to ensure full staffing during peak times, invents jobs to keep these people busy in between times. But when the rush comes, the original intention of these jobs is forgotten and they are sincerely believed to be essential. There is too much work for the department to handle, so more staff are engaged.

I have mentioned in an earlier chapter how the very existence of a computer within an organization can lead to the proliferation of paper. Insufficient thought may also result in its being used to perpetuate procedures that are utterly pointless.

A story told to me as true in this connection concerned a very large American organization that has factories all over the USA. Every month, each factory analysed its output by product and sent the figures to its area manager. At the area manager's office, a clerk consolidated the analyses from several factories (the products were identical) to produce overall statistics showing total output of each product. Finally, these figures were sent to head office, where a sizable staff was employed in dissecting the area figures to reveal the output of individual factories!

Do not be too sure that your organization, too, does not do things as absurd as these. It may well be that if you feel the time has come to think about a computer, your staff are snowed under with work. In these circumstances, it is fatally easy to overlook the significance of what is done. A computer dropped uncritically into such an environment can simply make inefficiency rather more expensive.

I think I have written enough to indicate that it is folly even to consider the possibility of installing a computer without first ascertaining whether or not existing methods of operation are sound or

M

whether less sophisticated methods would do the job just as well. There can never be any virtue in using a sledge-hammer to crack a walnut.

The formal investigation that precedes a decision to use (or not to use) a computer is known as a *feasibility study*. Before this is carried out, however, or at least concurrently with it, top management must be prepared to find the most realistic answers they can to two very searching questions.

First, '*What are the overall objectives of the organization?*' That is, where does it hope to go in the immediate future and, say, during the next 5–7 years? Second, '*How can these objectives be achieved?*' In other words, what broad strategy should be adopted? As I have already discussed both these points in an earlier chapter, I mention them here as a reminder in context.

The feasibility study

At least two men are required to carry out a feasibility study and often it is desirable to employ more. The question of who is best qualified to tackle this task is discussed later in this chapter. Meantime, let us look at what information the study should yield. Its first phase is designed to find out what *precisely* the organization is doing at present and how *precisely* this is being done. Among the questions to be answered are the following:

(*a*) Why are these procedures carried out; what is their purpose?

(*b*) Who carries them out? How is the company organized; what is the pattern of responsibility?

(*c*) What is the relationship between one procedure and another? In other words, how does the work of each section or department impinge upon that of the others?

(*d*) What data is collected and processed during these procedures?

(*e*) What is the volume of work? For example, how many invoices are processed each month, how big are they, or how many and what kinds of unit are manufactured?

(*f*) What percentage of error occurs in clerical work, or what percentage of scrap or rejection in manufacturing?

(*g*) What is the time-scale? For instance, how long a period elapses between receiving an order, acknowledging, and eventually fulfilling it? Between the issue of an invoice and payment by a debtor? Between the start and finish of a series of factory operations?

(h) How are people being used? Are highly-qualified people doing jobs unworthy of their calibre, or teenagers occupying highly responsible positions?

(i) What is the cost of each procedure?

(j) What kind of management information is yielded by existing procedures? Is this as much as is needed? Is the format suitable?

Though I doubt whether this list is exhaustive, it at least gives some indication of the lines along which such an inquiry should proceed.

Results of phase 1 of the feasibility study are often disconcerting because they reveal so many weaknesses, even in a business that seems to be well run. Typically, some of the areas of failure are as follows.

Duplication. The same information is written repeatedly on a number of different documents. The amount of error is too high and labour is used uneconomically.

When the O & M Department of the Bristol Engine Division of Rolls-Royce Ltd carried out a feasibility study for computerized control of the engineering development of the Olympus 593 (Concorde) engine, they found much duplication. Procedures such as the drawing up of manufacturing schedules and the issue of operating instructions for fabrication (only two examples of many) involved repeated copying of the same detail. When a new system was devised, a great deal of labour—some clerical, some much more highly qualified—was obviated and errors that had arisen during transcription and had slowed down and confused the entire operation were eliminated.

Excessive delay between the opening and closing of transactions. It may be found, for example, that orders lie around unacknowledged for days; that bottlenecks frequently occur as a result of unnecessarily elaborate procedures or a pattern of responsibility that gives the power of decision only to one man who is often unavoidably absent.

Misuse of highly qualified labour. Poor organization or an overload of paperwork may mean that highly qualified men and women are performing tasks that ought to be handled by clerks.

Lack of control. In the absence of any coherent system for feeding back information on work in progress, there is no real control over what goes on within the company. The manager of an American-owned factory in Scotland told me that he would like to purchase more components in the UK but that: 'When I ring up and ask them how an order is coming along, they can't tell me. I often suspect they don't even know whether or not they have started on it. I can't run my own operation properly when I have no idea of the delivery times of important suppliers—or indeed, if the goods will be delivered at all'. Lack of an adequate control system in one jobbing shop I visited had meant that customers (probably quite innocently, perhaps not) picked up jobs as they were completed but before any documents had been prepared and a good many items were never invoiced at all. During the first month of a computer system's coming into operation, £6,000 more was invoiced than in the preceding month, though over-all production had not risen.

Under-utilization of resources. Machines of all kinds, from keyboard calculators to lathes, may be severely under-utilized. Poor planning or lack of forward information results in inability to forecast demand for capacity or to smooth out work flow. As a result, expensive machines and their equally costly operator are sometimes idle, sometimes grossly overloaded and required to work overtime. Lack of suitable techniques for machine loading, even when demand can be forecast, may have equally disastrous results.

Wasteful procurement of raw materials and other stores. This may arise as the result of having no standardization; in consequence stock control is difficult, undue space is occupied, and the organization cannot avail itself of bulk-buying discounts. One engineering manufacturing company that looked into this question found that 14 different types of steel bar were held in stores when 2 would have been sufficient to fulfil all its needs.

Lack of other management information. Much of this information may technically be available but cannot be retrieved because it is effectively hidden away in files or in documents whose analysis is precluded by lack of time and labour. In other cases, valuable information that could easily be obtained is lost because no provision is made for the inclusion of the 'raw material' in routine documents. One firm of publishers that began to analyse invoices at a computer service bureau included a check on individual salesmen's performance and discovered that two of its men were consistently selling at a loss.

These are but some examples of the sort of findings that may emerge as the result of the first phase of a feasibility study. You will probably have noticed that it is similar in form and purpose—though probably larger in scale—to a standard O & M investigation. At the risk of annoying you, I must stress again a point I have already made: the importance during this study of recording what really, as distinct from what theoretically, happens. Often any resemblance between working methods and those laid down in procedure manuals is purely coincidental.

The second phase of your feasibility study will be directed towards finding methods for improving, extending, or replacing existing routines. Always remember, however, that you must keep very firmly in mind that management information should be a primary, not a secondary, product of the new procedures so that these cannot be designed until you have decided what information is needed.

Your purpose in instigating this study was to find out whether a computer would provide the best means of increasing profitability within your organization. Having the concept of a computer by now well established in your mind, you must be particularly aware of the danger of introducing an unconscious bias in your findings. Such a bias, unrecognized, can be very dangerous, for it can result in an unnecessarily elaborate and expensive (and therefore economically unsound) recommendation for solution to the problems you have discovered.

You must therefore always make sure that it is not desirable to effect the desired improvements by using more traditional methods. Labour costs, for example, can often be as drastically cut by redesigning forms as by mechanization of any kind, especially if the machine concerned is a computer. And it may be that you can institute all the required improvements merely by revamping existing methods and using a computer service bureau.

Solutions like these admittedly lack glamour and it therefore sometimes requires some courage to recommend them. But it may be a consolation to reflect that costs will be but a fraction of those you will incur in installing your own computer and you will avoid the necessity to recruit trained staff and all the other upheavals inevitably induced by computerization.

Table 7.1 summarizes the findings of a feasibility study made by a company whose major weakness lay in invoicing and the functions associated with this. The organization concerned was in fact a group of small companies each of which had originally been independent

Tasks to be done	Present system	Present system enlarged and streamlined	Electronic invoicing machine A	Electronic invoicing machine B	Electronic invoicing machine C	Desk-size computer I	Desk-size computer II	Desk-size computer III	Visible record computer X	Visible record computer Y	Visible record computer Z
Update customer history	clerical	clerical	clerical	clerical	clerical	clerical	clerical	clerical	clerical	clerical	*
Update representative history	clerical	clerical	clerical	clerical	clerical	clerical	clerical	clerical	clerical	clerical	*
Produce invoice	clerical† and desk calculator	desk calc.†	*	*	*	*	*	*	*	*	*
Update stock control records	clerical and analysing m/c†	clerical and analysing m/c†	*	clerical and analysing m/c†	*	*	clerical and analysing m/c†	*	*	*	*
Produce sales statistics	analysing m/c†	analysing m/c†	*	analysing m/c†	*	*	analysing m/c†	*	*	*	*
Management control	none	none	none	none	partial	partial	none	partial	partial	partial	complete
Labels for cartons		electro mechanical addressing equipment†									
Sales ledger	keyb'd acc'g m/c†	keyb'd acc'g m/c†	keyb'd acc'g m/c†	keyb'd acc'g m/c†	keyb'd acc'g m/c†	keyb'd acc'g m/c†		*	*	*	*

Number of staff for all above operations	18	20	20	21	22	21	21	21	22	22	23/25
Staff saving under new system	5	3	3	2	1	2	2	2	1	1	N/A
Overtime required	little if any				at some peak periods				at all peak periods		
Investment already made in equipment	£9,200	£9,200	£9,200	£9,200	£9,200	£9,200	£9,200	£9,200	£9,200	£9,200	£9,200
Estimated proceeds of trade-in of existing equipment	£6,000 guaranteed	£5,000	£5,500	£5,500	£2,000	£6,000	£6,000	£2,000	£5,000	—	—
Cost of new equipment	£19,050	£15,700	£23,000	£14,000	£12,090	£15,500	£22,450	£11,090	£21,090	£10,041†	—
Estimated average stationery cost	£1,500	£1,500	£1,500	£1,500	£1,500	£1,500	£1,500	£1,500	£1,500	£1,500	£1,500
Total initial cost	£23,750	£20,900	£28,200	£19,200	£19,290	£20,200	£17,950	£19,790	£17,590	£20,745	£10,700

NOTE. * = Carried out by machine named at head of column.   † = Equipment already purchased or on order before extension of existing system.

Table 7.1

and at the time of the study shared the same headquarters offices. On joining the group, each company had been allowed to retain its existing accounting systems, while its products (which were similar to those made by the parent company) were simply included in the manufacturing spectrum.

You will notice that a thoroughly realistic assessment has been made, not only of the relative efficiency of various methods but of their total cost in relation to benefits expected. In this case, the findings were overwhelmingly in favour of a 'visible record' computer (see page 7). This system has now been operating for over two years with outstanding success.

Let us, however, now suppose that the findings of phase 2 of your feasibility study point unequivocally towards the use of an in-house computer. The next step is to select a suitable system, and to estimate as accurately as possible what this is likely to cost.

WHAT A COMPUTER INSTALLATION COSTS. By this time, you have probably made tentative investigations into computer capital costs. As a result, it seems that the kind of configuration you will need may cost you, say £200,000 or the equivalent in rental. (The considerations involved in deciding whether to purchase or rent are discussed later in this chapter.)

But don't let this fool you. Manufacturers' prices relate only to the computer configuration itself and such software as is available to go with it. When software is not charged for on an itemized basis, it is realistic to assume that it is covered in the price of the hardware.

To this you must add the cost of data-preparation equipment, which could amount to some 40 per cent of what you pay for the computer itself; the expense involved in preparing suitable premises —building, where necessary, air-conditioning, false floors, and fire protection measures; in recruiting and/or training technical staff; and in the preparation of your own programs.

It is realistic to assume that these ancillaries will together add up to a sum equal to more than the cost of the computer configuration. You must also be prepared to accept the fact that extensive experience has shown final costs to amount to more than was anticipated in almost every case. To think of installing a computer when funds are available only to cover the costs originally estimated is therefore to invite trouble.

On the credit side of the ledger is the fact that, at the time of writing, the government will give a grant of 20 per cent towards the cost of the computer configuration if this is used to promote the efficiency of a business. No subsidy, is, however, offered for any of the ancillary costs listed in the preceding paragraphs. In this connection, one executive who has had long and varied experierce with computers told me he thought the government would have done a better service if it had offered grants for software development. There is a good deal to be said for this viewpoint.

In assessing costs, you will gain a realistic answer only by comparing these with the value of the benefits you hope to achieve. Yet almost inevitably it will not be possible for some of the most significant of these to be estimated precisely in terms of money. You may, for example, accept unhesitatingly that the new management information obtainable by using a computer will put you in an incomparably better position vis-à-vis your competitors. But what will this mean in terms of turnover or profitability?

At a recent conference held by the British Computer Society on Production Control and the Computer (I have referred to this also in chapter 5, page 98), a member of the large and sophisticated audience asked a speaker—who had emphasized the importance of realism in costing—whether he knew any formula for estimating the 'intangible' benefits of computerized production control. Back came the uncompromising answer: 'I do not. And I have never met anyone who knew such a formula.' No-one among the 1,000-odd people in the hall was prepared to disagree with this verdict.

It therefore seems that an element of faith is inevitable when you are planning to install a computer. This, however, does not absolve you from doing everything you can to do an accurate costing, as I have pointed out already and discuss further on page 208.

I will deal with costing more fully later in this chapter. Meantime, let us move on to the question of which computer you will choose.

Which computer?

To choose the right computer for the job is not easy. For it involves, as I have already said, consideration not only of today's needs but those likely to occur within the coming three to five years at least. Aside from this, it is realistic to assume in the light of wide experience among many types of user that once your computer is working smoothly many applications that were not originally envisaged will suggest themselves. It is not at all an uncommon experience for an organization that has introduced a computer against stiff opposition in some quarters to find these same protesters banging vehemently on the door of the computer room, begging to use the system.

All right. You agree that the choice of a suitable system is difficult. But this gives you no excuse at all for ducking the issue by relying entirely upon manufacturers. I might as well be candid and say here that if you, as a manager, contemplate installation of a computer and have not bothered first to educate yourself at least in the fundamentals of the subject, you need your head examined! On the other hand, if you are a senior manager, particularly in a small or medium-size business, it is unlikely you have had time or inclination to equip yourself with the considerable body of technical knowledge that is required to evaluate the finer points of computer design and performance. So where do you go from here?

There are three possible courses of action. First, recognizing that a computer project is an exercise of critical importance, you may search within your organization for a manager capable of assimilating and applying the necessary know-how to make an informed judgement; and be prepared to vote time and money for his systematic training. Second, you may recruit into the company a man already qualified and entrust the job to him. The third possibility is to employ reputable consultants.

Many people believe that the first of these lines of action is the one most likely to bring success. Systems design (upon which choice of a computer depends considerably) can be done properly only by one who has an intimate knowledge of the workings and requirements of the user organization and has established a satisfactory relationship with its senior management. Often the design of the system is a job more complex in detail and significant in relation to final results than which computer is chosen. Where it is not possible to find inside the company a man suitable or available for the job, it may be advisable to use a two-man team made up of one outside consultant or newly recruited specialist and one well established senior manager. In either case, you will need a support team whose members are drawn from different parts of your organization and represent different levels of management.

I have deferred discussion of the pros and cons of using consultants during this phase until later in this chapter. Meantime, let us assume that you, the user organization, have decided to assume responsibility for selecting the computer and see how you can best set about this task.

Here I feel it necessary to stress again how important it is to precede any consideration of computers in general or a specific system by a thorough investigation; and to produce from this investigation a comprehensive report. Whether this feasibility study has been carried out by your own organization or by an outside agency is not as important as the fact that it was carried out by a body that has no axe to grind.

By some quirk—perhaps a result of the highly technical nature of their products or their impressive body of know-how—computer manufacturers' representatives are widely regarded as different animals from the men who offer, say, typewriters or even electronic invoicing machines. Certainly computer salesmen have good technical qualifications, have been well and carefully trained, and sometimes are widely experienced. But one must not forget that their organizations—like those who send other salesmen—are in business to sell a product.

Aside from this, the overheads of computer manufacturers are very high indeed. It is thus unlikely that they have available suitable resources to carry out thoroughly a study of this kind on a purely speculative basis; for this could, at best, bring no return at all and at worst be used by the prospective customer as a basis for soliciting rival quotations. (Oh yes! It has been done.)

I think I should make it clear that I do not intend to convey any implication that computer manufacturers are less than scrupulously honest; or to suggest that their services are not immensely valuable to the user, once he has selected their systems. All I am trying to say is simply that, on the grounds of common sense alone, it seems inadvisable to employ an interested party to make a survey whose value lies in complete impartiality. A bias may be completely unconscious. But I think you will agree that it is almost impossible to work wholeheartedly for any organization and remain entirely unprejudiced. For this reason, it is wise also to expect some bias if any outsider you employ has worked exclusively and for long with one computer manufacturer of with one make or machine.

After this digression we will return to the problem of how you, or a representative of your organization, goes about selecting a computer.

Armed with a detailed report of the findings of the feasibility study, the prospective computer user first takes a broad look at the field with the object of eliminating any manufacturer who, for one reason or another, seems unlikely to be able to supply a suitable system. What could these reasons be? Most likely, perhaps (at least until now), has been a gap between series when an existing range is more or less obsolescent as far as a new user is concerned and a new series has either not yet appeared or is not sufficiently proved in the field to make its use attractive to an inexperienced organization. Another factor might result from the fact that the definition of 'computer' is somewhat loose and some systems that conform to this description are too limited or in some other way unsuitable for the proposed applications.

In the past, some prospective users have omitted this preliminary elimination contest and have invited as many as five or six computer manufacturers to submit tenders. This seems to me to be both unfair and wasteful. No manufacturer can submit a proposal until his representative has had fairly prolonged discussions with the prospective customer. This is expensive, not only for the manufacturer but for the customer, who must be prepared to set aside a good deal of time for this purpose.

Recent amalgamations among computer manufacturers suggest that in future the choice will be considerably narrowed. Nevertheless, I will not withdraw a general caution against burdening all concerned with unnecessary work.

It is probably fair to state that, at this point in time, at least when smallish systems are involved and applications are fairly run-of-the-mill, the technical differences between the computers produced by one maker and another are smaller than they have been in the past. This is partly the result of the enormous cost of hardware research and development which has compelled many manufacturers to share in some degree with others the fruits of this work and allow them to manufacture or sell certain parts of the equipment under licence. It is also attributable to the ever-growing importance of *compatibility*. This tends to be an ambiguous term, as you will see later, but I use it here to mean the capability of exchange of information between one user's system and another.

I would not like to suggest that all makers' systems are much of a muchness as I believe this is an over-simplification. But more than ever, the importance of the emphasis lies on software. The final choice of a system will be governed, in many cases, less by any doubt whether a rival system can handle the job but the efficiency of software in a particular field.

Most computers are, through hardware or software design, markedly more efficient in some ways than in others. It is therefore up to the user to relate this efficiency to the pattern of his own requirements so that ultimately he will derive maximum benefit from his computer's good features and suffer a minimum of inconvenience from its lesser efficiency in other areas.

HARDWARE EVALUATION. The best way to rationalize one's hardware requirements is to create a yardstick whose calibrations are based upon the nature and bulk of the work the system is intended to handle. Not everybody in the organization will agree, of course, on what hardware requirements are in relation to this work. The programmers, for example, will probably put a generous-size internal store at the head of the list because this feature provides them with plenty of leeway. The systems men, on the other hand, may feel that the biggest, fastest random-access device available within the price range should take pride of place.

Top management, who must ultimately assume responsibility for the profitability of the computer system, will have to try to establish a balance between the ideal and the feasible: a system that, while not cramping the technical men unduly and leaving a realistic amount of capacity for applications expansion, will still peg down hardware cost to a realistic level.

One company I met tackled this problem by getting the permanent steering committee, which it had formed to see the computer project through, to set a percentage value on each of several hardware features after reconciling the conflicting demands of the various interests involved.

I reproduce the result of these deliberations in Table 7.2. It is most

Table 7.2   Computer hardware evaluation by a specific company.

Hardware feature	Importance in relation to applications (% of total configuration)
Internal storage capacity and access speed	35
Random-access and multi-programming capability	20
Number and type of input devices available	15
Number and type of output devices available	15
Number and type of magnetic tapes that can be used	10
Number of channels (a factor that affects the total number of peripherals that can be used)	5
	100%

important that you should appreciate that *the figures cited here are in no way absolute*. They are simply one company's assessment of the relative importance of various hardware features in relation to its own, very specific requirements. I therefore include the Table merely to indicate how this kind of exercise can rationalize one's approach to hardware evaluation.

The relatively low value put upon the last four factors here is less an indication that these were unimportant than that the prospective purchasers felt it unlikely they would encounter any difficulty in finding a system that could operate sufficient and suitable peripherals of acceptable speeds. Overwhelmingly this assessment reveals that the crucial factors were the performance and capacity of the central processor.

At the time the study was made, third-generation computers had not yet appeared, though they were known to be mooted. Examination of manufacturers' proposals indicated that none of the random-access storage devices currently available entirely filled the bill. The system they eventually chose therefore met the requirement for the central processor in regard to capacity, speed, and multi-programming capability but substituted high-speed magnetic tapes for random-access devices.

This unavoidable substitution did, as they had foreseen, prove something of a handicap. It made considerable demands upon the ingenuity of the programmers and reduced throughput because it lengthened processing time. In theory, perhaps, they should have waited until suitable random-access devices came along. But it was a matter of urgency that a workable computer system begin operation with the least possible delay.

Time has proved this decision to be right. The company tackled the challenge and emerged triumphant. I mention this because you, too, may find yourself in the same position. Half-an-hour's talk with any enthusiastic computer man can convince you that any machine on the market now is a real old clunker! But if one falls into the temptation of waiting until something better comes along, one is likely never to get around to the job at all.

But I must backtrack to the original feasibility study made by this organization. Having placed the weightings shown in Table 7.2 on the various hardware features, they decided to prepare another Table which would indicate the importance in their eyes of various other aspects of the project.

'Cost/performance ratio' is an assessment of a system's capabilities in relation to its cost. Thus, if two systems, one at £200,000, the other at £250,000 had similar capabilities, the first would be said to have a better cost/performance ratio. Similarly, the cost/performance ratio of third-generation computers is very much better than that of second-generation systems.

Table 7.3 Evaluation of features and services offered by manufacturers for one company.

Features/Services	Value to user (% of total)
Cost/performance ratio	55
Manufacturer support	15
Flexibility	10
Peripherals	10
Manufacturer's qualifications	5
Modernity of the system	5
	100%

'Manufacturer support' refers to several factors: these include the availability of technical advice as part of the standard service to customers and the quality of this advice; the availability of time on similar configurations prior to installation for program testing and after installation for use when breakdown occurred; software; and maintenance facilities.

This particular user company was sophisticated (both in computer and other terms) and it did not therefore feel the need of a great deal of technical advice. Another organization, particularly one new to computers, might find this a much more important feature.

Software is today of more importance to the user than it was at the time this feasibility study was in progress; a good operating system, for example, is almost always indispensable for a system of any size. Other software the manufacturer would be expected to provide would be a repertoire of sub-routines such as sort and merge which save the user-programmer from individually writing features likely to be included in many programs; and package programs for some fairly standard applications.

To these particular users, though, good maintenance facilities, and the availability of a standby machine and of a system for program-testing before their own computer arrived were the most important of the facilities grouped under the heading of manufacturer support.

'Flexibility' relates to the possibility of changing the hardware configuration after delivery should this be found necessary. This was possible in a limited way in second-generation systems but is entirely feasible with third-generation computers, where this facility may pretty well be taken for granted.

The factor named as 'peripherals' in Table 7.3 relates to the availability of sophisticated peripherals for use with the system. As it happened, none of the items like optical readers had any relevance to the requirements of this user, so this boils down to the random-access equipment which, of course, eventually turned out not to be available.

'Manufacturer's qualifications' is, in a sense, a feature of manufacturer support, for it relates to whether or not the company has had useful experience in the applications the user proposes to put onto the computer. These users were, in many ways, breaking new ground when they designed their systems and therefore put a low rating on qualifications since they considered it unlikely a manufacturer could be expected to offer much help in this area. Had the application been less new and untried, these users might have set a higher premium on this factor.

The low rating on modernity reflects the fact that, at the time the feasibility study was made, the prospective purchasers were well aware that current systems were becoming obsolescent. But, as I have already mentioned, it was the urgent need to get a viable system going that carried the day.

Again I must ask you to bear in mind that there is nothing absolute in any of these ratings; they simply reflect the ideas of one user organization. Yours might be entirely different.

At this point, you must be careful not to lose sight of your primary objective. That is, you should remember that the aim of the exercise is to discover which of a number of computer systems will do the best job for you—not to hold a competition for manufacturers. Since you are soliciting their suggestions rather than giving them an IQ test, you should help them—and yourself, of course—by providing them with as much relevant information as you can.

On your side you will, of course, give each the systems specification (the broad description of your needs) you have already prepared. You should also give a fair idea of the kind of money you are prepared to spend on hardware. You should name an approximate date for hardware and software delivery, indicating whether or not you regard this as reasonably flexible; set a date within which you expect to receive the proposal; and name the points on which you expect the manufacturer to provide you with information. These points include the following:

(a) Complete specification of the configuration, broken down into individual items of hardware with purchase price and rental charge for each.

(b) Suggestions of how any existing equipment may be used in this connection.

(c) Trade-in terms, if any, for surplus existing equipment.

(d) Details of shift loading—i.e., how many shifts will be needed to work the proposed system. (Talks with experienced users suggest that if *initial* applications are likely to occupy more than one shift, it will cost you little, if anything, more in the long run to have a more powerful configuration that can do the work in one shift. This is because of the high cost of employing duplicate shifts of staff.)

(e) A definition of what is meant by 'normal operating time', i.e., how much time is expected to be required for routine maintenance.

(f) Estimated cost of maintenance and of spares required.

(g) Estimated costs of consumable items such as cards, paper tape, and continuous stationery.

(h) Requirements for power supply and current stabilization. It is usually necessary to provide equipment for automatic smoothing of fluctuations in voltage that occur from time to time when electricity is drawn from the mains because these variations may seriously upset the computer.

(i) Details of the temperature, humidity, and other environmental requirements.

(j) Full specification of software and date of availability. If the software concerned is untried or not yet completed, you are justified in regarding a quoted delivery date as purely notional!

(k) Suggestions about what programming language(s) may be required and estimates of how long basic training for programmers will take.

(l) Details of the availability and maintenance of back-up services. These include facilities for the training of programmers; and the

N

availability of manufacturer's staff to help out initially with programming, etc.

(*m*) How much free program-testing time is offered and how much will be charged for this facility if the free entitlement is exhausted; and the location of the system on which testing time is available. When the proposed system is a new model, these facilities may not be available at all. Alternatively, it is sometimes possible by using simulation techniques (i.e., reproducing in one computer the conditions that obtain in another type) to test programs on a different kind of system.

(*n*) Advice on the type and number of data-preparation machines required; and an estimate of cost.

ANALYSING MANUFACTURERS' PROPOSALS. It is possible that, for one reason or another, none of the proposals you receive from manufacturers will adhere closely to the limit you set on price. If every one deviates in the same direction from your figure, you can probably safely assume that you over- or under-estimated. But if there is a wide variation in either direction by only one manufacturer, do not automatically discard his proposal on this score. The suggestion may be either more or less realistic than the others. The proposal will, like the others, give reasons for the configuration suggested, so you should examine these as carefully as the others.

In the past, manufacturers were frequently accused of over-selling; that is, persuading customers to buy too much hardware capacity. This may sometimes have been the result of over-optimism in the assessment of the customer's ability to utilize the system.

Currently, however, the reverse is often true and quite a number of users discover while they are still programming their first applications that the system they have ordered is inadequate. The most common deficiency is in memory capacity.

Unless you are aware of this situation, which is due in part no doubt to cut-throat competition leading to a desire to quote the lowest possible prices, you may come unstuck. Though the design of a computer allows the addition of extra increments of memory (provided, of course, your initial configuration did not have the maximum) this necessity can incur unforeseen costs in the order of tens of thousands of pounds. Difficulties may also arise because the programmers have tried to squeeze a quart into a pint pot; it may be a while before they arrive at the conclusion that this cannot be done. Meanwhile, a good deal of time and effort has been wasted.

On the whole, hardware today accounts for a smaller proportion of total cost than it did in the past. This, plus the fact that in a successful installation the amount of work put onto the system may be expected to rise by something like 30 per cent per annum, suggests that it is as well not to be too conservative about your requirements.

This brings us to consideration of the important factors of *expandability* and *compatibility*.

Expandability. Today's computers are designed to allow expansion so that the user may, without substituting another system, accommodate growing requirements. This expansion may, as I have already indicated, take the form of adding extra increments of internal storage. Alternatively, or in addition, it may involve the use of extra peripherals or substituting faster peripherals for those included in the original configuration.

Thus, the modest size of the initial workload may allow a single slow card or paper-tape reader to be used; but an increase in the number of applications may demand the use of a faster reader or the addition of others. A decision to add scientific applications might make it desirable to use a paper-tape reader as well as a card reader. An expanded application may demand the addition of random-access files.

The internal memory (core store) cannot be expanded indefinitely because the design of the central processor precludes this. A manufacturer should always indicate not only the capacity of the basic memory but how far this can be expanded and the size of the increments. Typically, a basic store of 8K (see chapter 2) can be expanded, first to 16K and perhaps subsequently to the limit of 32K. But one cannot break down these increments and turn the initial 8K store into a 12K one. The size and number of the increments of internal storage that can be added vary from one manufacturer, and often one model in a series, to the other.

When it comes to peripherals, there is less limitation. Most systems make provision for the addition of as many peripherals as any user can conceivably need. But it is important to understand that the greater the number of peripherals the bigger the control job assigned to the central processor and the smaller its available capacity for work demanded by applications programs. It is not therefore wise to assume that one can go on adding peripherals *ad lib* without materially affecting other aspects of the system.

To implement this concept of expansion as conveniently and as cheaply as possible, computers are built with a number of *channels* or pathways to the central processor for use by the peripherals. Each channel is typically capable of handling several *control units* which in turn can service a number of peripherals. Thus, a channel might offer a capacity for, say, eight control units each of which could, in turn, handle two or more peripherals of like kind. So the addition of a single disc control unit would permit the system to utilize two or more disc handlers, or a tape control unit could look after several magnetic tape decks. But a requirement for more of these handlers or decks would require the addition of a further control unit.

When the units concerned are designed to handle remote terminals, their capacity is higher. It is unlikely, for example, that a communications controller would incorporate less capacity than was needed for eight remote terminals; and most have a higher capability than this.

These control units and the peripherals they handle are often referred to as *sub-systems*. This indicates that local organization of the work of the peripherals is done by the control unit and that the complex can therefore logically be regarded as self-contained because it receives only broad directions from the central processor and breaks these down further. A proposed configuration might, therefore, include a disc or a tape or a communications sub-system, or all or any combination of these according to estimated requirements.

Compatibility. Compatibility, as I mentioned earlier, tends to be an ambiguous word. It is sometimes taken to refer to the capability of one computer to handle data processed or passed to it by another. Thus, a British Rail computer installation which processes the payroll for a very large number of employees extracts during this work details of individual contributions to an insurance company, several building societies, and the National Union of Railwaymen. Each of these organizations owns or uses a different computer, but the magnetic tapes prepared by the British Rail system can be put straight onto these other machines without intermediate processing. Thus, these users are presented with data in a very convenient form.

Compatible computers may also be linked directly to one another. Thus it is possible, for example, to link a Univac 9000 Series computer to an IBM System/360 model and vice versa. Compatibility used as a description of terminals or peripherals means that these can be connected to various makes and models of central processor with insignificant modifications.

Compatibility of this order is becoming so universal with third-generation computers and associated equipment that it can generally be taken for granted. In many cases, therefore, this consideration does not enter at all into choice of a computer.

What is far more important to you when you are trying to select the best computer is *compatibility within one maker's range*. This means the capability to transfer programs written for one system onto another, larger system by the same maker. This is a facility whose importance cannot be over-estimated.

But, you may say, there is not the slightest prospect in the fore-seeable future of our wishing to use a larger system. Our feasibility study has made it clear that we shall require a third-generation system of minimum size and use this for only one shift. There is ample capacity for expansion within this.

My reply to this is, 'Don't be too sure'. In the past, incompatibility has raised serious barriers to progress since it has entailed complete re-programming of every routine run on the first system.

This can be a mammoth task. True, the necessity to rewrite gives an opportunity for incorporating improvements whose nature may be suggested by on-the-job experience or the enhanced capability of the larger system; but the job is slow and tedious. And the investment represented by the usually very large number of man-hours devoted to writing the original programs is largely wasted. Aside from this, it may also be necessary to teach the programmers a new language.

Manufacturers are sometimes inclined to treat the question of compatibility at this level rather glibly. Only subsequent investigation (too late) reveals that this is not as complete as the user believed. I therefore urge you as a matter of policy to investigate this question with some care before you select a system.

When a user is moving from a second-generation to a third-generation computer, there is little he can do about incompatibility other than grin and bear it. The technological differences that exist between the generations are profound, the improvements and inno-vations in third-generation engineering design so significant that it simply would not have been feasible for manufacturers to contem-plate compatibility. All the user can do is to take account of re-programming costs when he draws up his estimates. He can also be careful that he does not purchase a system that will lead him into this situation again.

Does this make sense when some people are already talking about fourth-generation computers? I think it does. I believe that, in the business world at least, there are very few users yet capable of exploiting to the full anything more than a fraction of the potential inherent in third-generation systems. It therefore seems most unlikely that progress will be hampered if you assume that a third-generation system will fulfil all your foreseeable needs within the next few years —and that is as far as most of us care to plan. Aside from this, investment in third-generation systems by users is so heavy that it seems reasonable to suppose that manufacturers will solve the compatibility problem before they launch yet another generation.

HARDWARE COMPARISON. To compare the merits of two or more rival makes or models of car, one of which you intend eventually to purchase and drive, is not too difficult a task. The car is a single, indivisible unit (except for the optional extras which seldom affect overall performance) and your own experience as a driver is sufficient to allow you to determine whether or not a vehicle will suit your particular requirements. It is not necessary either for you to examine or to employ someone else to examine technical detail such as, say, the finer points of gearbox design.

A comparison of two or more computer hardware specifications is far more difficult. The computer is a collection of units. How this collection is made up depends entirely upon what tasks you require the configuration to do—tasks whose nature and combination has not been predetermined by the manufacturer except in the very broadest way.

This means that you will often be placed in a position where you are comparing two or more computer systems whose make-up is quite different. As a result, each will tackle a given task in a different way. This implies you will have to 'peer into the engine' with far more perspicacity than you need when you are choosing a car.

I am not going to suggest that you, as an average manager, should try to gain sufficient technical knowledge fully to understand and evaluate the many factors that affect the performance of computer hardware. Here, a little learning can be a dangerous thing, for it is easy for a layman to latch onto some point he believes he has grasped and to over-emphasize its importance or misunderstand its significance in assessing the overall performance.

Just the same, it is you and your colleagues who will sign the cheque and whose reputation will stand or fall in accordance with the outcome of the computer project. It is therefore up to you to demand that the technically qualified person on whom you have placed the onus of comparison of rival computers should do his job conscientiously. This implies that you must require him to submit to you a full report (not necessarily in writing) in terms you can understand. He should explain what factors have influenced his recommendation and why he considers these important. It is also up to you to listen carefully—and to have the courage to ask questions if you do not understand!

COMPUTER COMMUNICATIONS. In chapter 3, I pointed out that it is already technically feasible to design and operate a computer system where all but the very lowest levels of data processing are carried out at a central point, information being supplied to this from outlying branches through remote terminals or satellites.

Any organization intending to replace an existing computer by a more modern system, or any about to install its first computer, must, I believe, consider the possibility of using a communications facility. This may sound a rather absurd statement if you are a small organization and currently occupy only one set of offices or a single factory. But when you buy a computer you should be trying to project your plans several years ahead.

At present, communications is one of the areas in which growth and development is fastest. Aside from this, there is in the business world a strong trend towards an increase in the size of organizations. A company that is now small and self-contained may well, within a very short time, be faced with a choice of amalgamating with others, expanding its own scope considerably, or going out of business. And growth may well lead to a demand for data links of one kind or another.

For an organization that is already scattered over a number of locations, the use of communications links may be a possibility at present or in the fairly near future. If you are a senior manager in a company of this kind, I believe you should consider, at the time you purchase a computer, what kind of possibilities exist. This is important, not only in selection of hardware but in planning the pattern of management responsibility.

There are several possibilities open to you here:

Complete decentralization. Self-contained data-processing systems will be installed at several different and geographically separate points. Each branch office, factory, or warehouse will have a system, varying in size and configuration according to local requirements.

Probably one computer will also be installed at head office. Its tasks will include work such as the maintenance of a share register and the production of dividend warrants and the compilation of financial accounts from data already processed up to a predetermined point and in an agreed format at local level. If this head office computer is a powerful one, it may also be used as a service bureau for handling problems too big or unsuitable for the branch computer systems.

Complete centralization. In a set-up of this kind, an all-purpose central computer system will process all work originated at local level. This system may be fed by the following:

(*a*) Simple, inexpensive terminals linked directly to the central computer.
(*b*) Terminals linked to the computer centre but not directly to the system—e.g., paper-tape-to-paper-tape transmission facilities. In a case like this, paper-tape might well be originated as a by-product of work on keyboard accounting or invoicing machines
(*c*) 'Raw' data derived from documents sent to the centre by conventional methods such as road or rail transport.

Partial centralization. The system may comprise a powerful central computer with a satellite at each branch office, factory, or warehouse. All processing that can be carried out locally will be done on the spot by the satellite, but it will draw on the power of the large system for big jobs. It will also transmit some partially processed data into the larger system for use in head-office accounting systems.

There are variations on these basic themes. In a sizable organization with some large branches and a number of smaller local offices, for example, it may be desirable to place satellites at branch offices and simpler terminals in the smaller, outlying locations. Each branch satellite could control its own group of terminals which will have direct access only to it; but the branch computer itself can be put on-line to the central installation.

An interesting possibility for those who prefer complete decentralization might be to have no computer at head office but to use a service bureau, either of the conventional type or a 'utility' (see chapter 10). This utility, which provides a user with a terminal on-line to a very powerful bureau machine, might also be employed at some branches by installing terminals there in addition to local data-processing facilities.

Terminals used on a system need not be of a type used for data processing but may be instruments used for process-control applications. The Eastern Gas Board, for example, will use a network that includes data-processing terminals and instruments that monitor gas distribution at certain points over the area.

Many considerations will influence the decision on which kind of communications network to use. Among these are the fact that high-speed data-transmission lines are costly to rent and not always easy to get. A number of alternative types of data-transmission facility with different speeds is now available through the GPO. But I would urge you, in your own interests, as soon as you begin seriously to contemplate the use of any data-transmission facility, to contact your local telephone manager. Some at least of the existing difficulty in obtaining data transmission lines is due to delays in application for them. Apart from supplying the service itself, the GPO provides the 'modems' (the 'black boxes' interposed between the transmission lines and the terminals and/or computer that uses them) and must approve all other equipment used on its lines.

The idea of high-speed data transmission is attractive, both to management who equate it with efficiency, and to the computer men who see it as a technically elegant contributor to systems design. But the supposition that speed equals efficiency can lead to much un-necessary expenditure. If speed offers no genuine contribution to efficiency (i.e., if it makes no practical difference whether action is taken within two minutes or two hours or half a day), one is simply wasting money.

As a concept, technical elegance can be dangerously seductive and I would urge you to be on guard against it, not only in this connection but in others. It is fatally easy to fall in love with sophisticated technical developments and neglect to consider cheaper though less glamorous alternatives. In some cases, for example, on-line communication might be replaced by a set-up that involved local production of paper-tape and its transmission by slow paper-tape-to-paper-tape links. Though this may not be aesthetically as attractive, it is an alluring alternative in terms of cost.

These are but some of the technical and economic considerations involved in using computer communications. I shall now move on to consider that very important element: human reaction.

When you consider the merits of centralization versus decentralization, it is essential to take into account the effect your decision will have on the people on whom you depend most heavily: your management and executive staff. The introduction of complete centralization into an organization that until now has been structured in such a way as to give a high degree of local autonomy may have a devastating effect.

There are powerful arguments in favour of total centralization. Among these are the fact that the organization has an opportunity of installing one powerful computer system, of recruiting and/or training only one set of technical staff which is geographically adjacent to the company's key executives. On the other hand, a set-up like this inevitably makes local managers feel that they are little better than head-office puppets because many aspects of their control function have ceased to exist.

Probably partial centralization provides the most acceptable answer for many organizations. One group whose name I am not at liberty to quote has found this a very happy solution. Visible-record computers are being installed at depots in several large towns in the UK. These produce invoices and implement a stock-control system at local level. Relevant details of invoices are automatically punched by these small computers into paper tape which is later used by a powerful head-office computer to produce sales statistics and other reports and analyses. Initially sent overland, the paper-tape will later be transmitted to the computer by medium-speed data links. In setting up a system like this, the organization has preserved for branch managers much of their autonomy. Decisions on the pattern of stock control, for example, will be made at this level as will discount allowances made to customers. At the same time, it takes advantage of the benefits offered by a powerful computing system which is also used for many other head office applications.

Another argument in favour of retaining computing power at local level is that this pattern provides room for a more flexible pattern of expansion, since local systems can, when necessary, be altered to meet increased local demand. An increase in workload on a large central installation could prove more expensive and raise difficulties as regards software. A local computer gives the people on the spot a chance to develop computer expertise. When all this know-how is located at a distant point, there is less scope for developing fresh talent at local level and, of course, less opportunity for the able and ambitious. Where there is some overlap in local applications, know-how developed in one installation can be applied to the benefit of the others. A set-up where different people have an opportunity to try out their ideas and can freely exchange information may be of considerable benefit.

SOFTWARE EVALUATION. Good software, as I have pointed out before, is at least as important to the modern computer user as good hardware. I also mentioned in chapter 3 that it is, in the opinion of every expert on this subject I have consulted, generally quite impossible for any but outstandingly sophisticated users to evaluate software directly.

This does not, however, mean that you as a prospective computer user must simply cross your fingers and hope for the best. You must, in fact, do everything you can to evaluate software indirectly—preferably by consulting existing users and then trying it out on your own applications. Even this is not entirely foolproof—what is?—but it is about the only feasible possibility at present.

Manufacturers put their most impressive brainpower to work on software development and invest very large sums of money in it. The magnitude of their task can be gauged by the fact that one manufacturer at least has candidly admitted that it is only after four years' work by a large team that software concepts first formulated when the hardware it is designed for was launched have been translated into working reality. This is by no means an atypical case.

In spite of all this effort, much remains to be done to improve the efficiency of software, particularly for large systems. I hope, therefore, that you will not feel I am 'knocking' manufacturers when I urge you to be both cautious and persistent in your attempts realistically to evaluate the potential of computer software.

In doing this, you will be better advised to consult existing users than manufacturers. It is a reflection of the reaction of human nature to the bitter competition in the computer market that every manufacturer seems to be well primed with convincing evidence of how a rival's software fails to perform. After a few conversations like this, one can easily gain the impression that all software currently available is monstrously inefficient if not virtually useless! This is rubbish, of course. While few fail to admit, when pressed, that there is still considerable room for improvement, software now offered does, in fact, work.

Software difficulties cannot, however, always be blamed on the manufacturer. One honest customer I met admitted that the manufacturer's software he was using (and which was, as it happened, relatively simple) caused difficulty because his demands upon it were too heavy. Difficulties may also arise from the discovery of an area in which the software concerned has not yet been fully tested (see chapter 3). These problems, made much of by rivals and other users in the surprisingly small and gossipy computer world, are invariably eliminated or circumvented eventually.

Your most useful course therefore is to get into touch with existing users of the kind of software your system will require. This, inevitably, will involve investigation by a specialist, but will undoubtedly be a good investment. Awareness of areas of intractable difficulty before a project is under way may result in re-thinking the approach to certain problems—while there is still time.

During the time when your decision is pending, manufacturers will naturally invite you to attend demonstrations of their computers at work. These demonstrations will, if at all possible, involve programs resembling one of your own major applications. There is, however, a possibility of being misled if your organization does not provide the job specification; for unless each demonstration is applied to the same problem you have no accurate yardstick for comparing performances.

There may be important differences that are not immediately apparent between the ways in which two superficially similar results are achieved. One program, for example, may be more efficient than another in an area particularly pertinent to your needs. Another, though satisfactory in isolation, may make excessively heavy demands upon, say, core-store capacity, which could slow up the throughput during multi-programming. Though you, as a manager, will probably want to attend these demonstrations personally, you should always bring an unprejudiced computer expert along with you.

WHAT KIND OF INPUT? All modern computer systems offer a choice of input media. This leaves you to decide between the merits both of these as media and in relation to the machines used to prepare the data for the computer. As a decision, this is highly important, though this point is not always fully recognized. A correct choice can have considerable impact upon system efficiency. Aside from this, the average user may have to allocate as much as 40 to 50 per cent of his total outlay on hardware to data-preparation equipment, while the maintenance and staffing of this forms a sizable proportion of running costs.

As things are at present, the choice lies principally between paper-tape and punched cards as input media, though indications are that magnetic-tape data-preparation methods are gaining ground. Other possibilities include various types of optical or magnetic character reader. (Brief descriptions of all these are given in chapter 2.)

Although data preparation on either cards or paper-tape involves the punching of holes by means of a keyboard of some kind, several factors contribute to create important differences between the two.

For many years, there was a strong bias in favour of 80-column cards. This, however, can be attributed less to their inherent virtues than to the fact that the earliest (and certainly most aggressive) makers of computers for business applications were established manufacturers of punched-card equipment. The fact that cards could continue to be used on computers constituted a good selling point; and, of course, the thoughts of all concerned tended to be orientated towards the punched-card approach.

One point in favour of cards that continues to carry weight with users of computers without magnetic storage media is that these, unlike paper tape, can be sorted electro-mechanically independently of the computer in conventional punched-card equipment. Contemporary users of computers without magnetic storage devices are therefore automatically confined to punched cards as an input medium, as every business application sooner or later demands some data sorting. (The exception is users of visible-record computers who can hand-sort the magnetic-stripe ledger cards used in these machines.)

What other advantages can punched cards offer over perforated paper-tape? The chief of these is, I think, flexibility. Since paper-tape is produced in a continuous length, it is not easy to amend. A single incorrect card in a pack can soon be abstracted and replaced. Punched cards also constitute a very inexpensive form of external 'memory'. It may, for example, be more economic to retain quite large data files on cards when these are to be used only occasionally than to maintain the same data on magnetic-tape. The fact that the file can be updated without the use of the computer may also be of value in this context, as is the fact that the cards can be interpreted. This electro-mechanical operation involves reading the punched matter and reproducing key detail in print on the card surface. The cards can therefore be used in a conventional indexing system.

Among the drawbacks of cards as an input medium are: the blanks are far more expensive than an equivalent quantity of paper-tape; they tend to be awkward to handle—a pack can quite easily be dropped; and they occupy a lot of storage space. An individual card may be lost from a sequence without this being apparent.

Punched cards may be prepared as the by-product of a conventional machine operation such as ledger accounting. An automatic punch may today be attached to many makes of keyboard machine. But this is more bulky and clumsy than a paper-tape punch that performs the same function. It cannot be built into the console of a desk but remains essentially a separate unit connected by a cable.

Cards, on the other hand, are generally more satisfactory than paper-tape for use in automatic data-collection systems. More robust than tape, they are more suitable for handling by shop-floor workers and can be distributed as individual units.

Probably one of the major reasons for the trend in favour of punched paper-tape is the ease with which it can be physically transported from one place to another. Paper-tape is also a convenient medium for transmitting data from remote points at slow to medium speed.

When paper-tape is used, no limit is imposed on the length of the data to be entered for each transaction whereas, with cards, entries occupying more space than can be squeezed into 80 columns must be carried over to a second or even third card. And very short entries waste not only an area of the card itself but, to some degree, slow the preparation and processing since the blank areas must still pass through preparation and reading machines before the next card can be fed in. With paper-tape, there is no gap between one entry and the next and these may vary in length.

Among the disadvantages of paper-tape is the fact that data recorded on it cannot be sorted except in a computer and it is therefore in this way less flexible than cards. Short lengths of paper-tape can more easily be lost than an equivalent pack of cards and tape is more easily torn. Though a variety of ingenious filing systems has been devised for the short lengths of punched tape that are required for some applications, tape is not, on the whole, as easily handled as cards.

For cards, only quite a narrow range of data-preparation equipment is available and this is supplied only by two makers in the UK. As—at the time of writing and for some years past—demand usually exceeds supply, a prospective user may well have to wait for a year or more before equipment on order is delivered.

The market for equipment for punching paper-tape, on the other hand, is fiercely competitive and a great deal of alternative equipment is available. Many of the machines in this category, as distinct from that used for cards, are multi-purpose, and can produce a printed copy as tape is prepared.

Aside from these various points of comparison, there are more technical considerations relating to the way the data can be actually handled by the computer and which may influence a decision one way or the other.

The special type of magnetic tape used in data-preparation equipment offers many of the advantages of paper-tape—e.g., physical ease of handling (the reels are roughly comparable in size to those used on modern dictating equipment) and facilities for entering records of variable length. One of its drawbacks is that nothing recorded on it can be recognized by the human eye, whereas the holes on tape or cards can quite easily be read visually. Thus magnetic tape separated from its label cannot easily be identified as to content; nor can it be broken into short lengths, so is not as versatile as a filing medium.

The capital cost of optical readers and magnetic-ink character-recognition (MICR) equipment is very high and their use is therefore precluded for many companies at present. Aside from this, they impose fairly stringent restrictions on the format of input data and the type and size of paper that it is recorded upon. Their use at the moment is therefore confined to applications where these restrictions do not cause inconvenience.

How successfully optical reading equipment can be utilized depends to a considerable degree upon the ingenuity of forms designers. The art lies in devising a method where information not previously handled in this way can be formatted to take advantages of the benefits—which include very high speeds—of automatic reading. A single optical or MICR reader can take the place of a whole army of girls who would otherwise have to punch data from source documents into cards or tape or record it on magnetic-tape data-preparation equipment.

What, therefore, are the points to be considered when settling for input method and equipment? First, a careful review of overall requirements; second, an examination in some depth of which type of data preparation is most likely to meet these needs. Some facilities offered only by one type of equipment (for example, the ability of a card punch automatically to enter at maximum speed certain fixed information on every card) may be of considerable value in reducing the time and cost of data preparation. Sometimes an external factor, such as the fact that paper-tape is easily conveyed from place to place, may be overriding.

The director of a service bureau which specializes in data preparation and offers an advisory service on this subject told me that often insufficient thought is given to some of the aspects of input data preparation which, though apparently trivial, in fact significantly affect overall cost. Even a small trick of programming, which, for example, allows data that would otherwise occupy two card columns to be contained in one, can be significant when tens of thousands of cards are punched each month. It may be possible, for example, to use the computer itself to insert an item like a serial number, or the 'end of field' markers which are equivalent to punctuation in data handling by the computer. My informant claims that he has saved clients sums of money as large as £35,000 per annum by incorporating such apparently minor refinements as these.

Programmers who know little or nothing of the mechanics of keyboard operation may unwittingly slow down productivity in data preparation by including codes incorporating characters that are inconvenient in machine terms. (Any typist will tell you that frequent use of isolated capitals will reduce her productivity because it demands constant use of the shiftlock; similar considerations apply to data-preparation equipment.) Aware of this, they could just have used a character that is more easily recorded.

When considering the subject of data preparation, it is useful to appreciate that this falls into two phases. There is the one-off initial preparation which is involved in the preparation of entries for master files to be held ultimately on magnetic tape or discs or drums; and day-to-day data preparation for applications.

A medium judged to be most suitable for day-to-day use will not necessarily be the best for setting up files. The restricted amount of information that can be recorded on a single punched card, while no disadvantage in daily work, may slow the data preparation of master files, for example. This is one of the considerations which may make it worthwhile to sub-contract the job of preparing the master file to a service bureau (see chapter 10).

Before leaving the subject of data preparation, I should like to draw two more points to your attention: first, the importance of adequately training your keypunch or other keyboard operators; second, the vital part that form design plays in overall efficiency of data preparation.

Though great pains are taken to see that all other staff directly connected with a computer project are properly trained, many organizations neglect their data-preparation operators in this respect. And manufacturers who provide facilities for other types of training will confine their instruction for keyboard operators to machine functions. In consequence, most data-prep girls work with only two fingers—a method as inefficient on data-prep equipment as it is on a typewriter.

A British organization, Keyboard Training Ltd of London, which is at the time of writing one of a few of its kind, specializes in the initial training of new operators and the re-training of experienced girls. Results have repeatedly demonstrated that productivity of experienced operators is generally more than doubled after training because of higher speeds and lower error rates. Courses, normally held on customers' premises, only last two weeks and are offered at moderate cost. (Operator personality and welfare is discussed in chapter 8.)

The design of forms used as source documents for data preparation requires considerable skill, for it demands reconciling the requirements of those who complete the forms and those who transcribe the content into machine language. Among the factors that must be considered is the necessity to make the form as simple and un-ambiguous as possible so that it can easily be filled in and none of the wanted detail omitted. At the same time, the order in which the detail is entered must correspond to that in which it is punched into a card or tape. When the form concerned is one which has been used for years by people who do not easily change their ways, it is desirable to maintain a resemblance to the original layout if this is at all feasible in the light of other considerations. When the form is to be completed by a new method—say, on a typewriter instead of by hand—care must be taken to ensure that its layout is efficient in terms of machine utilization. Line spacing, for example, must conform to that of the machine, entries made at the head must be aligned to eliminated 'fiddling' movements. I think I have said enough to convince you that my contention that form design requires considerable skill and is of considerable significance is true.

Computer consultants

I was surprised to find, while gathering background material for this book, both formally and at random during other assignments, that very few of the computer users I met had employed consultants.

o

Furthermore (though I confess my research in this area was not statistically based or entirely methodical) there seemed on the whole to be considerable dislike or even hostility towards consultants among those I questioned.

Opinions on the subject fell into two categories. There were those who dismissed all consultants with contempt as rogues and charlatans —and, of course, supported their contention with a wealth of evidence that was seldom first-hand. Others agreed that consultants might well perform a useful function for other people but believed their own organization could muster sufficient expertise to make outside help unnecessary.

While I am prepared to make no special plea for consultants and perfectly willing to admit that unscrupulous and/or incompetent practitioners exist, I think these attitudes are too arbitrary. I have no doubt that reputable and high-calibre consultants, properly used, can perform a very valuable function. Having written a book (7.1) on the subject of UK management consultants in general, much of whose content could apply as much to computer consultants as to other types, I do not propose to go here into the subject in too great depth. Nevertheless, I think some discussion is necessary of points that relate specifically to the use of consultant firms in connection with the installation and operation of a computer project.

Summed up very briefly, here are some of the arguments in favour of using consultants.

(a) Unbiased minds are applied to the problem. When you are deeply involved in anything, you often cannot see the wood for the trees. A difficulty that looks insuperable to one on the spot can sometimes be solved quite easily by an outsider.

(b) Internal difficulties are reconciled. Consultants should never be made solely responsible for breaking the news of impending computerization to an organization's staff. But it is axiomatic that many who will not believe a word said by people who are close to them will accept the same information or advice proffered by a stranger. Consultants may be able to help in reconciling differences of opinion and resolving personality clashes among the members of a board of directors, provided they are demonstrably not a tool of one individual or faction.

(c) They have expertise in the technical field and experience to back this. Breadth of experience in the specialized areas of computing and, perhaps, also in one particular aspect of it such as its application in your own industry, can be immensely valuable as can a seasoned consultant's broad experience in other applications and in the handling of people.

(d) They help in the recruitment and evaluation of technical staff. Good consultants should be able to sort out the sheep from the goats, at least on the basis of qualifications. An organization with little knowledge in the computer field can fall prey to a fast talker. Only the employing company, on the other hand, can decide whether an applicant is personally acceptable—a very important ingredient in success.

(e) They will liaise between you and the computer manufacturer. This can be a very time-consuming task and it certainly demands considerable specialized knowledge. If you are learning on the job as far as computers go, you could make a horrible hash of your dealings with manufacturers who, like anyone else, usually behave better when faced by a determined individual who knows his onions. The consultant should also be able to assess and explain to you whether problems cited by manufacturers are genuine or not.

(f) Management objectives can be clarified. This, as I have stressed, is by no means an easy task and therefore one that is too often evaded. A consultant, by acting as guide, catalyst, and adviser, may break a hold-up in this area and elicit more information than the company itself could unaided.

FINDING A CONSULTANT. One reason for the poor opinion that many people have of consultants is probably that news of failure and difficulty usually spreads more widely and more quickly than news of success. Failure may be due to many causes of which incompetence or dishonesty on the part of a consultant firm is only one.

There certainly are, if not rogues and charlatans, at least a good many inefficient practitioners in this field. Typically, these are people who have put in fairly lengthy service in a technical or semi-technical capacity with one or more computer manufacturers and believe this qualifies them to act as consultants. Such people's knowledge is often limited and biased. Often they have little or no practical knowledge of the real problems of business management. Yet this knowledge is, I believe, an essential qualification for any consultant who deals with commercial or industrial data-processing applications.

Practices set up by such people are generally under-capitalized, and since they are neither more nor less ethical than the rest of us, they may yield to the temptation to let their hunger for business colour their recommendations. One cannot get rich by advising an organization whom one thought of as a client not to install a computer! (In parenthesis, may I plead with you to restrain the annoyance you may feel as a result of disappointment when a consultant advises you it is not in your interest to computerize. After all, he has not only lost an assignment but has saved you a great deal of expenditure and possibly heartache.)

I do not want to imply either that the very small consultant firm is inherently incompetent or that a big firm is inherently efficient, for this would not be true. The foregoing observations are only part of a list of possible dangers to look for.

How does one recognize a dubious consultant? One may immediately become suspicious if he puts paid advertisements in newspapers or journals. Professional firms are not permitted to advertise their services at all (which, in my opinion, is a pity). If they infringed this rule, they would be expelled from professional bodies and the members of their staffs who are also professionals—accountants, engineers and so on—would also immediately be in trouble. This stricture does not, however, refer to their mention in or writing of editorial matter in journals. This is an entirely different kettle of fish.

A dubious practitioner is often overwhelmingly certain of fast, easy success which he will often promise to achieve at a cost significantly lower than that incurred by employing a more conservative firm. He will apparently be prepared to put in a lot of preliminary work without charge. He is glib, and may attempt to reassure you that you have nothing to worry about because he will look after everything.

He may find plausible excuses, either for failing to submit the names of previous clients whom you might contact for an opinion on his work (after, of course, the client company has given permission for its name to be cited—a stricture observed also by reputable firms of consultants), or for failing to render a proper written report after a preliminary investigation, or for not getting down to brass tacks in his recommendations.

Much as I would like to, I cannot recommend any completely satisfactory method for finding and identifying a satisfactory computer consultant, except by asking other businessmen. The professional associations are always afraid of appearing to favour one or other of their members, so they will do nothing more than supply a list. While inclusion in this list is virtually a guarantee of respectability, it cannot guarantee that the firm in question has the depth of up-to-date knowledge that should be at the command of computer consultants.

When you talk to other businessmen who have used consultants, you should place more weight on the evidence of what they (and you) believe the consultants have achieved than on their opinion of the firm they have used. One quirk I turned up during investigation for my book on management consultants was that, even when the consultants had undeniably done a very good job, the client, though freely admitting this, was not particularly enthusiastic about the consultants. There seems to be a tendency, once the exercise has been successfully concluded and the last bill paid, for clients to believe they could have done the job just as well themselves.

This belief is, in a sense, a measure of the consultants' success, since any reputable firm aims to guide and teach the client so that when it withdraws the client is standing confidently on his own feet. It does seem rather hard luck on the consultant, though, that when he has done this successfully the client believes he was redundant in the first place.

HOW TO USE CONSULTANTS. I will now assume that you have obtained the names of one or more firms of computer consultants whom you feel confident can probably do a good job for you. It is very important for you at this stage to appreciate that much of the quality of the work will inevitably depend directly upon you and your staff. No doctor can do much unless his patient has some faith, is prepared to help himself, and co-operates to the full. The same is true of a consultant. Your role as a client therefore can never be passive. From the outset, you must regard the assignment as a joint exercise in which you as well as the consultants become heavily involved.

This implies two-way exchange of opinions. As a client, you must not forget that you are the employer of the consultants. While listening carefully to the consultant's advice and studying carefully the reports he compiles for you, you will also protest if, for example, you believe conclusions have been based upon wrong assumptions or if you disagree strongly with a recommendation. If the consultant's arguments support his viewpoint convincingly, well and good. If not, you must decide whether you are prepared to yield gracefully or dismiss the consultants. I would advise you against trying to force a consultant into a line of action which he regards as inadvisable, for it is unlikely that in such circumstances he will achieve optimal results.

As much depends upon the establishment of *rapport* and mutual confidence between consultant and client as upon the purely technical aspects of the job.

'What kind of circumstances might lead you to suggest that a client would do well to reconsider the idea of an in-house computer?' I put this question to Mr Christopher Bostock, managing director of a highly reputable and successful firm of consultants. 'Supposing a client said, "I want to automate my clerical procedures" but was apparently quite uninterested in the management information aspects of the exercise and resisted discussion of these.'

'We are quite direct with our clients,' said Mr Bostock. 'In a case like this, we would tell the client we are not aware of any modern computer installation which either does, or can be expected to, pay for itself on clerical work alone. We would tell him that he has some hope that if he has a relatively large amount of clerical work he might break even as against manual or keyboard accounting methods; and that in, say three to four years' time, he might be paying no more for this work than he is paying now. The only exception to this rule would be an organization whose work is almost exclusively clerical and is very large in volume.'

Mr Bostock went on to emphasize that a consultant should test the reaction of the client management to subjects like systems integration and the use of scientific management techniques. 'I believe one should work from the outset towards some sort of integrated data processing and you can often integrate a whole series of relatively small individual procedures from the start. But if you don't get any spark of reaction from the client management—in other words, if they say they've read about this kind of thing and are sure it isn't for them, their business isn't like that—then I think you've got to consider very seriously whether they should use a computer at all. Because there is little likelihood that they will get the pay-off that alone justifies the cost and upheaval of installing a computer.'

This, then, constitutes two reasons for not recommending a computer: inherent inability to make the system pay; and intractable attitudes towards new techniques on the part of client management. Another possibility is that only one aspect of an organization's operations justifies the use of a computer. In this case, a consultant would advise the use of a service bureau.

Called in from the outset, the consultants will follow the course I have outlined earlier in this chapter: feasibility study (four to eight weeks, on average); specification writing (two to four weeks)—

provided, of course, the findings justify installation of a computer. After the choice has been made, the consultants will help and guide their client through all the stages of systems design, staff selection and recruitment, training, programming, and installation of the system. Normally, they will probably remain—though possibly on a one-visit-a-week basis rather than in-house—until the initial applications are satisfactorily running.

As a client, you must help the consultants to resist the temptation of taking too much into their own hands—and temptation it is. If a consultant does his job properly within an average business, he should be able to withdraw, by stages perhaps, after three months. But this may not be easy because a consultant is, after all, human. At the earlier stages, his role is the all-knowledgeable computer specialist; later, he becomes temporary data-processing manager. As such, he runs a department. But if he has acted wisely, the people he has selected and helped to train begin to know more about the job than he does.

Gradually, the consultant will begin to move downwards in the hierarchy. When the client's data-processing manager is run in, he may for a while become chief systems analyst because help is needed in systems design. Bit by bit, he must relinquish responsibility until he finally fades out of the picture. Eventually, the new computer team will scarcely notice his absence. This is as it should be. If people go wrong, it is because the consultant has assumed a dominant role for too long so that, when he goes, the computer team feels it has lost its boss. He has behaved like a father who cannot bring himself to stand back when his son is approaching maturity and allow him to learn by personal experience, but stands at his elbow all the time.

Even as a first-time computer user, you may find yourself among the companies who do not find it necessary to employ a consultant in the initial stages. One manufacturing company I met, Brintons, the carpet manufacturers of Kidderminster, considered quite correctly that they were qualified to carry out their own feasibility study and did not call in consultants until they wanted advice on which computer system to use (7.2). After the consultants had helped them to make the decision, they stayed on to help through subsequent stages of the project.

One of the interesting features of this project was that although Brintons had a well established and efficient O & M department, they were prepared to spend money to have some of this department's staff trained by the consultants in the special techniques of computer systems design. As the consultants are particularly advanced in this subject, the investment paid off well. I should perhaps caution you here that, on the whole, too little thought has been given to rationalization of the systems design function. It would not therefore be wise to assume that every consultant firm could make a significant contribution in this area.

It is also quite feasible to employ consultants to handle only some highly specialized computer application—an integrated production control system, say, or an operational research problem. If you are competent to design and program your own routine data-processing work, there is no need for the consultants' assignment to overlap into this area.

The one request that any consultant dreads is an urgent plea by a company to extricate it from some horrible mess that has resulted from its own incompetent attempts to install a computer system. It is a thankless task for, in such circumstances, the consultant is seldom able to do more than a basic salvage job—that is, get some sort of system going, though this may be only barely adequate. It is not unknown for the luckless consultant to be confronted by a computer system that has already been installed and, in addition to remaining unused, is totally unsuited for the tasks which its owners hope it will perform. In consequence, unless a change of computer is feasible, a great deal of money and effort will probably be needed to write or rewrite programs which, in happier circumstances, should have given rise to no difficulty.

So let me urge you that in circumstances where you feel a choice of system or an applications job may be beyond you, to seek assistance before you have time to get into a serious muddle.

Before leaving the subject of consultants I must warn you that, however you use these, you cannot expect to obtain their services cheaply. (I will resist the temptation to discuss whether or not consultants' fees are too high—a subject of endless and fruitless controversy—and say merely that in my opinion they are not usually excessive when the client knows how profitably to utilize these specialists.) The minimum an average-size company could expect to spend in fees for an assignment that began with a feasibility study and carried on right through the project would be around £5,000. It could quite easily be two to three times this amount.

When considering whether or not you can afford to spend this, you must see it in relation to the sums you will inevitably lay out on hardware and all the other contingent equipment and functions. You must also consider the cost, in terms of morale and reputation as well as money, of even partial failure in a major computer application.

I will reiterate what I said at the beginning of this section: it is not my intention to urge you to employ consultants. But I think that some of you at least will find it worth while to weigh up the pros and cons of using them before embarking on your computer project.

Rental or purchase?

The points I am going to discuss here relate principally to the non-financial aspects of rental versus purchase of a computer system, since I deal with the question of costs in a later section.

Rental is usually based on the number of shifts that you work the installation. You may therefore reasonably expect that the amount you pay in rental will rise fairly soon if you are utilizing the system as much as you hope.

This charging system may seem irrelevant. But the less the machine is used, the less servicing is required and—equally important to the manufacturer—the greater the leeway in the times fixed for routine maintenance. This makes the organization of servicing facilities easier since, in small to medium-size installations, it is normal practice to make one engineer responsible for routine maintenance of several installations in the same geographical area. Another factor is that when your computer is used for only one shift it becomes available for use as a standby machine for other customers or for program testing by the manufacturers on behalf of other customers. This may be a valuable facility when the computer is a fairly new model and few installations have yet been made. Even when this is not the case, a manufacturer always tries to arrange geographically convenient standby facilities for customers in case disaster or serious breakdown occurs.

As a customer you will not, of course, be forced to allow any other organization, including the manufacturer, to use your installation. But the camaraderie that always exists between computer people and the minor nature of the inconvenience caused by agreeing to such an arrangement will probably combine to make this idea fully acceptable.

One argument sometimes advanced in favour of rental is that it gives one a chance to exchange an initial system for a larger or otherwise different one at less cost than would be entailed by purchase. This could be a valid argument if you feel unable to predict with any certainty how your organization will develop during the next few years. In other cases, the decision will revolve round whether it is better to purchase a rather larger system than is currently needed; or to rent, say, a system with the maximum available memory capacity in the expectation of exchanging it for a larger central processor in the fairly near future.

On the whole, the pros and cons for rental versus purchase of a computer system are very similar to those that are raised when any other kind of capital equipment is involved. Purchase may be cheaper in terms of total expenditure if the equipment has a longer effective working life than the time taken for expenditure on rental to reach parity with purchase price. On the other hand, there is a risk of being saddled with obsolescent equipment or a system whose size is inadequate. It is seldom easy to sell a second-hand computer, so you would be wise not to count upon this possibility.

What price 'patriotic' gestures?

When choosing a computer, should one buy British at all costs? Or should one concentrate simply on finding the best system for the job?

Some people feel they should actively demonstrate and encourage a patriotic attitude by refusing seriously to consider any but a 'British' computer. Others have a good reason for finding it politic to buy British. Plenty of organizations, of course, buy a British system because it will do their job at least as well as a system emanating from an American or other foreign company.

Some of you, however, may share my feeling that the best way to be patriotic is to operate a company as efficiently as possible and thereby, directly or indirectly, to contribute towards improvement of the UK economy. If a computer emanating from a foreign-owned company is demonstrably superior to anything available from a British manufacturer, it therefore seems better to make the decision in favour of the non-British system.

The foregoing remarks are based on the commonly held belief that it is possible accurately to determine the 'nationality' of any computer. (This is why I have worded my sentences rather carefully.) To designate a computer as British or American is as absurd in many ways as to pretend that the average Englishman or American can trace his origins back to a completely pure-bred strain.

Let me support this by applying a few criteria. Can we assume that the team that designed the computer is drawn from the nationals of only one country? This is unlikely these days, to put it mildly. In any enterprise where the possession of a first-class brain is an overriding necessity, one generally finds a richly heterogeneous collection of nationalities.

How about components and the manufacturing or assembly processes? The electronics industry is very international in character, and most manufacturers use components from many sources. Many manufacture as well as purchase in lands other than their country of origin, giving employment to many of the nationals of the foreign country in the process. Several American computer companies manufacture here and export a high percentage of their output—made by British workmen—to earn foreign currency for this country. On the other side of the fence, much so-called British equipment incorporates components and know-how obtained from overseas.

Let us try again with marketing and servicing. Both these functions are performed in this country for foreign companies by British nationals. The managing directors of many 'American' companies in this country are Britons, as are most of their executives and staff.

In spite of all this, there have been occasions when a choice, for unassailable reasons, must lie in favour of an American computer system but the decision has gone in favour of British. This has happened even when the chance of the latter's adequately performing. the tasks set for it are slim—to put it kindly.

I do not believe that British computer systems are inherently inferior to American. But there are areas in which, at present anyhow, American expertise is ahead of British, and a disinterested consensus acknowledges this. When one system or one manufacturer is unquestionably superior to others in a specified field, there should surely be no serious dilemma, especially if the project is large-scale. Failure costs far more, both in prestige and in money, than any of us can afford these days.

Paper-handling equipment

One item you must not overlook when budgeting for your computer installation is equipment for the automatic handling of continuous stationery after it comes off the output printer. There is little point in producing large numbers of forms at high speed if there is a serious bottleneck in their distribution.

What kind of equipment you will require depends very largely on the kind of stationery you use and what your applications are

Possibilities include: a machine for removal of single-use carbons and/or the separation of sets of forms into individual continuous webs; form bursters, which break webs of stationery into individual forms or sets of forms at horizontal perforations; and automatic guillotines which perform a similar function by cutting. Precision-built, widely adjustable, capable of operating at high speeds, these machines are not cheap and you can probably expect to spend at least a couple of thousand pounds on them, possibly far more.

If you have already mechanized your mailroom, you will probably need no extra machinery for folding or inserting computer-produced documents like invoices into envelopes. But if you do not possess any equipment of this kind, you will probably need at least a folding machine. Inserters, unlike simple folding machines, tend to be expensive. They are not, however, always such a luxury as might appear, for they save untold hours of tiring and tedious labour; and can sometimes also be used for other applications such as the dispatch of catalogues or direct mail circulars.

Costing and financing your project

Costs associated with your computer project in its initial stages can be grouped under two broad heads: tangibles and intangibles.

The tangibles category includes: the computer system itself, including all its peripherals; data-preparation equipment; continuous stationery and other paper-handling devices; storage equipment for items like punched cards, magnetic discs, and magnetic tapes; expendables, such as stationery, cards, or paper-tape; the furniture and other fittings used in the computer room itself and in surrounding offices. On the building side of the operation come structural alterations to existing accommodation, including the installation of false floors and sound-proofing materials or the construction of new premises; the purchase and installation of air-conditioning equipment with its attendant ducting; the purchase and installation of equipment for detection and/or prevention of fire; and, possibly, provision of extra telephone or loudspeaking intercom systems.

Costs that may be included under my heading of intangibles include: the possible provision of extra management and other staff to do the day-to-day tasks that cannot be handled by company members engaged on the feasibility study and associated activities; consultants' fees, if any; recruitment and training of a data-processing manager, systems analysts, computer operators, and data-preparation staff; fees paid to bureaux for the setting up of master files; travel expenses and other items connected with the use of distant computer systems for program testing; estimated cost of time spent during the systems-design and program-testing period and of running your existing system in parallel with the computer system until this is operating smoothly.

Two equally good reasons preclude my examining here the details of how all this should be financed. First, I have no personal knowledge of the subject: the best I could do would be to inform you at second hand without providing any evaluation of the suggestions made. Secondly, government policy and legislation change so frequently that anything I could tell you about subjects like investment grants and tax allowances might well be out of date before these words appear in print.

I must therefore confine myself to a few very general remarks. The possible methods of financing include outright purchase from existing cash resources, through a bank loan or by new capital issues; by hire purchase; by leasing; or by rental through the manufacturer. Although there is a tendency to think first of tax considerations when working out the advantages of one method or another, it is even more important to calculate the return on capital employed. To obtain realistic results you should use one of the 'scientific' methods such as discounted cash flow or return on capital investment. (Such calculations could be done by a 'package' program at a computer service bureau.)

I will once again urge you to make every effort to evaluate realistically how capital and running costs are likely to balance out against benefits expected; and to make provision for the extra costs that, in the initial period at any rate, will almost certainly be incurred. You may find it very helpful when attempting to do these sums to consult other users of systems similar to your own. Though their experience will not be entirely relevant, it may give you some useful guidelines, particularly in anticipating the areas in which extras are likely to occur.

Installing the computer

Although there are exceptions, you will normally expect an interval of 9 to 18 months to elapse before the computer system you have ordered is due to arrive. And, if things go to pattern, delivery may well not be until a month or more after the scheduled date

Manufacturers do not deliver late simply because they are inefficient (though this may sometimes happen) but principally because a very large number of the factors involved are partially or wholly outside their control. Thus, while you may openly offer them no leeway, you might make mental reservations about when delivery will actually occur.

During the interim period, a great deal of activity will take place. You will recruit your staff—mainly from inside your own organization, I hope (see chapter 8). You will organize education and training, not only for the specialists but for all levels of management. Having got your computer team through any initial training, you will see that systems design and programming begin with as little delay as possible. At the same time, you will be organizing, supervising, and chasing all the physical arrangements connected with the constructional end of the project.

It will be almost impossible to co-ordinate all this activity and have even a sporting chance of reaching your target by the time the computer arrives unless you draw up a clear, detailed, and realistic time-table. In fact, you would be very well-advised to use the PERT method which I have outlined in chapter 6.

As you may well be employing some kinds of people you have never employed before, I would like to pause for a moment to discuss what this is likely to involve—where you must be prepared, perhaps, to afford more latitude than is normally given to staff and where you can afford to be firm.

I think it is incorrect to suppose that the specialists who are responsible for systems design, programming, and the other more esoteric aspects of computer systems planning cannot be disciplined by the setting of productivity targets and deadlines. People who are not—or do not consider themselves—very creative often feel there is something mysterious about the process of creation. In particular, they believe that it cannot be disciplined and must be permitted to proceed at its 'natural' speed. This may be true about some aspects of creativity, but I think one should keep a sense of proportion and not allow oneself to be overawed or bamboozled. Most of the people engaged on computer work have a considerably higher IQ than the rest of the population; but, bright as they are, they possess exactly the same failings as the rest of us and are not above directing this superior intelligence towards having an easy life.

There are wayward geniuses in this as in any other field. But these rare beings are a race apart and you are not likely to employ one.

Much more common are individuals who are endowed with a higher than average intelligence and a reasonable degree of creativity who are, by preference, unamenable to discipline; they try to escape the consequences of mental laziness by a pose of outrage when some peasant (you!) expects them to produce results by a predetermined date.

Some people genuinely cannot work under any real pressure. There are others, by no means rare (whom I would advise you to seek out), who are strongly stimulated by a deadline and always give their best when subjected to the right degree of stress. Do not for a moment think that this kind of person is intellectually inferior to the woollier individual I have described in the preceding paragraph. In fact, I would suggest he is to be admired and respected for the self-discipline he applies.

In setting a time-table, your task is to name deadlines that are realistic but not so tight as to impose an unbearable strain. The kind of person who works best under stress will, when he finds it necessary, create his own tensions by dawdling about if he feels you have given him too long. This should not bother you too much, though you should keep a watchful eye on him by asking him to report on his progress from time to time. Ultimately, though, what counts is results.

You will find that very few computer people will conform to conventional disciplinary routines. You will waste your time, for example, if you try to compel them to arrive punctually in the morning. On the other hand, many are night owls who appear to be torpid during much of the early hours of the working day but improve as time goes by. Long after everyone else has gone home, they will work steadily with a remarkable depth of concentration.

The notion that bright young men and women cannot reasonably be expected to produce to a time-table has been neatly exploded by one company I met. This employs a large number of scientists and engineers of outstanding ability on a number of concurrent research and development projects. For each project, a team is made up combining a number of individuals with varying fields of expertise and, if the company's operations are to be profitable, it is essential that each of these men is used as productively as possible. This problem has been successfully solved by using the PERT technique, which does much to ensure that each project is completed as near to a predetermined date as possible.

The manufacturer of the computer you have ordered will help you to design a PERT network. You may find that, as well as using time analysis, it will be useful to employ cost analysis to control and monitor expenditure during this period. In addition to the direct benefits you are likely to reap as a result of employing PERT, you will have an opportunity (if this is a new experience for you) of getting the 'feel' of computer work.

WHICH PROGRAM FIRST? There is no easy or rule-of-thumb answer to the question of which, of a number of applications scheduled for the computer over, say, the first two years, should receive priority.

Sometimes choice is dictated by expediency. Where it has been found hard to sell the idea of computerization to senior managers, the data-processing manager and the executive to whom he reports may well decide that the best strategy is to put first onto the system the application which will yield results most easily recognized as valuable because of clear savings in time, cost, or labour. This may sound a somewhat naïve approach, but it often works well. A computer project whose major benefit will lie in the implementation of a complex integrated system may not become fully operational for a long period after delivery of the hardware. During this time, the somewhat shaky faith of the board of directors (who, after all, also have to face searching and not always kindly questions from their friends outside the organization and from the shareholders) may be further undermined. So it may be politic to begin computerization with a payroll program which, though unexciting, simplifies and speeds what may have been a troublesome job and releases, say, a number of keyboard machines and their operators.

The question of expediency may also arise when an existing system is in danger of breaking down through an overload of work, staff shortages, or other factors.

Where there is strong and confident support from senior management, the better policy may be to tackle the hardest job first. John Summers & Co. Ltd, the big steel company, purchased a computer system largely to implement a highly complex control system for the production of various types of sheet steel product. This was a very tough assignment in computer terms. Nevertheless, the data-processing team and the senior managers felt that, as this was the area in which the biggest benefit was to be achieved, it was best to tackle it right away. 'Anything else we plan to do subsequently will seem easy,' the data-processing manager told me.

Scheduling the order in which programs are to be put onto the computer can be particularly difficult when the final result is to be a complex integrated system. For this implies that every aspect of a group of routines interlocks with others. At the same time, practical considerations preclude the simultaneous computerization of several applications of vital importance to the company's operations.

In such cases, very careful planning is necessary. After deciding the order in which it is feasible to write, test, and implement these programs, it will be necessary to devise methods whereby only some sections of each are used initially, the rest remaining in abeyance. Later, the links that lock the various sections together will be added.

This activity is rather like constructing a grid in piece-meal fashion. Ideally, one would interweave the various structural members during manufacture. But when this is impracticable, one must approach the question of design in a different way. One possibility would be to preform all the vertical members in such a way that they will subsequently engage with the horizontal members when these are finished. Another is to make up several small, self-contained sections which are subsequently locked together to form a larger structure.

What I am trying to say is that good results can be achieved only when the designers envisage the total structure from the beginning. Unless they do this, they will have to try to create an integrated structure from an assorted and probably mis-matched collection of parts.

PARALLEL RUNNING. Unless the applications for the computer are entirely new to your organization—i.e., you have never used these routines in any form before—some period of parallel running is often necessary. That is, source data used in existing procedures is also used in the computer system which processes it as though this dry run were the real thing. Meanwhile, the old procedures are still treated as 'live'. This allows the computer team carefully to check every aspect and to solve any problems that may arise without disrupting day-to-day work.

In the past, parallel running often went on for months. Today, it is shortened to a minimum, and for good reason. It is, for a start, very expensive. When punched-card systems or keyboard accounting machines have been used in the past, the running costs of these will be added to the cost of the computer. Parallel running for any length of time is also bad for morale. It suggests either that the computer people do not know their job or that management has

P

little faith in the new system. Those operating the old procedures are hardly in a position to produce their best work when they know these will shortly be obsolete.

Careful planning should allow almost complete testing of the initial programs before your own computer arrives. This should, unless some unforeseen difficulty is met, reduce the parallel running period to a matter of a week or two.

I have met organizations who have abolished parallel running completely. One firm in particular took a deep breath and went straight into its computer system without a break, the changeover being carried out during a weekend. As it happened, everything went beautifully, but I think they were pushing their luck a bit. Had anything gone seriously awry, there would have been disastrous disruption of day-to-day work. Customers, for example, could not have been provided with routine accounting documents and a backlog, with all the attendant difficulties this implies, would very quickly have built up.

What can happen when unforeseen difficulties arise is illustrated by the experience of a smallish manufacturing company who, having decided for the first time to handle its own marketing, judged that this was the moment to install a computer. Since no previous system for sales order processing was in existence, an entirely new, computer-orientated one was designed.

It was sheer bad luck that the small computer this company had purchased was a 'rogue'—a phenomenon which many car-owners have encountered. The machine developed fault after fault. No sooner had the engineers put one right than it recurred or a fresh one started. A service engineer was virtually in residence and worked intolerably long hours in an attempt to solve the problems satisfactorily.

Since the other arrangements for marketing had been set up, distributors had been stocked, and so on, and there was no alternative method of handling documentation, very serious difficulties arose. These were aggravated by the fact that no suitable stand-by system was available in the vicinity and the only possibility was to undertake a daily journey of some 50 miles. Nor could the troublesome computer easily be replaced, as no spare machine was available. By the time this did arrive, the unhappy owners of the system were approaching bankruptcy.

This was sheer bad luck. The machine in question had been successfully installed for other users and no serious technical faults had developed. Nevertheless, it is always unwise to assume it would never happen to you. The moral of this story is that you cannot be too careful. With the wisdom of hindsight it was maddeningly easy for the user company to see that its planning had been unrealistic. It should have ensured that the computer system was working properly before the distribution arrangements were put into effect. To launch a new sales plan and a new computer system to handle the administrative end of this simultaneously was too risky. The expense of running a dummy system for a while would have had to be taken into account; but this would have been trivial compared with the cost of what actually happened.

Summary

The following points have been mentioned in this chapter:

(*a*) What looks like a good case for installing a computer does not always turn out this way. A computer will not, in itself, solve any problems for a business that is badly managed.

(*b*) An investigation known as a feasibility study must always precede any decision whether or not to use a computer. This study is in two phases, the first of which is designed to find out what is actually being done within an organization, the second to ascertain what improvements could be made and how these can be implemented. It is not wise to invite a computer manufacturer to carry out this study.

(*c*) Once it has been decided that a computer is required, a selection must be made between a number of alternative systems. Two or more manufacturers are asked to submit detailed proposals of the kind of system they will supply. Since these will differ considerably, one must devise a common yardstick which will compare one with another in the light of the user's specific requirements. Only in this way is it possible realistically to appraise the merits and drawbacks of alternative systems.

(*d*) Software evaluation is a notoriously difficult task, even for a computer specialist. For most users, therefore, the only possibility is to find out from other user organizations how well a manufacturer's software works on the job.

(*e*) Too little attention is often paid to weighing the considerations involved in alternative methods of input and training data-preparation machine operators. Yet this is an area in which sloppiness can prejudice the overall efficiency of a computer scheme and raise its cost.

(*f*) Computer consultants may be very helpful to an organization by guiding it through the feasibility study and all the subsequent phases of computer selection and installation. But care must be taken to find good consultants and they must be used intelligently by the client company. A consultant asked to pull an organization out of a muddle caused by its own incompetent attempts to install a computer may be able to do little to help.

(*g*) Estimating the probable cost of launching a computer project is not an easy job. Care must be taken, not only to include every factor and examine alternative methods of financing, but also to assess return on capital on a realistic basis.

(*h*) The use of the PERT method outlined in chapter 6 will help in the organization and control of a computer scheme during the pre-installation phases.

(*i*) Consideration must be given to the order in which applications are to be put onto the computer and parallel running time of the old and new system must be cut down as far as possible.

References
7.1 TATHAM, L. *The efficiency experts*. Business Publications Ltd, 1964.
7.2 TATHAM, L. Optimizing Brintons carpet production. *Data Systems*.

8. Computers and people

The success of any computer project, however ambitious or however modest it may be, depends directly and crucially on people—on the human element in all its aspects. I feel I cannot over-emphasize the importance of this point.

Currently, hardware has reached a high stage of development in terms of both performance and reliability. Software, as we have seen, can cause tough difficulties but these are being overcome and are met mostly in projects where new ground is being broken and advanced techniques being pioneered.

Yet far too many quite modest computer projects achieve very qualified success or fail outright. This is primarily due to human failure of one kind or another within the user's organization. One might imagine that the more sophisticated computers become, the smaller the human contribution. In fact, I believe the reverse to be the case.

It is pretty obvious to anyone that the attitudes, abilities, and qualifications of those directly associated with the computer itself—systems analysts, programmers, the data-processing manager, for example—can make or break the project. It is, perhaps, less apparent how profoundly the attitudes and actions of the managers of the organization, from the top downward, can influence the final outcome.

Yet the enthusiasm, scepticism, or indifference of every and any senior manager percolates right through any organization. Poor attitudes, even though never overtly expressed, will always be reflected, more or less accurately, right through the company hierarchy. Any individual who habitually visits a large number of commercial and industrial organizations in a journalistic or consultant capacity will tell you that one can pretty accurately gauge what the chief executive of a company is like after five minutes in the reception area. This impression is gained by an amalgam of subtle factors which include the attitude of the person who takes your name, the expressions and even gait of those who walk through the hall, and similar small but significant signs.

Ultimately, then, responsibility for the success of a computer project lies fairly and squarely with top management. This means, of course, that as a senior manager you must become personally involved from the outset. This does not imply that all the board members should roll up their sleeves and start writing programs or take courses in systems analysis. Their job is in many ways far more difficult than this.

Senior managers have to steer a well-judged course between merciless driving and constant interference. While respecting the specialists they employ, they cannot afford to live in the fool's paradise that surrounds those who rely blindly upon experts. It is senior management's job to direct, not submit to, the computer project and to bring to this important task at least as much expertise as they would apply to directing any other major undertaking.

Direction cannot, of course, be undertaken without education. But what form should this education take? Its major objective must be to gain a broad understanding of the areas in which computers can and cannot be usefully applied. It must include an appreciation of the role of modern, computer-based management techniques. Ideally it should, I believe, also yield some understanding of what computer specialists are like as human beings; what makes them tick. The members of the computer team, in fact, are mysterious creatures only to those who are too lazy or too nervous to make their acquaintance.

Properly designed and run, introductory computer courses can be immensely helpful to top management. They will probably be two to five days in duration and should be concerned with broad issues. A good appreciation course gives senior managers sufficient insight to enable them to make wise policy decisions, take an intelligent interest in the project, and evaluate with sympathy the efforts of those directly involved in getting the computer scheme off the ground and implementing it.

A management induction course that devotes two out of five days to an exercise in programming in Cobol or network analysis does not, in my opinion, fulfil its function adequately. Though there is much to be said for a short exercise that enables a layman to get the 'feel' of computer work, too much emphasis should not be laid on this aspect.

Many computer manufacturers now offer introductory courses for managers and executives. Inevitably, these will to some degree be orientated towards the manufacturer's own hardware and philosophy. Although I am not suggesting you will be inundated with propaganda, you should be aware that some of the material presented to you will relate specifically to this company's products and ideas rather than to the computer field in general.

Many independent organizations such as management consultant firms and educational establishments of various kinds also offer introductory courses. The National Computing Centre has recently set up a three-day residential course in data-processing appreciation for working directors and senior management *without* previous experience in data processing (NCC emphasize this last point). Held normally on Mondays to Wednesdays at different parts of England and Scotland, the course includes a practical exercise in evaluation, a feasibility study, and a visit to a computer installation. The cost is 180 guineas per head (150 to NCC members) and in 1968 six were held.

I feel I must caution you against indiscriminate attendance at the many seminars, symposia, conferences, and other gatherings the purpose of which is to offer education to businessmen. My own experience has demonstrated that some of these are highly unsatisfactory. Among the causes for criticism are lecturers whose knowledge is badly out of date, speakers who have no idea of how to put their subject across interestingly, failure to live up to the titles listed in the advance programme, and too great a discrepancy between the standards of knowledge assumed by the speakers. Thus, one speaker may offer the audience what amounts to a child's guide to computers while the next talks incomprehensibly about some recondite aspects of computer file organization. I once attended a symposium in which an advertised speaker made almost no reference to the subject which the advance programme gave as the topic of his lecture. As this talk was, for me, the highlight of the conference, I felt cheated.

As few businessmen have time to waste and nobody likes to throw 15 to 25 guineas down the drain (the fee range for a one-day event including lunch), I suggest it may be profitable to investigate—via the grapevine, perhaps—the status and reputation of the sponsoring organization, the calibre of its guest speakers, if any, and whether it has any clear idea of the audience it is aiming at. This last is particularly important, as too mixed an audience (in terms of knowledge level) results in an attempt to please everybody and, often, profit to none.

Having received your introductory, and possibly some other subsequent, education in computery, you will feel a little more confident about establishing communications with your own computer team. May I, however, beg you to swallow your pride when you find there is something you do not understand and ask for elucidation? Understandably, you may feel reluctant to ask what you feel is a disgracefully elementary question. But if you fail to do this, you can easily become blinded with science or completely misunderstand what you are told.

I will pass on to you one very useful tip I have gained from years of experience as a journalist (and even more years as a female!): I have never met anybody who objected to answering even the simplest of questions or betrayed that he thought me a fool for asking it. Most people enjoy passing on information; almost everybody, properly drawn out, enjoys talking about his job. So you will not lose face if you ask your data-processing manager to clarify some point; but you will lose his respect if you pretend you have understood, for sooner or later you will unwittingly reveal your ignorance and be labelled as a fraud.

Timing, of course, is important. You would not necessarily want to hold up an entire meeting for explanation of a term that everyone else appears perfectly to understand. On the other hand, my own experience suggests that, provided the diversion is not too long, several people may well be grateful to you for your question because it saved them from asking it! The more candid of them may well confess this to you later.

Basic human attitudes

Yourself introduced to the subject of computers, you should be in a position to tackle the delicate problem of introducing the idea of a computer project to your organization at large. I think you are more likely to do this job well when you recognize the nature and extent of the fear of computers that many people feel. This fear is often not overt, but lurks below the surface of consciousness.

Fear is infectious. It manifests itself in ways that include mental apathy, panic flight, sullen despair, or a mulish refusal to co-operate. You must do all you can to see that none of these undesirable reactions occurs in your workpeople.

Though familiarity does not breed contempt in those who work with computers or at least know something about how they work, it certainly dispels mystique because the limitations become at least as apparent as the potential. But to many other people, even the well-educated, a computer is utterly mysterious and an object of real fear. Because the expression of apprehension is sometimes naïve, it is easy to under-estimate its seriousness and extent.

The irrational fear of computers is fed by many sources. It started with that unfortunate phrase, 'electronic brain', which has unnerving undertones of superhuman knowingness and efficiency. Regrettably, it is still used by the popular press, but I beg you as a manager to refrain from employing such a dangerously emotive term.

In science fiction stories in print, in films, and on television, the computer frequently figures either as a sort of demi-god or as a dreaded, all-powerful villain. To the knowledgeable, these fictional gods and monsters look about as terrifying as a white-sheeted 'ghost' appears in the light of day. For the less informed, fear is not easily dispelled.

The writers who invent and the people who visualize these productions are, consciously or not, shrewdly exploiting a very real and deep contemporary neurosis—the growing sense of impotence in industrial man in an environment that is becoming ever larger, more complex, and more impersonal. The fear aroused by the computers that figure in science fiction is therefore a good deal more disturbing than the agreeable reaction to the more traditional type of spine-chiller which relies for its horror on mediaeval phobias and superstitions.

Responsible, factual TV and film documentaries which examine far-out experiments in computer science can reinforce fear. For they deprive us of even the slender comfort of writing off the subject as imaginative nonsense. Can you truthfully maintain that you are entirely unmoved by the phrase *machine intelligence*? (This subject is being intensively investigated, particularly at Edinburgh University, where computers have already been taught to learn by experience.)

Real though it is, fear like this is often deeply buried and therefore unrecognized by its victims. Far more tangible and immediate is the apprehension aroused by the possibility of losing one's employment or, at best, one's status. Such fear is very vivid for those who have reached the age of 40 or more. First, they associate computers only with the young and bright; second, they continue to believe that computers are used principally to eliminate clerical work and are therefore likely to cause widespread redundancy.

To people like this, the word 'computer' may be a synonym for privation and humiliation. Placed in the past by management in comfortable positions of minor authority that they could reasonably have expected to hold until retirement, they may not have flexed their mental processes for a long time. They see themselves thrown onto a job market where experience, maturity, and a sense of responsibility count as nothing against youth and high academic qualification. If the organization's attitude is paternalistic, they suspect they will be moved to some inessential, harmless job to rot quietly away until they may formally be put out to grass with a pension.

I would like to plead with all the eloquence at my command for a constructive and sympathetic attitude towards men and women in vulnerable positions within your own organization. Later in this chapter, I outline some possibilities for employing these in ways that fruitfully exploit their abilities. Meantime, how do you introduce the explosive subject of computerization?

Introducing the computer

As a conscientious manager, you recognize the existence and nature of fear and have resolved to do everything you can to allay this from the outset. How do you go about this? The only effective way to dispel the kind of general unease I have mentioned is to try to replace it by genuine, informed interest and personal identification with the computer scheme. To achieve this end, you will inform your employees, in acceptable and understandable terms but without patronage, about the nature and function of computers in general and how the computer will be used within the company in particular.

You must lay strong emphasis on the way the computer will extend rather than devalue human effectiveness. You must encourage people to ask questions at every stage; and however naïve these sound, you must answer them seriously and without condescension. One ill-timed witticism at someone else's expense can set you back a very long way. You need not, of course, be deadly serious. But see that if you use humour there is no trace of sting in it.

Education like this must, of course, be given on a face-to-face basis, though it may often usefully be supplemented by films. These should be chosen with an eye to stressing the practical and everyday rather than the 'far out' applications of computers. A film showing how computers direct missiles, for example, is worse than useless.

Specific fears can be dispelled only by the exercise of complete candour from the start. Above all, everybody wants to know what will happen to him. Any attempt you make to fob your audience off with generalities or half-truths is an invitation to irrevocable disaster because it destroys the confidence that is all-important to success.

Your first exercise in candour will be the making of an announcement, as early as possible, of plans to launch the feasibility study. Some very pertinent comments on the bad results—and the futility— of attempting to conceal plans for a computer are made in a little book by Enid Mumford (8.1). Though this was published in 1964, her remarks have lost none of their relevance. The book is a collection of annotated case histories, only the names of the organizations and a few details being fictional.

Relating the story of 'Carters', Miss Mumford notes that everyone except the board of directors and the company secretary was kept in ignorance of the fact that the computer was coming. But:

> An attitude survey was carried out at Carters three months before the computer arrived. It was found that although staff were supposedly ignorant of the firm's plans to install a computer, many were unfavourably disposed to the idea of office automation.

By its policy of secrecy, management lost the opportunity of reducing this resistance by 'selling' the idea of a computer to the staff. Writing of another computer user, Miss Mumford says:

> When the original decision was taken, the company put a notice on the board saying that a computer had been ordered and gave assurance of job security. This degree of communication with the staff proved quite inadequate to meet the need for information in the areas affected by the computer; much hostility resulted so 'the idea was never accepted and we had a £25,000 computer standing idle'.

The speed of the average organizational grapevine as a communications medium assures that no secret can be kept for long without absurdly elaborate (and probably impractical) precautions. It does not, for example, take much perspicacity to guess the import of questions asked during a feasibility study. You should therefore consider the pros and cons of making an announcement before this study is begun. This, after outlining the scope of the exercise, might point out that the outcome is uncertain; and that, even if the decision were in favour of a computer, 18 months (or whatever period you wish to name) will elapse before its impact will be felt substantially, giving plenty of time to see that no-one gets hurt during reorganization.

The choice of the right method of communication is at least as important as choice of content. Commenting wryly on the company that chose to put a notice on its bulletin board, Miss Mumford writes:

> Managements are very often under the impression that they have given information to their employees although the employees themselves are unaware that they have received any.

Effective communication is emphatically a two-way exercise. And your best chance of establishing good relationships and getting to know what people really think is to encourage questions, the challenging of assumptions, the voicing of apprehensions (in private, where necessary), and freedom of discussion. Any ideas submitted must receive serious and careful consideration and rejections be accompanied by a full and honest explanation.

If bulletin-board notices are inadequate, so is an article or series of articles in the house magazine. The average person reads little (especially if he feels management is trying to reach him) and frequently misconstrues what he reads. Though an article can usefully amplify information given by word of mouth, or be used to report progress on an already accepted project, it can never substitute for two-way exchange of speech.

Spoken communication, then, is a must; and top management must be seen to be involved from the first. They must personally introduce the computer scheme, speaking as people who are themselves vitally concerned and interested.

On this occasion, it may be helpful to invite a member of your consultant firm, if you are using one, or a computer company representative or some other specialist to speak about the computer itself and to answer questions. It is important that this person has the gift of putting his subject across well, otherwise he will damage your cause by boring or irritating your audience.

Your own attitudes are very important, too. The average worker, whatever his job, appreciates a manager who has 'no side', who succeeds in conveying the right kind and degree of friendliness, and does not adopt a superior attitude. You will do yourself no harm if you reveal that you, too, have plenty to learn. I do beg you though to avoid the dreadful out-of-place geniality which some managers naïvely suppose will endear them to their employees. No adult enjoys being treated like a child at a Punch and Judy show.

I have been supposing that this presentation is done at a meeting. The timing of this is important. You will not put your audience in a receptive frame of mind if you invite them to come along in their free time, even if you do offer them cake and buns. You should therefore arrange this occasion during working hours.

Middle management can be your most useful ally or your most effective obstructer. I think therefore you may find it politic to take middle management into your confidence about the computer plans a short time before you make the general announcement. This will give the managers a chance to voice doubts and difficulties among their peers; and it demonstrates that you have sufficient confidence in them to divulge your plans in advance. Prestige, which otherwise might be in danger, is maintained. Properly briefed, aware of top management's reliance upon them, middle managers can help a great deal by answering questions and encouraging constructive attitudes among the rest of the staff.

It is just as important that the rank and file should see that middle management is aligned with senior management. This makes it clear that there is no 'them against us' attitude but a unanimous identification with the project and desire to help it run smoothly.

Anyone inside the organization who has already been selected for some task in connection with the computer project should be identified and seen to receive support. Details of what kind of people are to be recruited from outside—a chief programmer, perhaps—should also be given with an explanation of why they are needed.

Above all, you must give as full an account as you can of how existing jobs are likely to be affected by the computer. This is naturally the subject closest to everyone's heart and a point where confidence may be permanently gained or lost. You must be strictly truthful. Glib general assurances are worse than useless to people who feel their jobs may be in peril. It is better, if necessary, to admit that you cannot say exactly what will happen in some job areas than to try to dodge this issue. At the same time, you must give an assurance—and faithfully implement this at the earliest possible moment—that full and careful personal consideration will be given to every individual as soon as the situation is clarified.

You must have done your homework about redundancy, if this is expected to arise. Make it clear that announcements will always be made in plenty of time to allow re-employable people who become redundant to find other jobs within or outside the organization.

If your policy is to permit rundown by natural wastage, keep a careful eye on the personnel or other department responsible for labour recruitment. It is not uncommon for these, though well aware that staff requirements will soon be reduced or modified, to continue recruitment along the old lines as though nothing had happened.

Admittedly, some inconvenience may well occur through allowing a rundown of staff. But recruitment in a situation like this seems indefensible. Where existing systems must be staffed, it should be possible to employ 'temporaries', to farm out some work to a bureau, or to induce those due for retirement to stay on a little longer as stop-gaps.

Finding computer staff inside the company

One good confidence and morale booster is the knowledge that the computer team will include as many existing employees as possible. This line of action also helps solve the problems raised by the apparently chronic shortage of qualified programmers, systems analysts, data-preparation machine operators, and other computer personnel.

Finding computer staff within an organization which already uses punched cards is seldom difficult. But to recruit suitable people from inside a company where the level of qualification and ability appears to be relatively low sounds like a counsel of perfection. In fact, it is far more often feasible than might at first appear.

A surprisingly large number of people, particularly those in dull, routine or undemanding jobs, are like icebergs, in that much of their real ability remains submerged and undeveloped in their working environment. Abilities, whose existence is often unknown even to their possessors, quite frequently come to light as a result of taking aptitude tests for computer programming, systems analysis, and other jobs.

Shorn of their superficial glamour, many of the tasks associated with computers are revealed as fairly routine in character. Those who have been successful in clerical jobs may therefore prove suitable for others that demand the same patient attention to detail.

During the past few years, I have talked to a good many organizations about this question of internal recruitment for computer jobs. As far as I can determine without systematic research, there is a growing tendency to do this, as a matter of policy, not of expediency.

It is being increasingly appreciated that knowledge of the organization itself, its personalities and activities, and a feeling of identification with these, are more valuable than computer experience. Given people with a reasonable measure of the right kind of aptitudes who will be carefully guided, it is more satisfactory to train these in computer techniques than to try to teach outsiders the intricacies of the business.

The data-processing manager of one wholesale grocery firm I met, when looking for a systems designer from outside, aimed not for a qualified systems analyst but for a young man who knew the grocery business well. Having satisfied himself that the most suitable applicant possessed the potential to design systems, he engaged him for the job and the company, of course, saw that he received a suitable training. This policy paid off very well and the selection of applicants was wider than if the company had advertised simply for a chief systems analyst. The computer jobs themselves were not very complex, but the grocery business takes a long time to learn.

I think in this situation it is important always to bear in mind that the object of installing the computer is to increase the profitability of the business. It is too easy to get so immersed as to regard the computer operation as an end in itself and to forget that it is simply a tool to improve the management function. The object of the computer staff is to serve the management, not the machine—a point that is sometimes overlooked.

FINDING PROGRAMMERS. Among those who, to my personal knowledge, have become successful computer programmers are a warehouse clerk, a storeman, a travel agency clerk, the manager of an off licence, a junior bookkeeper, and a taxi driver. Some of these are writing quite complex programs. None had had any previous experience in an area anything like this, or was even aware of aptitude before volunteering to take a test. Some were over 40 before they began to learn the new job.

Programming still tends, at least in the eyes of the layman, to be a 'prestige' job. This is true at the top levels. But today, thanks to better computer design (which reduces the need for ingenuity in programming), to the assembler, and to high-level languages, many of the lesser programming jobs can be done by people with quite modest mathematical ability and education.

The time, effort, and ability required to learn basic programming has steadily decreased. Typically, assembler language for a small computer system is learned in three to four weeks by a person of suitable aptitude, and six months' on-the-job experience under the guidance of a qualified programmer will produce a useful member of the programming staff for an average company whose applications lie in the data-processing field.

Other factors that help are the availability of package programs which minimize the amount of work to be done by a user's own staff; and the modular system of design which, in elaborate programs, permits the stratification of work to some degree so that some levels can be tackled by programmers of modest ability.

What are the human and other qualities required to make a successful computer programmer? To find out, we must look at what the job entails.

The programmer is the final link in the chain of communication between the ultimate user and the computer itself. His function is to translate the user's intentions, as expressed by the systems designer, into a series of logical, precise, and unambiguous instructions for the computer. Or, to put it another way, he has to do the thinking for the electronic idiot in his charge.

At the highest level, programming allows much room for creativity, as it may demand ingenious use of the computer system to achieve the desired ends at all, if these are complex. At other levels, however, it is clear that the principal demand on the programmer is an ability to think clearly and logically and the patience to attend meticulously to detail.

Basically the programmer must be machine-orientated (to use a currently fashionable term). That is, his job is, in a sense to serve the computer. It is not up to him to outline management's intentions but to take these as his starting point. Only when these intentions are unclear or there is some fault in logic is he likely to question them.

Dealing as he does with a machine that works exclusively with figures, dependent absolutely upon logic, he must have at least some mathematical background. This need not be particularly impressive —O-level maths may be quite adequate as a starting point for a junior job. Given the faculty sometimes described as 'a feeling for figures' and ambition, it will not be difficult for him to fill, through evening classes or some other form of instruction, any gaps in his knowledge and to move to higher things if he wishes.

Though life is obviously easier for his colleagues if the programmer is a good mixer, he need not be conspicuously successful in this area as his work is, on the whole, rather impersonal; but he must be capable of working as a member of a team.

Whether or not a man or woman possesses the two basic characteristics, an ability to think logically and an aptitude for figures, can be discovered by using formal tests. There is a number of these in use, of which the most popular is probably the programmer test set designed by IBM (and available also to non-users of IBM equipment). Whatever the test, it must be properly applied and is usually administered by the computer manufacturer or by a consultant if the user company employs one.

I think one should be careful, though, not to rely slavishly upon test results, particularly when these are (as intended) completed within a prescribed time. The tests are designed to find people who will make good programmers and normally a score of 80 per cent or so is required for a pass.

Within a user company, however, this stringency may not always be necessary or desirable. I have met more than one organization whose programming was done successfully by men and women who achieved scores of only 60 to 65 per cent in aptitude tests. One data-processing manager required a higher score than this but did not stick to the time limits prescribed by the test. 'There was nothing too complicated about our programs and we were not in a frantic rush to get the work onto the computer,' he told me. 'I was anxious to recruit from inside, so I selected people who are a bit older than most programmers. They work more slowly, but they do the job quite satisfactorily'.

I do not suggest that you should overrule the advice of a specialist who tells you there are no suitable candidates for programmer training within your organization; but simply that you make sure he does not set his sights too high when he reaches this conclusion. Your requirement is for people who will be able to handle your job satisfactorily. While you might be asking for trouble if you employed too many programmers whose abilities were marginal, it is often possible to use some in this category, provided they are carefully supervised. What you lose in technical ability you gain by having a staff which knows the organization and is not as likely as newcomers to be lured away by promises of a higher salary.

TRAINING PROGRAMMERS. Normally, you will expect the manufacturer of your computer system to train what you mutually agree is a reasonable number of programmers. This training, however, will be

Q

basic and must be followed by several months' on-the-job training under the supervision of a qualified and experienced programmer before the person can be considered sufficiently trained to work alone. Sometimes the senior programmer is a manager who has been given, at company expense, a more comprehensive training. In other cases, he will have been recruited from outside sources.

Perhaps I should warn you of the dangers of the many so-called computer training schools run by organizations independent of manufacturers or recognized education authorities. Many of these schools are, I am afraid, manifestations of the eagerness of sharp operators to climb onto the computer bandwagon.

One of the greatest sins of these dubious schools is to accept for training people who simply do not possess the required degree of basic ability. One typical case that came to my own attention was that of a girl who attended a full course at one of these institutions and emerged with a diploma. Subsequent testing of her programming ability by a person who had no axe whatever to grind revealed that she was wholly unqualified even to do the simplest kind of programming.

Because word has got around about these schools, their 'graduates' are generally regarded with suspicion and in consequence find it difficult to obtain jobs, in spite of the much-talked-of shortage of programmers. This seems harsh, particularly to the unlucky trainee who has probably paid a substantial fee for his tuition. But generally, even if he or she has real aptitude, the course has provided little or no on-the-job experience. Even if his basic training has been adequate, he is therefore far from qualified in the technical sense; and may well also be handicapped by total lack of knowledge of commerce or industry.

One cannot therefore altogether blame potential employers for turning down these 'graduates'. They cannot be used in a senior capacity, and the employer often prefers to obtain, probably at lower cost, suitable school-leavers for training if he has to recruit from outside.

Not all independent programmer-training organizations are, of course, suspect. But I think you should be on your guard.

FINDING SYSTEMS ANALYSTS AND DESIGNERS. Good systems analysis and design are probably the most important factor (at least from the technical viewpoint) in ensuring the success of a computer project. A sizable proportion of the known failures of computer schemes—

that is, unworkability, dissatisfaction in one form or another or plain unprofitability—both here and in the USA has been attributed to poor or inadequate work on the systems side.

There is, in fact, a trend towards placing increasing importance on the role of the systems designer as opposed to the programmer. And it is certainly true that a properly designed and methodically documented system can often reduce the programmer's job to little more than a coding function. Perhaps it is this that makes a good many programmers ambitious to become systems designers.

Some organizations do not draw a line between the functions of systems work and programming, believing that those who analyse existing systems and devise new ones should also be responsible for programming. Others are strongly opposed to this and believe there should be a clear division between the two functions. The programmer, they point out, is machine-orientated; the systems man must be problem-orientated. Though this may sound a quibble, the distinction is, in fact, an important one. The aim must always be to utilize the computer to handle a problem, not to bend a problem to fit the computer. Some argue, in fact, that the less the systems man knows about computing, the better he will be able to do his job. This is rather an extreme view. What may weigh more is that the systems man needs the kind of personality that is often not possessed by the professional programmer.

There are two aspects of systems work: analysis and design. These can sometimes be handled by different teams, sometimes done by the same team. An entire systems exercise covers four phases. First, to investigate and formulate management requirements. Second, to examine and describe existing procedures. Next comes an investigation to establish whether or not the existing systems fulfil management's new requirements; and if not, how they can be modified. Finally, new systems must be designed and described in a way that is absolutely clear to provide a brief for the programmers.

What kind of person can best perform these tasks? A good listener, for a start; for the systems man has to elicit information from people who are not always very good at explaining and often resist the idea of change. He must also be a persuasive communicator, for he will probably have to sell new ideas fairly hard before they are accepted.

To be efficient is not enough. The systems man must be liked and trusted, a diplomat but not a liar. He must be experienced enough to know that working systems seldom bear much resemblance to those laid down in procedure manuals. He will therefore tend to be sceptical about what he is told, though he will never allow himself to appear critical of those who give him the inside information he needs.

A systems man responsible for eliciting information from top management must possess sufficient stature to earn their respect. If management regard him as an underling, it will be almost impossible for him to do his job satisfactorily. Often it will be he who must force the pace: cajole management to formulate its requirements, compel it to look ahead, put up his own ideas where he feels these may be relevant. He may have to precipitate decisions that reconcile conflicting requirements.

Aside from these personal qualities, the systems man needs a really sound working knowledge of how this particular business at least operates—and preferably, something about business in general. He must be aware of the value of new management techniques and, perhaps, be prepared to outline to top management how these may usefully be applied by them. Though he needs no profound technical knowledge of computers, he should, I believe, have a broad and sound understanding of the subject so that he can appreciate what makes sense in computer terms and what is impracticable.

A good systems man will therefore need enough experience and expertise to dissect existing methods and to design new procedures plus a thorough knowledge of business methods in general, a broad appreciation of the capabilities and limitations of computers, and an ability to get along well with all sorts and conditions of people.

Is this type of person likely to be found inside a company that has not previously used a computer? Much depends on how the organization has been run until now. A concern that has a good O & M or management services department will probably find the men it needs without difficulty, though they will possibly need some further training. Others, particularly those where there has been little continuity of management or few co-ordinated attempts to ensure efficient working, may have to go outside, at least for their chief systems man.

Whether or not relatively poorly qualified people can be used in any aspect of systems work is a matter of some controversy. Some people think that using less than highly qualified personnel is an invitation to disaster; others, like Robin Gibson, who was for some years training manager for English Electric Computers Ltd, believe that it is perfectly feasible to use relatively inexperienced people for systems analysis, provided that they are properly trained and supervised.

Clearly, a good deal depends upon the quality of the team leader and upon how ambitious and complex the systems in question are. In run-of-the-mill business applications, however, there seems to be no reason to disqualify people with fairly limited ability and qualifications at least in the more routine aspects of systems analysis.

Men and women who have worked for some years in supervisory jobs with the organization and are liked and respected may be well suited for systems analysis. Often they are accustomed to coping patiently with a mass of detail; they know how to handle people; and are usually more aware than anyone else of what actually happens within a department as distinct from what is supposed to happen.

At the design end of the exercise, an ability to think logically is of great importance. What is needed is the type of mind that can see beyond detail and perceive a pattern; that can take a broad approach and can consider the functions of an organization in relation to one another and establish the connections that make integration possible. For these reasons, it is usually necessary to employ a person in a fairly high management position to handle systems design—as opposed to systems analysis.

The results of systems analysis and the blueprints for new systems are not, at present, expressed in formal codes as computer programs are, though various attempts have been made to work out languages that will precisely describe business procedures. At the time of writing, none of these has been wholly successful and the traditional flow-chart method is generally used. The ultimate aim is to find a code which will itself act as a program and can be fed into the computer via a compiler like a high-level language. Urwick Diebold, the computer consultants, are currently working on a system like this in conjunction with the National Computing Centre. Known as Systematics, this endeavours to describe in clear and completely unambiguous terms the procedures used in various aspects of commerce and industry.

Although most people are aware of the difficulties already arising from a shortage of programming expertise, there seems, on the whole, far less concern about a similar scarcity of systems analysts and designers. Yet of the two, it is almost certainly the latter that is potentially more disastrous. The National Computing Centre, for example, referred in 1967 to 'the crisis in systems analysis which is crippling the full development of the use of computers by British industry, a shortage that could reach 12,000 by 1970'.

In an effort to help plug this gap as soon as possible, NCC, in conjunction with major computer manufacturers, users, consultants' and educationalists, has produced a syllabus for systems training and has developed this into a complete course package. The package contains complete sets of lecture notes, case studies, a business game, and many visual aids. It is designed to allow training establishments, technical colleges, and individual companies to teach systems analysis efficiently and in as short a time as possible. Taken on a full-time basis, it is six weeks long and the package is sold at £500.

To reduce any difficulty which may arise from those of different backgrounds being mixed during the systems training, NCC has also developed two preliminary modules. One of these two-week courses is to teach people already knowledgeable about computers (particularly programmers) something of the fundamentals of business management. The other, of similar length, covers the fundamentals of electronic data-processing for trainees who have business knowledge but know little or nothing about computers. Later, NCC hopes also to develop an advanced systems course for use two years or more after the basic six-week course and on-the-job experience.

I had hoped to be able to include here some opinions on the value of the NCC six-week basic systems course from some of the growing number of organizations who have been using it. But, unfortunately, it is still too early for this, since none feels it would be fair to comment in depth until sufficient time has elapsed for the virtues or shortcomings of the course to be assessed. Nevertheless, a few general comments were made by those I approached.

Two or three user organizations pointed out that the course cannot create a systems analyst—that is, it can do little for an individual without some natural aptitude. The course, they said, must also be considered as no more than the start of a training which continues through supervised, on-the-job experience (a view with which NCC entirely concurs).

One user, the National Coal Board, which has had long and wide experience in the computer field and does much internal training, points out that if any course like this is to be utilized to the full it should be developed by the teacher in the light of his own experience and, if possible, tailored to the special needs of the user organization. Thus, NCB has replaced the case history material contained in the standard NCC course by examples of NCB origin, and has supplemented the visual aids with material of its own.

While programming is, on the whole, a young person's job, systems analysis and design is often more successfully undertaken by those who have reached at least the age of 30. The personal qualifications required are more likely to be found in the mature individual who has had some of the corners rubbed off and appreciates the limited value of theory as opposed to practice. Actual experience within the user organization, or at least in a similar environment, is immensely useful—provided, of course, that ossification has not set in!

THE DATA-PROCESSING MANAGER. It is upon the efforts of the data-processing manager and upon his calibre as a human being that much of the success of a computer installation will depend. Great care must therefore be taken to select a suitable person.

There has, I think, been a tendency, particularly in the smaller organization new to computers, to put too much stress on the data-processing part of this man's title and too little on the manager. The computer user has, in fact, been on the lookout for a man who is thoroughly knowledgeable about computers and has sometimes failed to appreciate the importance of the managerial aspects of the job.

Yet, as I have emphasized, the success of any computer scheme depends critically upon how the human element is handled. Thus, the data-processing manager must be good with people. This implies success not only with the computer team of whom he is directly in charge but with those whose ideas he is implementing—the organization's senior managers.

What data-processing managers do in detail, the problems they meet, the qualifications they need, are discussed in a small but pithy book, *Data Processing Managers* (8.2), which I would strongly recommend you to read. Written by the education manager of the data-processing division of IBM United Kingdom, this book is based upon a study of a cross-section of 30 data-processing managers working in organizations of varying types and sizes. In one chapter, the author summarizes what the people he studied felt were important qualifications, and reported, in part:

> The way the data-processing manager carries out his job is affected by a number of factors—his position in the organization structure, the maturity of attitude towards computers on the part of his colleagues, the strength and outlook of his sponsoring manager [the manager to whom he reports], the type and rigidity of the organization structure, etc. Whatever the environment, the data processing manager is called upon to negotiate with a large number of associates within the organization in pursuing his job...

Certainly the ability to 'get on with people' was stressed by one-third of the managers as a highly necessary quality. Coupled with this was the importance of a facility for communication. The data processing manager is required to bridge the gap between the technicians and management and to translate proposals into realistic and acceptable terms. He must be able to present new ideas convincingly and clearly yet with tact to all levels of management. He must have the strength of purpose and temperament to adhere firmly and calmly to a proposition which he believes sound in the face of questioning and sometimes resistance. To these qualities must be added the familiar managerial attribute of stamina to meet the need, on occasion, to work long hours.

Summarizing the opinions of 24 of his sample managers who were asked for an impromptu assessment of the qualities required in their own successors, the author, R. J. Harper, lists the following:

Have the ability to get on with people; be a good communicator; be tactful yet firm, calm in the face of controversy; have planning and organizing ability; possess qualities of leadership necessary to handle a young, mobile specialist staff group; have the stamina to face occasional long hours; have the ability to grasp complex problems; be adaptable and flexible; possess a logical, simple, broad approach; have 'adequate' knowledge of computers and experience of systems analysis; and possess a good general experience and understanding of the organization to which he belongs.

You will notice that data-processing managers themselves believe that knowledge of the computer need only be 'adequate' though, as Mr Harper points out in his commentary, there was some diversity of opinion on this.

Well over two-thirds of the managers commented on the need for technical knowledge of systems analysis and of computers. They made these comments with varying degrees of stress. Some felt that adequate knowledge could be acquired quickly, that on balance it was of lesser importance among the attributes discussed. Others felt that a thorough knowledge of computers coupled with some years of *creative* [my italics] systems work was essential. This diversity in emphasis was not always reflected in the careers and backgrounds of the individual managers concerned.

Discussing, in his final chapter, what sort of person may make the most satisfactory data-processing manager, Mr Harper points out that the value of the skills already possessed by managers of punched-card installations, O & M men, programmers, or systems analysts (all of whom are potential candidates) must be weighed against managerial qualifications. While the latter may best be provided by an established functional manager with a wide understanding of the organization, its people and its needs,

> for a new installation it is essential that technical and administrative experience of computer management be introduced at a senior level within the data processing department. If it is decided to do this at the level of data processing manager, the particular expertise offered by the computer specialist from outside must be placed against his lack of established relationships and knowledge of the particular organization, its mode of work, its policies and its objectives. The correct solution to this problem will depend on individual circumstances, *not least on the ability of the sponsoring manager to provide active counsel and direction* [my italics]. Undoubtedly failure to reflect on these considerations has led in some instances to the inhibition of developments or to crises arising from ignorance of methods and techniques.

One point that must be settled at once is the precise position which the data-processing manager will hold within the organization. This is, of course, in turn dependent upon the way in which top management regards the computer operation. My own experience in talking to a large number of companies and other organizations who have installed their own computers suggests that the most satisfactory answer often is to regard the data-processing section as a service organization. That is, although the data-processing manager will obviously report to a senior (preferably a suitably educated director) his department will not be deemed to be 'owned' by any individual arm of the organization such as the accounts department. Instead, it will be regarded as a company facility—like the dispatch room or the print department—available without question to all who need it. When this policy is adopted, the computer seems to become more happily accepted, fewer internal frictions develop, and the system is more intelligently utilized than is otherwise possible. Everybody feels he has a stake in the computer centre.

As a computer user you will, of course, start off with one or more priorities. But once this application is off the ground, all claims for use of the system should receive equal consideration. It will not, in fact, be taken for granted that no-one gets a look in until all the accounting functions have been computerized. Instead, there will perhaps be (as there was in one local government I visited) a monthly meeting at which possible applications put forward by various departmental heads are discussed and allocated priority by agreement.

If this democratic approach is to work, the data-processing manager clearly cannot be regarded as an underling. He must be treated as an equal by the managers among whom he may sometimes have to arbitrate and must therefore possess both their confidence and their respect.

In this way—though not in others—the position of the data-processing manager vis-à-vis the top management of an organization poses similar questions as are asked about the standing of the public relations manager. Is he to be regarded as a member of the management team and taken into the confidence of the directors? Or is he merely to be a kind of ventriloquist's doll?

There can be little doubt that only the former can be acceptable. Regarded simply as a mouthpiece, the PR man is in no position satisfactorily to cope with the many sticky problems that are constantly thrust at him; and will probably succeed in antagonizing the very people whose help he needs—his own organization's top managers and his contacts in the outside world. But *au fait* with policy, trusted by the board, the PR man can effectively use his specialist knowledge and techniques to implement this policy.

The same is true, I believe, of the data-processing manager. This places an onus on management to select someone of suitable calibre who can be regarded as a member of the team.

COMPUTER OPERATORS. The duties of computer operators vary considerably according to the size of the installation. Whereas in a very large system there will probably be a computer operations manager, a chief operator, and several other operators, in a small one there will be only a senior operator and one or two beneath him, or her. In the latter case, the data-processing manager may well undertake the responsibility for planning, organization, and control of the use of the equipment in the computer installation, while the senior operator will look after day-to-day work scheduling and supervision.

Among the qualities desirable in any supervisory aspects of computer operation are an ability to organize well, to keep calm under stress, and to make snap decisions; self-reliance, a sense of responsibility, a good but not outstanding intelligence, common sense, and a methodical mind that is precise and attentive to detail are also valuable. In an ordinary operator, willingness to follow instructions, ability to keep records, and quick reactions are important. Physical stamina is needed, because many hours may be spent standing and the operator should be of a correct height comfortably to reach the equipment he or she looks after.

Less tangible but equally important in my opinion is to be the kind of person who likes machines and gets on well with them. Such individuals tend to establish the same sort of *rapport* with the computer as exists between a mother and child and develop a kind of sixth sense that tells them if something is amiss.

Normally there is no difficulty in finding computer operators in an organization that has previously used a punched-card installation, as existing personnel can be trained and promoted. In other cases, it may be necessary to recruit from outside, though every effort should be made to find people inside the company who have the right kind of potential.

DATA PREPARATION STAFF. Almost anyone can learn to operate the kind of keyboard machines that are used for data preparation. But not everyone will make a good operator.

The job demands somewhat paradoxical qualifications—a mentality that can accept conditions akin to those on a production line combined with a good deal more intelligence and education than are needed for most factory operations. Far more concentration is necessary than for purely manual work; yet manual dexterity is also essential.

At first thought, it might be supposed that intelligence, education, and the ability to concentrate are redundant. But the major requirements for a good punch operator are not only to read correctly but to interpret accurately what is read. In this sense, data preparation is closely akin to copy typing, an operation that a good deal of the time requires nothing more than the direct translation of visual stimuli into muscular response but also demands mental monitoring.

It is wise, therefore, to insist upon certain minimal qualifications for data-preparation machine operators. Some organizations accept no girl without a CSE Grade 2, others prefer some O-levels. Many use IBM aptitude tests, though more as a general guide in conjunction with other assessments rather than as an absolute yardstick.

In one organization noted for the quality of its data preparation, candidates for this job are given a simple test designed to discover whether they are reasonably intelligent and quick thinking. Success in this, plus a knowledge of typing—or even of piano playing or needlework—suggest the girl is a likely starter.

Personality is a relevant factor. Response to the team spirit—essential in a good data-prep unit—is not always to be found in women; nor is willing acceptance of the fairly strict disciplines that are necessary. Many companies believe that school-leavers make the most satisfactory recruits; others believe the very youngest are not as satisfactory as those in the 18–23 age group. One strong argument for starting young is the constant lowering of the marriage age. Chances are that the school leaver will have at least a year or two's work in her before she marries and has her first child.

Very few companies whom I questioned on this subject employed coloured keypunch operators. Objections cited included poor education and the belief that coloured girls move more slowly than their white sisters—a difficulty when bonuses are paid on output. The crux of the difficulty, however, seems to be a fear that, if it became necessary to sack a coloured girl, one would be accused of racial prejudice. I am sure this does happen sometimes. On the other hand, it seems regrettable if this prevents the employment of girls who could handle work of this kind.

How does one find—and keep—data-preparation girls? The prospect of promotion (where one can honestly offer it) seldom holds much attraction for girls with a temperament that can stand operating a keyboard all day. Money, of course, is a good incentive. One bureau operator who has a constant demand for operators finds all the recruits he needs by quoting in his advertisements typical wages earned by his operators (none of the existing girls had any objection to this practice). High productivity is encouraged by offering bonus payments for error-free output above an agreed basic minimum.

Another bureau operator in a district where punch operators were hard to find pulled in suitable applicants by advertising for copy typists. The girls, he discovered, were interested in the possibility of a job that required skills similar to those they already possessed but offered chances of higher earnings and higher prestige (association with a computer, however tenuous, still has a certain glamour).

Inhuman though the job of data preparation may seem to those with less modest ambition, personal pride plays a considerable part in making a good team. Girls who feel they are valued members of the computer team, who have been shown what happens when errors get into the system and are thus aware of the vital nature of their work, are better workers than those treated like battery hens.

It always seems strange to me that although data-preparation staff are at least as skilled and at least as valuable as audio-typists, they are very seldom half as pampered. While it is almost axiomatic these days that nothing is too good for the typing pool, data-prep departments are too often drab and depressing in appearance. Yet bright colours, attractive surroundings, give a real psychological uplift and involve very modest expenditure.

You may feel I have dwelled at rather excessive length on the question of data-preparation staff. But these are hard to find; and most computer operations would grind to a standstill without them. For this reason, their recruitment, welfare, and training (as I have outlined in an earlier chapter) should be a matter for careful thought.

Finally, I must emphasize the importance of good supervision in the data-prep department. This is necessary, not only to ensure high-quality work but to make certain that work is progressed methodically and that none is lost or leaves the department without verification.

Good supervisors are hard to find, for they combine something of the battleaxe with a strong ingredient of the mother-figure; are as acceptable to those in their charge as to those they report to.

You will probably be able to discover good punchroom supervisor material within your existing organization. On the whole, age, within fairly obvious limits, does not seem to matter too much. I have met successful supervisors varying in age from the early twenties to the late forties or even older. The young woman who, perhaps, has the makings of a supervisor but lacks confidence can often be developed by attendance at a general supervisors' training course where she learns some of the general techniques of personnel management. (The Industrial Society is one of the organizations that holds courses of this kind.) Experienced and already successful supervisors will probably need training only in the technical aspects of the new job.

Recruiting staff from outside

It takes a specialist to assess a specialist and if you are inexperienced in computers you will almost certainly come to grief if you try to recruit computer personnel without qualified advice. A number of agencies now specializes in recruiting computer staffs and it is therefore probably most satisfactory (having first ascertained what its reputation and performance is like) to put the job in the hands of one of these.

Remember, however, once again the importance of the human element. No outsider can judge with certainty whether or not a man's or woman's personality will prove acceptable to your organization. You cannot, therefore, afford to dissociate yourself from recruitment. You must use the agency (or consultants, if you employ them) only to carry out the preliminary sifting and ensure that candidates who reach you have appropriate technical experience and qualifications. You must give the casting vote.

Some bizarre things happen when a key computer man is ill-suited to the employing organization. I remember visiting one British company to collect material for an article on a different subject and, learning during conversation that they had a computer, asked for more detail.

To my surprise, the two fairly senior managers to whom I was talking first exchanged glances then admitted they knew nothing. Furthermore, it was plain neither was prepared to take me to the computer room. The data-processing manager, they finally admitted, was literally not on speaking terms with most of the managers and was heartily disliked (and vice-versa) all round. It is hard to believe that this organization was doing anything very significant with its computer.

The most superficial glance at display advertisements in any quality newspaper will demonstrate that competition for computer specialists of all kinds is intense. This implies that any bidder for this type of labour will get no better than he pays for—and without care may get considerably worse. Though people willing to accept low pay may occasionally offer themselves, these will either be inexperienced—in which case, they will soon get to know their own value as they gain experience at your expense—or unsatisfactory in some other way.

Sometimes, provided you are not counting on the person concerned to be a leader, inexperience is not a disadvantage, as long as you can offer suitable facilities for systematic training and development. On the other hand, you are optimistic if you imagine you will retain this person's services without recognizing his progress by increased financial rewards. The same, of course, is true of any really competent people you recruit from inside your organization.

It is never a good idea to attempt to represent a job as more exciting than it is. One of the major causes of dissatisfaction in a computer job is the limitations of the system, at least in those who are well qualified and ambitious.

As a new computer user, you may be tempted to grudge what seem to be the excessive salaries you have to pay for technical staff. But provided these are more or less in line with rates paid elsewhere, there is little you can do but bow to the fact that you are the buyer in a seller's market. It will not be much use to you to argue that the salary you are expected to pay a senior systems man is as much as you pay to your factory manager: it is just too bad. Maybe the factory manager should have a rise by now, anyhow.

Management attitudes to computer staff

One of the grievances most often voiced by managements is the very fast turnover that often occurs in computer staff. 'Computer people have no loyalty,' they protest. 'We pay them well, treat them well, yet they are always looking for new jobs. What is the matter with them? We have never had staff troubles before.'

This turnover problem is very difficult to solve at present. Many of the men and women associated with computers are very young, very bright, and deeply involved intellectually with the whole subject. And they are ambitious. Ask yourself if you were in their shoes with the world your oyster, what you would do. The offers of greater financial reward are a lure to those who are—or think they are—underpaid. But I believe that the challenge of a job that stretches them mentally is even more potent an incentive to move. I have been told on good authority that it is now a commonplace for computer staff working on fairly routine applications to become restless unless the hardware is upgraded once a year or so; and that it is getting increasingly hard to recruit experienced technical staff to work on systems without random-access files.

But there may be other factors, and one of these may be management attitudes. It cannot be denied that, owing to lack of foresight or a rather childish eagerness to get a computer scheme off the ground at the earliest possible moment, some organizations work their computer staffs to death during the initial period. Indeed, it is not uncommon to hear of constant all-night sessions with a few hours' dozing on couches in a near-by rest room (if one exists).

Admittedly, computer people are usually dedicated. But you are unwise if you deliberately exploit this dedication for you will know from your own experience that spontaneous involvement is very different from a situation where a pistol is held at your head. In a period of enforced rush, excitement and tension is at its height and everyone is carried along by the impetus. But later, when things have begun to run smoothly, the inevitable anti-climax comes. Exhaustion sets in and is accompanied by a general feeling of depression and dissatisfaction.

Do, therefore, curb your eagerness unless dire necessity dictates tremendous pressure on your computer staff. Though it is nice to be able to set speed records, it is even nicer to employ a contented team.

It is, I think, questionable whether management should expect loyalty of the traditional kind to be felt by computer staffs recruited from outside the organization. Though it would be unfair to suggest that all computer people feel themselves superior to ordinary office workers, the fact remains that their highly specialized job, which isolates them from much of the rough and tumble of company life, tends to make them feel like a race apart.

It might, therefore, be more realistic to expect only the kind of loyalty you will almost always get from computer people—complete devotion to the job and intellectual integrity. Loyalty of this kind involves little or no personal feeling for the organization itself. In any case, sentiment is usually alien to today's young people who are often cynical about paternalism of any variety, particularly its commercial manifestations. It therefore seems natural to them that when the job in hand ceases to make intellectual demands it should be exchanged for another without regret.

Though you would be unwise to exert pressure, it is not a bad thing to make unobtrusive attempts to involve your computer staff in any social activities that normally take place within your organization. Aloofness is not always due to a sense of superiority but to social ineptness, and therefore to mingle only with those who 'speak one's own language' is an easy way out. Though involvement with social activities will not solve the turnover problem, it will help everyone to form the kind of personal bonds that oil the wheels of working life and help people appreciate one another's viewpoints and problems. Even small gestures like introducing new members of the computer staff through the house magazine—or even, if you have no magazine, running a duplicated bulletin during the installation period—assists integration.

If you employ exceptionally talented and well qualified computer staff, you are always in danger of losing them during slack periods. In such cases, you may find it pays to release them from time to time to attend meetings, seminars, or educational courses in subjects that particularly interest them. Dr A. S. Douglas, when a member of a large consultant organization, remarked that people of this kind seem to have an irresistible urge to talk shop with their peers. Very natural! And conversations like this are often fruitful because they are mentally stimulating. To those who attend courses, this exchange of ideas may be one of the most valuable aspects—and one that may bear valuable fruit in your own organization.

Aside from this, about all you can usefully do, apart from the normal measures you take to try to keep your employees happy, is to try to ensure that continuity shall be preserved as far as possible through staff changes. You cannot, in fact, afford to regard any member of your computer team as a fixture or as indispensable. You must see, for example, that your data-processing manager formalizes as far as possible and records in detail all the work done in areas like systems design and programming. The use of and adherence to methods standardized through carefully designed operating manuals and of high-level programming languages will enable newcomers easily to pick up the threads. This is an important aspect of computer work, since no computer program normally remains unchanged for long. Sooner or later, changes within your organization, increasing knowledge of the computer staff, or enlargement of hardware configuration will necessitate program changes. And it is likely that these will have to be made by people other than the original designers. Without precautions, several man-weeks may be occupied in attempts to unravel a program—a task which is particularly frustrating and wasteful when the object is to make some quite small change.

What about staff redundancy?

When computers were first introduced for commercial work, it was generally anticipated that large-scale redundancy would be an inevitable result of their growing use. But these fears have not been realized, as John E. Hebden, Lecturer in Industrial Sociology at the University of Salford and member of a research team investigating the managerial and organizational implications of advanced usage, pointed out in 1967*. Of 331 firms with computer installations that had been contacted, only 13 had had any people lose jobs as a result of computerization; and in these companies, the average number was 10 people. In addition, particular factors existing in these companies had aggravated the situation.

In fact, said Mr Hebden, the overall effect of computers was not

*Speech at a conference of the Leeds & District Branch of the British Computer Society. (8.3)

R

to make people redundant and there was a shortage, not a surplus, of manpower. While Ministry of Labour figures estimated a reduction of 300,000 jobs in the decade 1964–74, office employment was expected to produce 700,000 new jobs so that 'during the next seven years we are going to be short of 400,000 people'.

Clerical redundancy, at least at the lower levels, is unlikely then to prove a problem for companies who install computers during the next few years. The area in which it seems possible difficulty may arise is in middle-aged middle management—men and women who, through no fault of theirs, have had no more than haphazard, on-the-job training for their existing work, have perhaps served the company for many years and are thoroughly set in their ways. Some of these are unsuitable for sending back to school; too old to be thrown onto the job market, yet too young to pension off. What can be done to help them when their jobs disappear?

Before offering some suggestions, I ought to point out that this problem is largely a temporary one that arises from the transitional period in which we are now. We are becoming more and more conscious of the necessity for management training and education at all levels. We have been warned repeatedly that it will be necessary to discard the idea that a single skill is enough to last a lifetime and be prepared to learn two or three during the course of a career. Managements have been advised to do all they can to encourage mental flexibility by moving employees from job to job; and should try to promote mental liveliness by offering training and educational facilities of all kinds and encouraging participation in these.

We are beginning, too, to appreciate what kinds of structural changes will occur within organizations, what skills will be demanded as a result of more widespread, more sophisticated computer usage, and can reasonably hope that the rising generation will be better equipped than we are to deal with these. (Mr Hebden, whom I quoted earlier, believes that the current pattern of entering an organization at the lowest grade and working upwards will be replaced by one of recruitment at various levels; and that the present broad band of middle management found in most companies now will tend to become narrower.)

All this is fine when one thinks about future planning, but poor comfort to the company confronted today with the problem of how to re-deploy redundant middle managers. What can be done now?

This problem must be given serious consideration by senior management at the earliest possible moment. For most organizations, at least one year elapses between a decision to install a computer and the system's beginning to operate, and often another goes by before the effect of the new methods begins to make itself fully felt. This gives leeway for thought. But it may also, in the general excitement engendered by preparations for the computer, offer a temptation to postpone consideration of a difficult human problem until this stares one in the face.

Some organizations will be able to find suitable jobs internally or among friendly neighbour organizations for middle managers displaced by the computer. Others may well be faced with a necessity to find new outlets. What kinds of job are these people capable of doing successfully?

When I was gathering material for an article about re-employment of the middle-aged and elderly, I dug out some interesting facts which cannot be disregarded when one is considering jobs for these people. One of the things one must recognize is that a person who has been in authority for some years (even if, in your eyes, his authority may seem petty) will not take easily to being a subordinate. He may succeed in adapting himself to this role when his immediate superior is approximately his own age; but will find it almost impossible to accept direction from someone much younger than himself.

Success is therefore unlikely if you put a middle-aged person under a younger supervisor, particularly when the older one already knows the environment. Difficulties are, perhaps, less likely to occur when a younger supervisor is technically skilled in an area where his older subordinate is ignorant. In this case, face-saving can be achieved by acknowledged respect for technical skill and know-how not possessed by the older man.

Everyone I questioned about jobs for older people emphasized the overriding importance of the time element. By this I mean they pointed out that no individual in these age groups is likely to perform well when a certain amount of work must be completed within a strict time limit. By the time we are middle-aged, our reactions are notably slower than they were.

The saving grace is that our judgement is often sounder because of experience and the poise gained during this. A middle-aged person can thus often compete very successfully with a youngster provided he is allowed to complete the work in his own time. Given this concession, he often does a better job and makes fewer errors than his less experienced companion.

It is this time element that sometimes makes re-training a disheartening business for all concerned. Interviews I had with a number of middle-aged men and women who had successfully been re-trained for computer work indicated that they had felt intolerably discouraged at first, specially while being trained side by side with youngsters. It needed, they told me, all their will-power and determination to stay the course during these early days. Facts which the younger people assimilated quite easily seemed obscure to them and they found they had to do extra homework to keep up. Eventually, though, persistence was rewarded and they made the grade.

If, therefore, you are faced by a necessity to re-train middle-aged men and women for computer programming or any other job, you should design a course of instruction different from that used for younger people. If the instructor himself is past his first youth, so much the better. But in any event, the course should be specifically orientated towards minimizing the problems of older people. (Incidentally, my own investigations suggested that the besetting difficulty for middle-aged men was arrogance; for middle-aged women, lack of self-confidence. Both, oddly enough, are also characteristics of extreme youth.)

When you are thinking about the redeployment of people displaced by a computer operation, you might well give careful consideration to the possibility of using these to provide better service, to others inside the organization and to customers. The complaint that the age of automation has seen the disappearance of personal service is universal and, on the whole, well justified. It is therefore no coincidence that organizations who pay the most careful attention to this aspect of their business usually get the most—and the best—customers. In this connection it is interesting that an increasing number of computer users I have talked to installed their machines with better customer service as a primary objective. In this case, though, they meant the 'mechanics' of service—quicker attention to orders, more accuracy in accounting documents, and so on.

The greater patience and emotional maturity that are often characteristic of increased age combine to qualify an older person very well for rendering painstaking, personal service of the type that is usually called old-fashioned (in the complimentary sense of the term). And, though present conditions tend to suggest the opposite, the average man or woman is usually genuinely glad to help other people.

A representative of British European Airways, for example, told me that booking clerks, relieved by the computer system of the sheer drudgery imposed by searching indexes and the nerve-racking necessity to watch an impatient queue while waiting interminably on the telephone, are happy to have time to pay fuller attention to customers —and have told the management this. In fact, this natural desire to be of service, inevitably submerged in any job that is difficult, exasperating or rushed, comes to the surface when circumstances allow.

Though it is obviously difficult for me as an outsider to suggest specific ways in which your organization could improve the service aspect of its operations, two general possibilities immediately suggest themselves.

One of these is to create a department to deal with the kind of queries usually handled as best she can by a harassed telephone switchboard operator. Such a department could not only help to sort out questions as to whom to go to for information on some specific subject (a question which, in my experience, a switchboard operator can seldom answer) but could take messages, keep internal directories up to date, and deal with all the dozens of other queries that come from both internal and external sources during the course of an average working day. In this way, it would be valuable to company personnel as well as outsiders.

Another department which would surely be welcomed by many customers is one to deal with complaints and queries on such subjects as accounts and the progress of orders. Normally, a request for information involves the caller in a series of transfers from one telephone extension to another or in a long wait while the right person is found or the details brought to light. Sometimes the person who could give an answer is away and a promise to ring back is not kept. Too often, in my experience, one overhears, through a half covered telephone, remarks that are not supposed to reach one's ears.

A department to deal with things like this would give the caller confidence that an answer would, in fact, be forthcoming and would be given him as soon as possible. It could also handle jobs like sending off catalogues or information sheets in answer to requests, with an accompanying letter if required—jobs that are normally done (or forgotten) by sales staff.

These are only two suggestions for areas in which customer service could be greatly improved in many organizations. A long-service middle-aged employee of suitable personality (make sure you do not use someone who has grown impatient and sharp-tongued with increasing age!) is particularly suited to run this kind of service as he or she is well acquainted with the departmental structure, personnel, products, and other aspects of the organization. No doubt you will be able to find other jobs of this kind that could usefully be done within your organization.

I would like to conclude this chapter with a plea for constructive action on behalf of older employees, and in particular middle managers, displaced from their jobs by the introduction of a computer system. It is a devastating blow to self-esteem to feel one has become useless; an appalling experience to be cast out into a labour market where it appears to be a crime to have reached any age over the early forties. If you pause for a moment to think seriously of how you would feel in similar circumstances, it will give you the incentive to use your ingenuity to see that this does not happen.

Summary

The following points have been mentioned in this chapter:

(a) The success of any computer project, however ambitious or modest, depends on the people associated with it. Top management's attitude contributes as much to success or failure as the efforts of the computer team.

(b) It is the responsibility of senior management to become personally involved in the computer scheme, to direct its progress with sympathy and intelligence. Broad knowledge about computers is essential if this is to be done properly. Many suitable introductory courses for top managers are now available.

(c) How the subject of coming computerization is broached within an organization is of crucial importance. Many people, aware of it or not, are scared of computers; many will be afraid of losing their jobs or being demoted. These facts must be recognized by senior management, who themselves must inform employees about the coming of the computer.

(d) The possibility of having a computer should probably be mentioned before the feasibility study begins. At this and all subsequent stages, senior management must be seen to be involved and must take care to ensure that proper, two-way communication with lower levels of management and other staff is established. Candour and face-to-face contact are essential if rumours and dissatisfaction are not to spread.

(e) There are a number of good arguments in favour of recruiting as many members as possible of the computer team from inside the organization. Often much unsuspected ability can be uncovered when people are invited to volunteer for these jobs.

(f) A suitable personality is as important as suitable ability and qualifications for many jobs associated with computers. Training courses are available to provide the necessary technical knowledge.

(g) In recruiting staff from outside, the organization which has not used a computer before will almost certainly require the services of an organization which can assess the technical qualifications of those who apply. But again personality (the suitability of which can be gauged only by the employing organization) is a very important factor.

(h) Computer staff, particularly those recruited from outside, are often criticized by company managements for their short stays and frequent moves from one job to another. It is important to understand the reasons for this, to integrate computer staff with the rest of the organization as well as possible, and to set up procedures that will minimize disruption when there are staff changes in the computer team.

(i) The introduction of a computer is unlikely to cause clerical redundancy on any large scale. It may, however, displace some middle-aged middle managers. Strong efforts should be made to find constructive employment for these.

References
8.1 MUMFORD, E. *Living with a computer*. Institute of Personnel Management, 1964.
8.2 HARPER, R. J. *Data processing managers*. Lyon, Grant and Green, 1967.
8.3 HEBDEN, J. E. *Data & Control Systems* (now *Data Systems*). March 1967.

9. Why computer installations fail

I did not originally intend to write a chapter devoted only to the depressing subject of computer failures. But after I had already completed the first draft of this book, I had lunch with a friend who is a senior computer consultant with a well known and respected firm and who said: 'You know I love my work and would not change it for any other. All the same, I sometimes feel depressed when I see companies today making exactly the same kinds of mistakes with their computers that others made ten or more years ago'. These mistakes, he added, could seldom—even in the days when hardware was neither so reliable nor so efficient as it is now—be attributed to machine inadequacy but were mainly the result of human errors of judgement.

This made me feel that it might be useful to sum up, in a single chapter, the cautions I have offered you elsewhere in this book. In this way, I can provide you with an easily accessible checklist of traps to avoid.

All the information given here crystallizes the experience of at least one unhappy organization, and more often, many. You might feel it was more authentic if I quoted names, particularly of those who accepted my invitation to talk to me specifically on the subject of failure. But no-one cares to publicize failure, and the people who talked frankly to me on this topic were prepared to do so only if they remained anonymous in print.

I can, however, tell you that my informants include data-processing managers, computer consultants, and senior and junior executives; and that a fair percentage of these had had experience dating back a number of years, and in several different organizations. The material in this chapter is based on what these told me and what I have learned from hundreds of interviews with computer user organizations in the normal course of my work during the past decade or so.

There can be no order of importance for errors of judgement any of which, alone or in combination with others, can be disastrously damaging. The sequence in which I have listed these causes of failure, therefore, should not be taken as an indication of an order of magnitude; nor is it intended to suggest that the earlier items I have named occur more frequently than the later.

ILL-DEFINED MANAGEMENT OBJECTIVES. The planning of management objectives for, say, the next five years is not an easy task. Nevertheless, this must be done before a computer is installed. Problems arise in two main areas: first, difficulty in deciding upon these objectives; second, their lucid communication to computer staff. Management, say computer people, is sometimes remarkably inarticulate.

If you find this problem intractable, you may think it worth while to seek the advice of consultants. Discussion with a reputable firm should enable you to formulate realistic objectives and to set these down clearly.

Subsequent difficulty could arise if your data-processing manager has little knowledge about business management. In this case, it may be worth while to invest a little time, effort, and money in providing basic explanation within your own organization or at an outside training course. Alternatively, you might find it advisable to replace him with a man whose background knowledge is sounder.

UNREALISTIC COST ESTIMATES. We agreed, did we not, at the beginning of this book that the only point of using a computer was to improve profitability? Yet, according to Roger Graham of ASAP Consultants (9.1), some 70 per cent of 2,500 installations made in this country have failed to be profitable.

Sometimes these disappointing results arise from nothing more sinister than unrealistic estimating. Among the areas where this is likely to occur are number and cost of staff, air-conditioning equipment, stationery, storage, and data preparation, says Mr Graham. The cost of the actual computer will probably amount to no more than 40 per cent of the total cost of installation, he asserts.

Estimates of staff reductions often go seriously awry, too. Many companies do not employ enough clerical staff in the first place to make staff reduction a justification for a computer. In addition to computer staff, more people are needed than is often anticipated for jobs like editing and controlling the source documents before they reach the computer department, says Mr Graham. And because computer output is comparatively cheap, more and more is asked for —which means more people are needed to read and interpret the reports thus produced.

Like others experienced in this field, Mr Graham concedes that many of the most important benefits brought by computerization are very hard to estimate. They are difficult to quantify and are not comparable with any achievable by alternative methods, because the features of a computer are unique.

Only experience, he concludes, can show where the real benefits lie; and this experience must be monitored:

> Management should insist that effective budgetary controls and audit procedures apply to *estimated savings* [my italics] as well as to costs. The assessment of such benefits is not easy, and should certainly not simply be the responsibility of the computer manager. But it must be attempted. By doing so, the real potential of the computer activity will be discovered.

Earlier in this same article, Mr Graham deplores the vagueness of such terms as 'better management information' or 'improved customer service'. It is the things like this that really matter and there should be nothing vague about them.

My own feeling is that lack of any attempt to put a price on these intangibles or to outline expected benefits in detail may well be due to mental laziness. If this sounds a harsh judgement, let me get personal for a moment and suppose you are trying to justify to yourself and your wife the cost of a motor mower to replace your hand-powered one.

You would certainly not be content with a phrase like 'better service'—particularly if you believed your wife suspected you of extravagance. You might, for example, point out that you could save the wages of a jobbing gardener because you could do the work yourself. If you were really enthusiastic, you might work out how much your wife could save out of her housekeeping allowance if the mower saved you enough time to cultivate vegetables.

It is really not too difficult to calculate in terms of money the benefits you are likely to gain, for example, from getting customers to pay their bills a month earlier than before because you send out statements more punctually; nor to estimate, by analysing past statistics, how much more you might sell if you could satisfy 10 per cent more incoming orders from stock. These figures will not be wholly accurate, of course. But unless you are quite ridiculously careless or optimistic, they should indicate at least the order of benefit you can expect with computerization.

Your task, then, before deciding to use or install a computer is to draw up as careful and realistic a balance sheet as you can of costs versus estimated savings and new benefits.

LACK OF FINESSE IN INTRODUCING THE COMPUTER. First confronted by the possibility of a computer's being used in their own organization, many people see this event as the beginning of the end as far as they are concerned. Lack of finesse in introducing this delicate subject may have dire results, as is illustrated by the following two anecdotes (both of which, I confess, may be apocryphal).

A managing director, anxious at all costs to avoid putting people out of work, informed his chief accountant baldly that the company would install a computer in two years' time. This, he said, should give everyone affected all the time needed to find another job. Next day, the entire accounts department handed in its resignation, convinced that the best possible course of action was to get out while the going was good.

The second story concerns a large manufacturing company who believed that shock tactics had the best chance of success. Accordingly, they installed a small experimental data-collection system in one part of the factory during one weekend. The first thing the labour force knew about this was seeing the machines on Monday morning. Retribution soon came. In the face of indignant protests and threats of strikes, the experiment was abandoned and the equipment quietly removed within a few days.

Whether or not these incidents actually occurred, they demonstrate the disastrous effects of clumsy handling of a potentially explosive issue. It is useful to remember that the introduction of a computer is often also the innovation of a different pattern of power. Cherished empires may be in danger of dissolution; and one key manager affected in this way can be unbelievably obstructive. Unease and unrest are horribly infectious.

NON-PARTICIPATION OF MANAGEMENT. A computer is not a cyst—a foreign object that, introduced into the body, can be isolated by encapsulation. It is the centre of an activity that, properly carried out, will influence almost every aspect of corporate life.

You as a manager, therefore, whether you are at the top or on a lower rung of the ladder, must not only be personally involved in the computer project but must be demonstrably involved from the outset.

This does not imply that you should be continually breathing down the necks of the data-processing people. But you should be prepared carefully to guide the course of the project, whose success will depend upon your efforts.

Apathy on your part will either kill the incentive of the computer team, lead to an open rift between the data-processing section and other members of your organization, or produce systems that fail to fulfil your company's real requirements or contribute effectively towards its profitability.

LACK OF UNDERSTANDING BETWEEN COMPANY MANAGERS AND THE COMPUTER TEAM. Breakdown of communications between the company's management and the computer team is probably most likely to occur when all the team, or at least its leading members, have been recruited from outside the organization. Because the computer people are often so young and senior managers frequently middle-aged, many of the difficulties that occur are due less to technical complexities than to the problems that inevitably arise between one human generation and another.

In a situation like this at its worst, top management secretly or openly regard the computer people as arrogant, undisciplined, and overpaid; and the data-processing team scarcely trouble to conceal their view that the management is a bunch of old fuddy-duddies who have not had a new idea for years and are far too dim-witted to have a hope of understanding what computers are all about. In the face of such attitudes, satisfactory co-operation is impossible.

As an independent observer, one can appreciate there may be a grain of truth on both sides. The problem is how to achieve a comfortable and productive working relationship.

This will be possible only when there is mutual respect. That is, management must appreciate the technical expertise required to initiate data-processing installation; and the computer people must recognize that it takes more talent and ability than may be immediately apparent successfully to manage a flourishing commercial or industrial enterprise.

It is up to you as a manager to take the lead. Try to ignore the long hair of the male programmers and the short skirts of the females. Take a long, slow look at an old snapshot of yourself in Oxford bags when you feel your blood pressure rising! Recollect that if you demonstrate sincere interest and a will to listen and comprehend, almost anyone—including the young—is delighted and flattered to be asked to talk about his job. If you persevere, you will gain a real insight into what is going on, what the problems are.

You will help to establish *rapport* if you take suitable opportunities to talk to the computer people about your own job. When discussing systems design, for example, try not to feel they are children who should be excluded from your grown-up conversation. When you want something done a certain way, take the trouble to fill in the background. Your listeners are above average intelligence. Your task is to arouse their interest, to make them feel that they in their way are as involved in the affairs of the organization as you are yourself.

POOR SYSTEMS ANALYSIS, DESIGN, AND PLANNING. Misjudgement in the analysis, design, and planning of systems is usually cited as one of the major causes of dissatisfaction, if not downright failure, in computer projects. Among the traps that await the unwary are the following:

Sloppy analysis work. Due to lack of appreciation of the importance of this function, insufficient time is allocated, and the number and calibre of staff are inadequate.

Naïvety. Systems people believe that methods laid down in procedure manuals correspond to those in actual use. In truth, any correlation between theory and practice is often strictly coincidental, particularly if the procedures in question have been in use for some years. It is important that systems analysts make it abundantly clear that their purpose is simply to find out what is actually done, not to pillory those who do it. Only by adopting this attitude can they collect realistic information for systems development.

Lack of experience or ability to design new systems. At their worst, these may lead to a direct, uncritical conversion of existing procedures into computer routines. Though it is foolish to assume that everything about an existing system is bad, it is equally shortsighted to assume that no improvements can be made, either from the viewpoint of general efficiency and/or the exploitation of computer techniques.

Without appreciation of the possibilities offered by a computer, opportunities for systems integration may be neglected. That is, routines that logically should be closely related during computer processing are handled as separate entities. As a result, there may be too much data preparation, too much processing time on the system, too much computer output, and a higher probability of error. In fact, the computer system may be little more than a faster version of obsolescent routines—a version that is a good deal more costly than what it replaced.

OVER-AMBITION. Once 'sold' on the advantages of installing a computer, it is easy to fall into the temptation of running before one can walk. Though it is vital to think big from the beginning, it is usually a mistake to rush headlong into the most complicated job, especially when your computer team is inexperienced. Unduly long postponement of the running of the first programs or intractable difficulty can be psychologically disastrous, not only to the computer team but to others in the organization. But even a modest success acts like a shot in the arm all round. It is therefore far more important at this stage to see that everyone is happy because a minor program is going well than to be in a position to boast about your computer system. Save this until later, by which time your pride will be fully justified.

UNDER-AMBITION. Whatever happens, you have made a sizable investment when you decide to use a computer within your organization. Any results you get are likely to be unsatisfactory by any criterion unless you are prepared from the outset to exploit computer techniques as fully as possible in relation to your own needs. It therefore pays to set your sights as high as you can. This may sound like a contradiction of the advice in the preceding paragraph. But there is a big difference between aiming low and starting modestly. Always aim as high as you can and design your systems as far as possible to contribute to your ultimate aims. This in no way precludes the cautious start advocated previously.

   Another aspect of under-ambition is a miserly approach to hardware. You can safely assume that if your initial applications are successful your horizons will widen and that within, say, two years of your first routines being put onto the system you will need to expand your hardware configuration. There is no need to purchase far more hardware than is needed at the time you get going; but it is important to think in terms of future expansion and make sure your initial system is capable of at least some expansion. If, for example, you have to choose between a central processor already equipped with as much core store as it can take and a larger processor with minimum memory capacity, you will be safer with the latter. Otherwise, you must be prepared to face frustration or substantial extra costs in the quite near future.

OVER-RELIANCE UPON COMPUTER TECHNOLOGY. If you have read the preceding chapters in this book, you are well aware that computers cannot work miracles. Are you equally aware that computer technology offers no substitute for systematic thought?

How this mistake occurs is well illustrated by a look at history when random-access storage devices first came onto the market. Computer specialists were naturally enchanted by this powerful new facility and, themselves inexperienced and anxious to sell it to management, waxed over-optimistic. In effect, management gained the impression that a random-access file could be used like a glory-hole into which one could toss any old data, yet be sure of immediate and orderly retrieval on demand at any future time.

Soon it became apparent that the system could not work like this. That the only realistic approach was to regard a random-access file as the electronic parallel of a particularly well organized manual filing system whose indexing allows you to pull out immediately anything you want.

Managements are still inclined to fall into this trap. Or, to put it another way, hopefully to imagine that computer technology offers an easy escape from the necessity for constructive, systematic thought. Beliefs like this will be particularly dangerous if they influence the design of ambitious projects involving large data banks.

Increasing sophistication in computer technology demands more, not less, thought and planning. Beware, therefore, of assuming that a computer system can clarify muddled or incomplete ideas; it will only make their deficiencies more glaringly apparent.

LACK OF CONFIDENCE IN THE COMPUTER. Two moral tales neatly illustrate the absurdities that can arise through distrust of the capabilities of a computer.

A bureau operator told me about a large organization that, quite correctly, decided his bureau could usefully and economically carry out certain routine jobs that had until then been done manually. Though simple, the jobs were very laborious and there was therefore a good chance that computerization would be worth while.

A program was written and the work put onto the machine with a minimum of difficulty. The print-outs were accepted and paid for by the customer without comment, so the bureau manager assumed that all was well. Months later he discovered, quite by chance, that his customer carefully filed all the print-outs but was also continuing to run the old system. All that was being done, in fact, was to create a pile of additional, useless and expensive paper.

The second tale came from the data-processing manager of another large organization which, by the time the story opened, had had considerable computer experience. My informant decided that his company could usefully apply rather sophisticated operational research techniques to solve a tough distribution problem. Success would bring substantial economies in running costs while giving more efficient distribution.

He had some difficulty in getting management to accept his proposal, but eventually they allowed him to go ahead. A thorough investigation was carried out; a program was written, tested and run with conspicuous success for several months. All the expected benefits materialized.

For senior management, however, the whole scheme was too clever by half. They were unable to grasp the mathematics used in the exercise and therefore distrusted the whole thing. 'It's very wonderful,' they admitted, 'but we'd feel much safer if we went back to the old system'. Which is exactly what happened.

Neither of these stories illustrates a stand-or-fall situation in a sense, because neither involved a company-wide project. But I think the point I am trying to make is clear without further comment.

RELIANCE UPON SELLING SURPLUS MACHINE TIME. Some organizations have believed themselves able to make profitable a computer installation that could not otherwise be justified by selling surplus machine time. Unless you have a really firm understanding with a specific user in your area (and he probably cannot be forced to adhere to this) you may find it very hard to sell surplus computer time.

Many people who buy computer time regularly want a whole spectrum of associated services—e.g., data preparation, systems advice, programming services. Aside from this, they may well want results at a fixed time every week or month. The exceptions are organizations who are already using a configuration identical to yours and literally want no more than a bit of extra computer capacity for overflow work.

The only way you are likely to make a go of selling surplus machine capacity is to set up a service bureau yourself and become your own first customer. But this is a venture that cannot be undertaken without careful prior investigation into the possibilities offered by your immediate neighbourhood.

Weetabix Ltd, the breakfast food manufacturers, is one organization that took this course of action. Owners or associates of a number of other companies, users of a tiny Univac system on which they were already doing some outside work, Weetabix decided to enlarge their installation by adding a second smallish but far more powerful third-generation Univac system.

Before deciding to operate a bureau, they carried out some careful research; and when results of this were found acceptable, made arrangements to provide subsidiary services. As I write, the operation has only just started, but seems to have every chance of success because there are few rival facilities in the neighbourhood and the bureau is treated as a separate entity which is expected to make its own profits. The parent company is therefore buying its time and services from the bureau.

I do not want to discourage you from selling computer time, for it may be very useful to do this, particularly during the early stages of a project when you are not in a position to use the computer's full capacity. I do, however, wish to caution you against too-easy acceptance of the belief that you can rely upon running your installation profitably by selling time.

Summary

The following reasons for failure or qualified success of a computer project have been discussed in this chapter:

(a) Ill-defined management objectives so that the computer is purchased with no clear long-term plan in view.

(b) Lack of realism in estimating costs and failure to estimate the value of intangible benefits with the result that the real extent of liability is unknown.

(c) Lack of finesse in introducing the computer into an organization, thus rousing needless fears and resentments.

(d) Non-participation of management in the computer project so that the team lacks informed guidance and may produce disappointing results.

(e) Poor communications between company managers and the computer team, leading to personal friction.

8

(*f*) Poor systems analysis, design, and planning with the result that the new systems are inaccurate or inadequate or redundant.

(*g*) Over-ambition on the part of management, producing undue difficulty and delay with the demoralization that accompanies these.

(*h*) Too-modest ambition on the part of management and, in consequence, a too-limited use of computer capability or too-early outgrowing of hardware capacity.

(*i*) Reliance upon computer technology as a substitute for constructive thought.

(*j*) Lack of confidence in the capability of the computer with the result that it is never fully exploited.

(*k*) Reliance for profitability of the installation upon the selling of surplus computer time when no proper prior investigation has been made, and in consequence failing to obtain the anticipated revenue.

Reference
9.1 GRAHAM, R. Why computers fail. *Financial Times*. 26 March 1968.

10. Computer service bureaux

Computer service bureaux have often been compared with launderettes. In fact, I think I have probably been guilty in the early days of using this analogy. I write 'guilty' because the comparison is a bad one. To suggest that source data can be equated with soiled linen, for example, is particularly unfortunate, since 'dirty' data simply clogs up the works of a computer.

If one needs a parallel, it would be more accurate to think of a computer service bureau (or data centre, as it may well be called today) as a jobbing shop where precision engineering is done. You, the customer, not only agree the product design with the shop manager but supply the raw material, and from these two he fabricates the final product. Success is dependent upon the quality of the raw material and of the product design, and upon the care and ingenuity that have gone into the manufacturing processes.

The computer service bureau has been a feature of the UK scene almost since the inception of business computing. The earliest centres were owned and operated by computer manufacturers who rightly regarded them as a sales aid and used them principally for demonstrating EDP techniques and providing facilities for customers awaiting delivery of machines. Later, bureau services were made available to anyone capable of using them.

Today, growth in the bureau business is spectacular. According to a market survey done in 1968 by International Computers Ltd, turnover has doubled over the last four years and may be expected to increase by at least 25 per cent per annum from 1968 to 1971 inclusive. The number of independent operators (e.g., owners who have no connection with computer manufacturers) has increased, as has the number of bureaux run by manufacturers as enterprises separate from the marketing of in-house computers. And, though batch-processing data centres will undoubtedly continue to be needed for many years, the possibilities offered by time-sharing, multi-access computer utilities are also rapidly being exploited. These utilities, which I will describe in more detail later in this chapter, provide subscriber-customers with direct access to a bureau computer via terminals located on the users' own premises. Users reach the computer as and when they need it through privately rented telephone lines or the public STD network.

Another of today's features is the specialist bureau which, operated on a batch-processing or (more often) a time-sharing basis, deals only with a certain type of application—the handling of stockbrokers' work, for example.

Batch-processing bureaux

Batch-processing computer service bureaux can be utilized in a variety of ways. Some of their customers are organizations who operate their own computers and use the data centre as a supplementary facility when their systems are temporarily or permanently over-loaded or provide insufficient capacity for certain applications.

For these, and for engineers, scientists, or technical men who need a computer only occasionally to process programs they have written themselves or are available as a package, the main requirement is simply for machine time and the services of the bureau's operators. Scientists, engineers, and others can also avail themselves of 'computer workshops'. These facilities, first set up by Elliott Automation some years ago and now operated by the bureau subsidiary of ICL, provide the computer only, the users themselves being responsible for programming and operating the machine. Rates, particularly in off-peak periods during the night, are very low.

Another way in which data centres, particularly those operated by manufacturers, are still frequently used is for program testing. Since every day that a user's newly-delivered computer stands idle represents a waste of money, many organizations get as near the final program-testing stage as they can before their own system arrives. When no configuration of the type they have ordered is conveniently available, manufacturers often provide software that enables the bureau computer to work in the same way as a different type or configuration of computer. By simulating conditions in the other system, they provide a valid environment for testing all but the final stages of the program.

The kind of customer who most concerns us here is the business-man who believes he can usefully employ a computer for processing some aspects of his work, but cannot or does not wish to install an in-house system. What can a service bureau do for him? And how can he use it most constructively?

If you have read the earlier chapters in this book, you know that there is little hope of computerizing any application, even at a service bureau, without careful thought and preparation. I do not mean that if you feel you may be able profitably to use a data centre for one or two restricted applications you will need to become as deeply involved as you would if you contemplated installing your own system. Nevertheless, the basic rule still holds good: you will get out of the computer results no better than can be provided by the data you put into it or the systems you have designed.

There is therefore not the slightest hope of using a service bureau profitably if you believe that all you need do is hand over a scruffy heap of papers, sit back, and await results. And if you are completely inexperienced in computer usage, you will almost certainly need some specialist advice during the preparation stages. For this reason, you will probably not be able usefully to purchase some machine time at low cost from a neighbouring user who has some processing capacity to spare but offers no subsidiary services.

Though the profits of a bureau operator are drawn principally from the computer time he sells, he has now appreciated, as a result of harsh experience, that time alone is insufficient for most users. Many therefore now offer, in addition to programming services, consultant advice which will help you to decide whether it is feasible to use a computer and, in that event, will guide you during the preparatory stages of the operation.

I think you would be optimistic if you expect to get high-calibre consultant advice, except perhaps at a very superficial level, free of charge. We have already discovered how hard it is to find systems analysts who really know their job. It has also, I hope, become clear that good systems work is an essential foundation for any successful computer procedure. Thus, though it is clearly in the interests of the bureau operator to see that you get something really useful for your money, it is not economically feasible for him to throw in a lot of subsidiary service without charging you for it. This charge may be expressed as a separate sum; or, if the service is minor in character, be included in overall job cost, so that you pay more for computer time to cover the cost of the other services you get.

Employing a bureau's advisory service is much like employing any other type of consultant. You should appreciate the advantages offered by an independent mind and experienced specialist advice applied to your problems. But you should evaluate the consultant's suggestions, not just accept them blindly. This, after all, is an exercise in co-operation. The bureau wants you as a customer and you need its services. Both parties have a stake in making things go well.

Quite possibly you will be advised that it is necessary to modify your existing systems. For example, the product identification code you currently use may not be suitable for a computer system; or, with additions, could be used to extract more information at negligible cost. Or your source documents might need revision because their present layout is inconvenient from a punch operator's viewpoint and without re-design may well incur substantial extra costs in data preparation.

Then there is the question of package programs. If slight modifications are needed to your existing systems in order to use a package, it is well worth while considering this possibility. For by using a ready-made package, you obviate most of the cost (normally some hundreds of pounds or more) of having a special program written for you; and the delays incurred by its production, testing, and correction. At the same time, you cash in on the experience that has already been acquired by the bureau or other sources in running the package program.

Do not, therefore, close your mind to the possibility that re-vamping of your existing systems may be well worth while. Though, like the rest of us, you may well believe that your present method is the best—or even the only possible—way of achieving your aims, you may be wrong. And this may give you a golden opportunity to re-think the basic aims of the procedure in question. It may well be, for example, that it is more elaborate than is necessary. As I have emphasized already, it is bad practice to employ a computer merely to speed up an existing system, particularly one that has fundamental defects.

I would advise you, too, to think if you can of your computerized system as being a potential beginning to further applications. I am not trying to 'sell' you computer bureau services. But the experience of many bureau users is that one application leads to another, and you do not want to be in a position of having to undo early work in order to extend to full advantage the use of a computer in an associated application.

Obviously you will have to keep the thing within bounds or you will find yourself embarking upon a full-scale feasibility study. On the other hand, give at least a glance to the possibility of future extension of your first application and design your system with this in mind.

If a program is written for you, whose property will it be? The answer is, yours. On the other hand a program written for you could be useful to other customers and may be of sufficient general value to make the bureau wish actively to promote its use elsewhere. Normally, you will make an agreement with the bureau so that you pay only a proportion of the overall cost of writing a program, and the bureau will hope to recover the remainder by allowing other customers to use it. They will not, however, make the program documentation available elsewhere unless you specifically authorize this.

One instance of an arrangement like this that worked well was when the North Kent Co-operative Society commissioned Randax-EDP, a central London bureau, to write a program for sales accounting at branches and stock control at a central warehouse. This program, with the original customer's consent, is now being used by several other co-operative societies.

If you are to get the best out of a service bureau, you channel all your dealings with it—or at least those concerned with one application—through a liaison officer appointed from your own staff. It will be this person's job to act as go-between between your organization and the bureau, and he or she alone should be permitted to handle the communications traffic in both directions. This helps enforce the discipline that computer usage always requires and does much to prevent muddles and misunderstandings.

One decision you will have to make is how you are to prepare the source data. Are you to handle this job yourself? Or will you ask the bureau to undertake it? Sometimes this is a question of economics, sometimes of convenience.

You might, for example, have the kind of application that allows the automatic punching of paper tape during daily routines. Typically, this can be done when the service computer is used for the analysis of accounting documents, the paper tape being a by-product of invoicing or customer ledger posting. This could involve exchanging your existing keyboard machine for one with an automatic paper tape punch. But if the machine is old, this may be advisable anyway (especially after decimalization of the coinage) and you will gain the benefit of automatic data preparation. Many companies are prepared to rent accounting machines with paper-tape punches.

On the other hand, you may wish to employ people who are out of a job because you are using a computer. In such cases, it may be possible to train these as card- or tape-punch operators. If they are past their first youth, they will not make the world's best operators. But if they do a useful task for you in handling work that would otherwise have to be done outside and you thereby fulfil a moral obligation, this may be well worth while.

If you do prepare your own data for the computer, you have the benefit of retaining the source documents within your own office. Otherwise you would, of course, have to send them away for punching. On the other hand, if you undertake this work, you must be prepared to impose high standards of accuracy, both in the data itself and the format in which it is recorded. Operators unaware of the rigours of data-processing requirements may unwittingly play ducks and drakes with the system by changing the data format. This creates havoc and expense when the work gets into the computer.

The bureau will, as a matter of course, draw your attention to any obvious errors in your source data or in the way it is prepared, whether they receive it in the form of documents, punched cards, or tape. But every error that gets through even to this point causes delays and it is therefore in your interest to eliminate as many as possible by imposing strict discipline during data or source-document preparation.

How long will it take the bureau to process your work? This depends principally on your own requirements. If the exercise is critical in terms of time—payroll, for example—you will obviously make certain that finished documents will always be made available at a predetermined time. In other instances, some leeway will be feasible.

If you want to get the best out of a computer (or any other) service bureau, do not insist upon unnecessarily early deadlines. You may think the bureau is unaware that your deadline is strictly sham and you would be quite happy in reality to wait another 48 hours. But sooner or later this intelligence will leak out; and though they will not penalize you, you will not be very popular either. Keep your urgent requests for jobs that really are urgent, and you will find you get good service.

I should like to have been able to give you some guidance about the costs you are likely to incur in using a computer service bureau for some of the most popular applications—say, sales analysis and maintenance of shareholders' register with dividend warrant production. The truth is that any figure I give you is likely to be quite useless. Bureau operators refuse, with one voice, to cite figures because even two applications which appear very similar often differ considerably in many of the details which influence ultimate cost.

I must therefore confine myself to saying that you will get an estimate of cost from the service bureau before the job begins. The way in which these costs are quoted will, as I have indicated, vary from one bureau to another and the total sum will, of course, be greatly influenced by whether or not you can use a package program or how elaborate or difficult a purpose-made program is to write. The amount of printing done is another factor that influences cost.

What kinds of work are you likely to hand to a batch-processing computer service bureau? Almost anything that can be treated as a self-contained operation and where you do not require print-outs more frequently than, say, once a day at the most. You may use the bureau for one-off jobs; sporadically; or at regular intervals; or in all these ways if you have more than one application. When you use the bureau regularly, say, once a week, you will probably pay slightly less per run than you would for occasional work. You will also probably be asked to sign a contract covering, for example, a year.

How the source data in the form of documents, punched cards, or paper-tape, and the finished print-outs are conveyed to and from the bureau is a matter of individual arrangement. Most bureaux have van deliveries within a specified radius. Other possibilities include your own company's vans, cars or lorries, post, passenger train, minicab, messenger, or the security firms such as Securicor.

In some cases, if both your organization and the bureau are on the Telex system, this could provide an answer, particularly for applications where the bulk of data for transmission is relatively small and results are required as soon as possible.

One of the major benefits offered by using a bureau is the ability to obtain, often with minor modification to existing routines, far more management information than can be made available by conventional methods. One of the most popular areas for exploitation of this is sales, where detailed analysis of day-to-day documents often yields valuable information about trends and patterns in sales and profitability of various products.

A good case in point was a small company I visited who manufacture and sell wooden doors of various kinds. For processing orders it uses an efficient but conventional system based on the use of a spirit duplicator and hand-typed invoices.

Partially completed invoices are passed to the operators of keyboard accounting machines with attached paper-tape punches. The girls, in one operation, update the customer ledger card, make an entry on a sales summary sheet, complete the invoice, and capture all the data required for sales analysis by computer. (The accounting machines are used also for other applications with the tape punch switched off.)

At the end of each working day, the summary sheet total is taken and punched into the paper tape and the completed length of tape removed from each accounting machine. Each month, all the paper tapes (which between them contain detail from about 2,500 invoices) are sent by post to an NCR data-processing centre in London.

Completed reports, which come back to the company by post 48 hours later, are analyzed by representative or sales-depot number and include the cost and selling price for each item, its value, and the percentage of gross profit this represents. Totals are given for each representative as well as grand totals. In a summary, also completed by the computer, analysis is on an item-by-item basis. Detail includes quantity, inter-company value (i.e., difference between factory cost and selling price), selling value, and gross profit.

Among the advantages gained by using the computer centre is the availability, for the first time, of combined accounts for sales and manufacturing operations. This not only obviates the keeping of two separate sets of records but allows constant review of the profit position in the sales company. Analysis of sales by representative enables the sales manager not only to keep track of individual performance but permits much faster payment of commissions.

The costs of this operation in mid-1967 were as follows: systems analysis and other work connected with the programming and setting up and initial implementation of the system, £250; rent of two NCR Class 31 accounting machines with automatic paper-tape punches, about £130 a month; data processing, varying slightly according to the number of lines printed, about £30 a month. I ought, perhaps, to emphasize that I have included these figures for general interest and they should not therefore be taken as a reliable indication of cost even of an operation that superficially appears to be similar. It is also possible that scales of charges have risen since 1967.

In the case of the North West Kent Co-operative Society to which I referred briefly earlier in this chapter, the Randax-EDP bureau was used after centralization of grocery warehousing and accounting— functions which had until then been handled locally by a number of individual societies. This rationalization in itself brought improvements not directly connected with use of the computer—for example, reduction in warehouse staff, lower transport costs, the benefits of bulk purchasing, and more modern handling equipment than could be justified when several small warehouses were used.

Data for the computer is prepared on Burroughs Sensimatic accounting machines with paper-tape punches from branch order forms filled in once a week by each local grocery manager and used in the warehouse as picking documents. Data recorded at this point includes branch code number, date, and code number and quantity of each commodity ordered. A similar procedure is followed for recording details of goods received into the warehouse, the supplier's advice note being used as a source document.

The bureau holds a master file containing full basic details, e.g., code number, description, manufacturer's and warehouse pack size, price, and gross profit on selling price, for each item held in the warehouse. Paper tape is brought in by a clerk to the computer centre at about noon each Friday. By 7 pm the same day, all the print-outs are ready for picking up by the Co-op's van driver who delivers them to the accounts office. These documents include the following:

(a) Branch invoices which, mailed to local managers on Saturday mornings, are available first thing Mondays, providing them with full information on all supplies received from the warehouse during the previous week.

(b) Full details of all goods received at the warehouse.

(c) Warehouse stock report. Information in this includes gross profit on each item, total issues made during the year to date, weekly average issues, issues in the week immediately past and for one, two, and three weeks prior to this; for each item, the number of packs received, number and value of balance held in stock, number of packs on order, and number of weeks' stocks this represents.

(d) Monthly report for each branch summarizing the month's invoices broken down into 40 analysis categories. Information on each commodity includes quantity received during the period, cumulative receipt for the year to date, gross profit in terms of cash and as a percentage, proportion of total sales as a percentage, and proportion of overall gross profit as a percentage. A stock summary at the foot of the report shows total stock held at the beginning of the year, stocks received during the current year to date, sales to date (fast turn-round of goods in this trade permit an assumption that stock ordered is stock sold) and present stock.

The benefits reaped as a combined result of centralization and use of the computer included savings in clerical labour (8 girls, including those used for data preparation, do work that needed 25 before) and punctual production of invoices which in the past were sometimes several weeks in arrears. Monthly summaries, not available under the old system, allow managers to keep an informed eye on their own trading results and to calculate—using the profit figures provided in the reports—how most advantageously to position the goods on their shelves. Warehouse buyers have figures that enable them to base decisions on accurate and up-to-date facts rather than guesses. During the first year of operation, warehouse savings were 25 per cent. The running cost of the bureau service worked out at about £1 per branch per week.

A good example of how a service bureau is used on a fairly frequent but irregular basis is afforded by the case of a medium-size building company who use an ICSL bureau (a subsidiary of International Computers Ltd) for processing a PERT program.

The company uses this for controlling the time element of contracts for building large housing estates and factories and for the allocation of labour resources for these. Typically, an exercise requires a preliminary processing immediately after the network has been drawn and data prepared, and two or three runs at irregular intervals thereafter as the project progresses. The total cost for a housing estate job, including the initial and all subsequent runs and data preparation, works out at about 30 shillings per house. Reports include: a list of activities sorted by department (area of responsibility or section of the project) and listed in order of scheduled start date and within this by total float time; bar chart showing start and stop time for each category of workman used on each house; and histograms and Tables showing labour utilization for 50 days in advance (a longer period could have been covered, if required). There is also a list of materials used on the project, shown as a daily total and on a cumulative basis.

Computer service bureaux with batch-processing systems are now used in scores of ways that cover almost every conceivable aspect of commercial and industrial operations from data processing to the solution of technical and scientific problems. Well distributed over England and the south of Scotland, these centres are now easily accessible to most businesses, whatever their location.

Bureaux with on-line terminals

When you use a bureau of the kind I have described above, you take your work to the computer. There is now another type of centre that operates a multi-access time-sharing system which effectively brings the computer to the user through a terminal situated on his own premises. This terminal, which may be a typewriter, a TV-type display device, a computer-driven plotter, or a smaller computer, is linked to the bureau's system via a privately rented telephone line. It allows its user to retrieve data from the central machine at any time, for as long or as short a period as he likes, and often without any human intervention at the bureau end. This offers a facility that can be tapped almost as easily as the electricity or water supply; hence, probably, the term 'computer utility' sometimes used to describe it.

Before describing in more detail how these utilities can be used, I would like to dispose of one problem that seems to make some people nervous—the alleged lack of security when a number of users who may be business rivals have access to the same computer system.

Fears of leakage of information are, however, groundless. Precautions taken by the bureau to prevent unauthorized access to data are stringent. Typically, each user has a machine code known only to himself, and exclusive use of a privately rented telephone wire. Software is designed to permit information channelled into or out of the system or held on magnetic files to become available only after a series of checks which, applied automatically, use codes unknown either to the terminal user or computer operators. No print-outs are produced at the bureau; results go back direct to the original terminal; and automatic lock-outs ensure that no terminal can operate except on its own channel.

This set-up, you will agree, compares very favourably with any kind of precautions the average company can realistically take to protect confidential information, either when it has its own computer centre or uses conventional methods. Unless the computer has remote, on-line terminals, the computer room staff have access to print-outs. Though I am not suggesting that any of these is untrustworthy or that measures such as security checks at gates and the destruction of paper by shredding or burning are necessarily ineffective, it must be admitted that such precautions are not unbreakable by an even moderately determined industrial spy, unaided by any electronic devices. The danger of leakage via an on-line terminal (which could easily be installed in a senior executive's office) linked to a service bureau computer is, in fact, much smaller than when less advanced methods of information handling are used.

Developments in the computer utility field are moving so fast that anything I can tell you now will probably be at least partly out of date by the time these words are set in type. Until very recently available for use almost exclusively by those who wished to process technical, mathematical, and scientific problems, utilities are already being extended in scope to allow their use for business data processing—a group of applications that implies a need for a high volume of fast input and output.

Later I shall describe one of the most advanced of these centres which is already beginning to operate in this country. Meantime, I will outline the advantages of an on-line terminal as used by W. S. Atkins & Partners, a large firm of consulting engineers who were the first UK company to exploit a system of this kind.

The bureau in question has a Univac 1107 computer situated in Birmingham and operated by Computer Services Birmingham, who have since changed their name to University Computing Company (Great Britain) Ltd. Atkins's terminal is located in the firm's headquarters at Epsom, Surrey, and is in itself a small computer, a Univac 1005 with magnetic tapes and an automatic plotter that is on-line to the 1005 but off-line to the 1107. This permits the 1107 to by-pass the comparatively slow plotter by recording data and instructions for it direct onto magnetic tape. After transmission has ended and the 1005 has been disconnected from the 1107, the magnetic tapes are used to drive the plotter. In this way, the amount of time used on the expensive 1107 is reduced to a minimum.

The 1005 is connected to Birmingham by an ordinary private telephone wire and transmission is at medium speed—that is, faster than is possible on a telegraph line but about half the speed achievable on a telephone-type line.

Interviewed by a reporter from the magazine, *Data Systems*, Mr R. J. Braithwaite, one of Atkins's senior planners, explained (10.1) that work handled through the terminal included strategic decision making, traffic studies, project and contract management, research and development, and almost every kind of engineering—civil, structural, nuclear, chemical, environmental, and electrical. Most of this work, he said, is best handled by a powerful computer; but various factors, including a workload of completely unpredictable size, preclude installation of a large in-house system. The terminal therefore offered a very attractive alternative.

The saving of time of valuable technical personnel was one big benefit. Atkins employs its own programmers and systems men, and when a conventional bureau was used up to 15 per cent of each programmer's time was wasted in travelling (the nearest suitable bureau is about one hour's journey distant). Facilities for experimentation which were made available by the data link were another important feature.

> Experimentation implies very close co-operation between teams of specialists ... We found it simply was not possible to develop programs effectively if one had to take the computer work outside the premises. We needed a flexible set-up which would give us a quick turn-round, preferably with direct access to the computer.

At the time the article was written, experiments were being made with the plotter. Applications included production of engineering detail drawings, perspective drawings, land surveys, diagrams showing results of traffic surveys, and bar charts and histograms used in planning utilization of labour resources.

Asked if he felt this pioneering experiment had been worth while, Mr Braithwaite said:

> There can be no doubt about that. We have access to a powerful computer any time we need it, but we pay only for the time we actually use. Of course, we have to rent the GPO line and there is the capital cost of the terminal itself. But these on-costs are small compared to the intrinsic costs of alternative possibilities. We waste no time travelling backwards and forwards to a bureau, or in waiting our turn for program testing. This means that we have excellent facilities for developing and running programs and as these facilities are in-house we have complete control over the operations.

To make the full resources of a powerful central computer available for business data-processing work and utilize the huge random-access storage facilities of such systems for applications of this kind poses a different kind of problem. Stated in its broadest terms, this demands the design of a system that will fulfil a number of very exacting requirements.

(*a*) Maximum utilization of the very expensive central computer. Unless this is exploited to best advantage, the operator will not be able to offer services at costs acceptable to customers.

(*b*) An ability to offer *all* the resources of the central system, including use of the random-access storage devices, to every one of a large number of terminal users. These resources must be available automatically on demand from the terminals without delay and at reasonable cost.

(*c*) Fast turn-round time on work. The advantages of a system like this are self-cancelling to a large degree if any significant delay occurs between acceptance of work and its processing and the return of results to terminal users.

(*d*) High input and output speeds at the terminal. Without these and the use of large, fast random-access stores, the utility would be of minor value for business data-processing applications. Data-transmission speeds must also, of course, be high.

(*e*) Availability, on demand from the terminal, of software such as high-level language compilers and of package programs. There must also be facilities for storage of users' own programs for calling in in the same way.

(*f*) Facilities for the testing of users' programs from the terminal.

This is an exceedingly hard nut for the computer men to crack.

One organization that has found a viable solution is University Computing Company of Dallas, Texas, whose subsidiary of the same name in this country opened a utility at the Euston Centre, London, at the end of 1968. I am aware that the following paragraphs sound like a testimonial to this company, but I can only answer that the system I describe is the most advanced of its kind in the world, demonstrably works (similar systems are already in use in the USA), and that I have no shares or other financial interest in the company!

UCC's main computer at the Euston Centre is a very large Univac 1108 whose peripherals include random-access storage devices with huge capacities. Terminals used with the system fall under two broad headings: small devices such as input/output typewriters (teletypes), automatic plotters and (later) TV-type display devices; and various makes of small computer. The latter category includes a model designed and made by UCC, Cope ·45, which is extremely fast.

A hierarchy of smaller computers and other devices is interposed between the terminal users and the 1108. This hardware and some extremely sophisticated software, both UCC products, act as a filter, relieving the 1108 of all the organizational and other work that can be handled at a lower level, passing on to the central system only jobs that it alone is capable of doing.

This arrangement places at the disposal of every terminal user the whole resources of the system. But the most sophisticated and expensive facilities are used (automatically) only when the application demands this. Costs are therefore kept down. And the system meets all the other requirements I have listed.

By the time you read these words, a dozen or more Cope .45 terminals will already be on-line to the 1108. Some of these terminals will be in European countries. One in Switzerland, for example, went on-line in November 1968.

The possibilities offered to you as a businessman by a system like this are exciting. For it places at your disposal some of the most sophisticated hardware yet developed (and the know-how that goes with it) at a realistic price. It seems possible that in the near future the availability of utilities like this will change the pattern of computer usage. Though, in many cases, it will be found desirable to maintain a self-owned and operated computer, the utility would supplement this. It is no coincidence that the earliest to avail themselves of computer utilities are mostly organizations who already have their own installations.

Market research done by International Computers Ltd suggests that the number of utilities will grow fast and steadily during coming years. It seems unlikely that they will supersede the 'conventional' computer bureaux now operating, however; instead they will exist side-by-side with these. UCC, for example, are also doing batch-processing work on a standard bureau basis at the Euston Centre.

So far I have mentioned only very briefly the type of utility that is dedicated to provide services to one group of users only. The SCAN and Centre-File services for stockbrokers, investment analysts, and others are examples of this. Problems associated with the setting up and operating of these are not quite as formidable as those that face the operator of an all-purpose utility, for the range of programs and services required is naturally more restricted and the pattern of usage more predictable.

Though there are not so far many utilities like this, the chances are that more will open. Centre-File, for example, has announced

T

plans for providing an on-line service to building societies. There would seem to be a potential in any type of trade, industry, or profession that embraces a sizable number of small or medium-size firms with common requirements and interests.

Computer services bureaux association

COSBA was founded in January 1968 to provide a collective voice for the computer bureau industry. There are two classes of membership: full membership, which is open to experienced and established companies operating as computer service bureaux or software houses; and associate membership for smaller companies and those in associated fields such as data preparation. Present membership represents some 30 companies who between them operate 55 bureaux throughout the UK and includes subsidiaries of major computer manufacturers in the UK.

The principal object of the Association is to establish and maintain a reputation for a high standard of integrity and professional competence. Among the mandatory requirements for all members are adherence to a number of standards which include the following:

(*a*) Impartial treatment of clients, subject to any special contract conditions.

(*b*) Assurance of continuity of service—including, if necessary, arranging alternative computing services at reasonable fees.

(*c*) Security—protection of confidential information and the taking of proper precautions against loss or destruction of files and programs.

(*d*) Agreements that are clear, concise, simply worded, and include a precise definition of work to be done, base price, and supplementary schedules covering all reasonable contingencies; accurate and realistic work and delivery schedules.

COSBA, whose headquarters are in London, will also undertake to give prospective bureau users unbiased advice on what kind of bureau could help them with specific applications.

Other service organizations

As one might expect in view of the general shortage of all kinds of computer staff and the high cost of machinery, various other types of bureau have been formed to handle such jobs as data preparation and program writing. Often these are used less as a substitute for in-company staff than as a valuable supplement at times when domestic resources are insufficient.

One of the best-known and most respected of the programming organizations is an all-woman company, Freelance Programmers Ltd. Staffed principally by women who work mostly from their own homes, it makes available to the computer world high-quality know-how which otherwise would have been lost owing to domestic commitments. The company insists that all its workers are properly qualified and experienced before they join and that, when necessary, they attend training courses to bring their knowledge up to date—an important proviso in such a fast-moving field.

There is a growing number of organizations which include programming in a range of service that covers software design and, sometimes, computer consultancy. Though many of these are reputable and well-run, caution suggests that you should investigate the background of any you intend to employ unless it is a member of COSBA. Non-membership does not, of course, imply that the company is a bad one, though membership confers respectability.

Data-preparation bureaux have grown up like mushrooms during the past few years. The service they provide is particularly useful for setting up master files, a job that often involves the punching of tens of thousands or even millions of cards or their equivalent in paper-tape. In such circumstances, it is seldom feasible to use one's own staff. Data-prep bureaux have also often been the salvation of organizations who find themselves temporarily under-staffed during holidays, sickness, or recruitment problems. Another source of work is computer service bureaux who do not themselves offer this service to customers.

The same precautions should be applied to the selection of a data-preparation bureau as to a programming or software house. If you have read the earlier chapters in this book, you need no warning about the difficulties that arise when the standard of data preparation is low. Among the undesirable practices that are followed in dubious bureaux are: employment of low-grade or poorly trained operators or of girls who hold full-time jobs in user organizations and are tired before they begin an evening shift at the bureau; inadequate supervision; and insufficient resources to adhere reasonably closely to agreed delivery dates. (Perhaps I should repeat here the warning I gave you against unnecessarily early deadlines.)

I would suggest that, before using any data-prep bureau whose prices are substantially lower than what you have been led to expect, you investigate its background. There may be a perfectly valid reason for its unusually favourable terms; and there may not.

A new kind of bureau recently opened by Rank-Xerox in London usefully exploits the company's high-speed electrostatic copier of continuous forms. Fed with computer print-out, it copies each sheet at reduced size and as many times as required, automatically collating the output into sets. These are later made up into neat volumes, which though much smaller than the original print-out tend to be more legible.

The main advantages are the speed with which the work is done and the compactness of the results which are easier to handle and file. One user found that over 400 volumes of management data, many of which contain hundreds of pages, can be made available through the bureau within a week. Previous methods required three weeks and they cost almost twice as much.

While on the subject of print-out, I can usefully mention that automatic cameras are now available for the microfilming, at high speed, of documents printed on continuous stationery in unburst form. Though I do not know any bureau that operates one of these, their rather high capital cost and high operating speed suggests that it will not be long before some enterprising operator installs one. The increasing cost of storage space is an encouragement to use microfilm as an alternative to original documents whenever possible.

Summary

The following points have been mentioned in this chapter:

(*a*) The number of computer service bureaux is rapidly increasing. At present, these fall into three broad categories: those using machines that operate in the batch processing mode and to which users carry their work; computer utilities which handle a wide range of problems on a powerful system and provide users with remote terminals situated in their own offices; bureaux of the preceding kind but which cater only for customers with one kind of application.

(*b*) Many service bureaux now offer a range of ancillary services which help the user to prepare his work for processing on their computers.

(*c*) The expense of using a bureau is greatly reduced by using a 'package' program, but this may demand some modification of the user's existing routines. This modification, however, may ultimately prove to be beneficial.

(d) Users of computer service bureaux and associated organizations such as data-preparation centres are protected by a recently formed bureau users' association whose members adhere to a code of ethics. Non-membership, however, need not imply that a bureau does not operate along lines similar to those laid down by the association.

(e) There are various other types of service organization who carry out programming, data preparation, and other work directly associated with computer usage.

Reference
10.1 Maintaining the lead at Epsom. *Data Systems.* December 1967.

Index

Index

Ackoff, Russell L, 135
Advertising agency
  accounting, 85
  TV time booking, 64
AEI Automation Ltd, 151, 155
Aerospace Industries Association, 144
Airlines (*see also* British European Airways):
  as pioneers in real-time computing, 64
ALGOL language, 44
APT machine tool system, 144–147
Arithmetic, binary, 10
ASAP Consultants Ltd, 253
Atkins, W. S. & Partners, 274–275
Autocodes (*see* Languages, assembly)

Banks, 19
Batch processing:
  definition and function, 30
  economics of, 33
  in service bureaux, 264–273
Beer, Stafford, 121
Bostock, Christopher, 202
Braithwaite, R. J., 274
Brintons Ltd, 203–204
British Computer Society, 98, 173, 245
British European Airways:
  real-time computing system, 32, 64
Burroughs accounting machines, 271

British Rail, 184
Budgets:
  control of, 94, 126
  planning, 95, 96
Building project control, 126–127, 272

Cambridge University, 118
Cards, punched (*see* Punched cards)
Cathode ray tube (CRT) terminals:
  Description and function, 34
  general use by management, 34–35
  indiscriminate demand for, 39
  use for depot location problems, 118
  use in hospitals, 70–71
  use for management planning, 130–133
Cattle feed formulation, 120
C.A.V. Ltd, 78, 102–108, 140
2C, L language, 146
Centralization of computing facilities, 38, 187–190
Central processor:
  general description and function, 8
Centre-File Ltd, 277
Check digit verification, 17
Clarke, Laurence, 157
Closed-loop systems:
  general description, 68
  process control applications, 149
COBOL language, 44, 45, 218

Compatibility in computer systems:
definition and importance of, 184–185
Compilers:
description and function, 42–43
Computer communications:
description and definition, 37
use in business, 187
Computers, analogue:
definition, 5
in process control, 152
Computers, digital:
definitions, 5–8
for mass data processing, 30
Computer staff (*see also* Data processing managers, programmers, Systems analysts):
control of, 210–211
management attitudes to, 243–245, 256–257
qualifications of, 227–243
recruitment of, 226–227, 241–242
Computers, visible record:
definition, 7
evaluation of, 170–172
for information storage, 193
warehouse application, 190
Configuration, computer:
definition, 8
representation on paper, 26, 65
Consultants, computer, 197–205
Control console functions, 11
Conversational mode, 36
Core store (*see* Memory, internal)
COSBA, 278
Cost/performance ratio, 178–179
Costing systems:
at C.A.V. Ltd, 103–106
general discussion, 92–95
Critical path analysis (*see* PERT)

Data banks:
description and function, 32
servicing by operating system, 46
use in hospital management, 69–70, 73

use in total management systems, 78
Data collection systems:
description and function, 139–141
Data preparation:
for service bureau work, 267–268
function of, 15
method comparison, 192–197
operator qualifications and training, 239–241
service bureaux, 279–280
Data processing manager:
responsibilities and qualifications, 235–238
Data transmission (*see also* Remote terminals, Post Office):
by Telex, 37
in service bureau applications, 269, 274–278
Post Office facilities, 38–39
Depot location problems, 118
Dialled Despatches Ltd pneumatic tube system, 112
Direct access (*see* Random access)
Direct digital control (DDC), 152
Distribution systems:
general discussion, 108–118
at William Timpson Ltd, 111–115
Dividend warrant preparation, 33
Douglas, Dr A. S., 244
Duplicators, offset litho, 107
Duplicators, spirit, 106

Eastern Gas Board, 156
Edinburgh University, 221
Elliott Automation Ltd, 264
Elliott Process Control Ltd, 157
English Electric-Leo-Marconi, 116
Exception reporting:
description and function, 58–60
emphasis on, 78
Expandability of computer systems, 10, 183
Exponential smoothing, 90, 107

Feasibility study:
  for business computers, 166–172
  for process control computers, 159–160
Feedback (*see* Closed-loop systems)
Fisher & Ludlow Ltd, 112
Financing computer projects, 208–209
Flowlink conveyor system, 112
Forrester, Professor, 68
Form design, 97, 197
FORTRAN language, 44–46
Freelance Programmers Ltd, 279
Frost, Peter F., 98

Gill, Professor Stanley, 38–39
GPO (*see* Post Office)
Graham, Roger, 253–254

Hardware, computer
  definition, 6
  development and evolution, 28–33
  evaluation of 177–182, 186–187
  in process control, 152–154
Harper, R. J., 235–237
Hebden, John E., 245
Hire purchase accounting, 84
Hitchcock, R. G., 75
Honeywell Computers Ltd, 26, 155
Hospitals:
  computer-based management systems for, 69–73
Humphries, J. D., 98

IBM (International Business Machines):
  aptitude tests for computer staff, 229, 239
  computer applications, 74, 151, 184
  PL/1 language, 45–46
  Wholesale IMPACT program, 90–91
ICL (International Computers Ltd):
  computer workshops, 264
  PROMPT program, 103

PROSPER program, 103
service bureau survey, 262
Illinois Institute of Technology Research, 144
Input:
  definition and function, 15–16
  equipment, 15–20, 152–153
  equipment evaluation, 192–197
  volumes, 28
Intangible benefits (of computerisation):
  as basis for pay-off, 55, 253
Integrated data processing systems:
  description and function, 57–58
  implementation of, 213
  planning for, 257–258
Integrated process control systems, 155–158
International Association of Department Stores, 108
International Federation for Information Processing, 137, 146
International Nickel, 151
Inventory control (*see* Stock control)

Jeffreys, Dr J. B., 108

Keyboard accounting machines:
  for data preparation, 267–268, 270
  for costing systems, 94
Keyboard Training Ltd, 197
Kimball tags, 139

Languages, computer:
  ALGOL, 44
  APT III, 144–147
  Assembly, 42
  COBOL, 44–45, 218
  FORTRAN, 44–46
  high-level, 42–43
  PL/1, 45–46
Language, machine:
  definition and description, 41
  necessity for, 15
Light-pen:
  description and function, 35–36

Light-Pen— *contd.*
  use in depot location problem, 118
  use in management planning, 130–133
Linear programming, 120
Liveware, 6

Machine intelligence, 221
Machine language (*see* Language, machine)
Magnetic discs, 13
Magnetic drums, 14
Magnetic ink character recognition, 19, 195
Magnetic stripe ledger cards, 7, 8
Magnetic tapes:
  computer, 12
  for data preparation, 18
Management accounting, 55–56
Management by exception (*see* Exception reporting)
Management education:
  at Tube Investments Ltd, 75
  for production control, 99
  on computers, 218–219
Management information:
  as aid to man-management, 61
  as primary product, 54
  distorted, 68–69
  early concepts of, 53
  on an exception basis, 58–60
  on production, 99
  on sales, 95–98
  total systems of, 66, 69, 78
Mark-sensing, 20
Marketing:
  general discussion, 95–98
  plans, 130
Masius Wynne-Williams, 85
Massachusetts Institute of Technology, 144
Mathematical models:
  description and function, 119–120
  in business planning, 129
  in process control, 150
Memory, external (*see also* Magnetic discs, drums, tapes):

definition, 12
lack of, 29
Memory, internal:
  as measure of computer capacity, 9–10, 192
  definition, 9–10
  expandability of, 10, 183
  requirements for compiling, 44–**45**
Microfilm:
  input equipment, 20
  output equipment, 25
Middle managers:
  existing functions of, 62, 67
  redundancy of, 250
Ministry of Labour, 246
Ministry of Technology (Mintech), 143, 147
Molins Machine Co. Ltd System 24, 147–149
Multi-programming, 30
Mumford, Enid, 223–234

NCR Ltd data centre, 270
Nanosecond, 10
National Computing Centre, 98, 219, 233–234
National Coal Board, 234
National Engineering Laboratory, 143, 146, 149
National Union of Railwaymen, 184
Network analysis (*see* PERT)
North Kent Co-operative Society, 267, 271–272
Numerical control of machine tools, 141–147 (*see also* APT language)

Operating systems:
  assessment of, 49
  description and function, 46–49
  necessity for, 179
Operational research:
  description and function, 134–136 (*see also* Linear programming; Mathematical models)
  in process control, 159

Optical readers:
  description and function, 18, 195
Order strategy, 91
Output (*see also* Printers):
  definition, 15–16
  equipment, 20–25, 153
  volumes, 28, 153

Paper-handling equipment, 207–208
Paper tape, punched:
  as a by-product of machine accounting, 16, 270–271
  as a filing medium, 29
  general description, 16
  in data transmission, 37, 189–190
  merits/demerits as an input medium, 193–194
Paper tape readers:
  as terminal devices, 36
  general description, 17
Parallel running (of computer/other systems), 213–214
Payroll, 29, 33, 88
  as basis for labour costing, 104–106
Peripherals (*see also* Memory, external, Remote terminals etc.):
  definition, 8
  functions, 26
  number handled by CPU, 183–184
  simultaneous use of, 29
PERT programs:
  description and function, 121–127
  for control of computer projects, 210
  for control of staff, 211
  through service bureaux, 272
PL/1 language, 45–46
2P, L language, 146
Planning:
  budget, 95–96
  general business, 127–133
  long range, 78
  marketing, 130
  production, 98–110, 130

Plotters, automatic:
  description and function, 24
  on process control computers, 149
  use by W. S. Atkins, 274
Post Office data transmission facilities, 38, 189, 275
Printers, output:
  description and function, 21–23
Process control, 149–158
Production control:
  at C.A.V. Ltd, 102–108
  at Tube Investments Ltd, 74–77
  by integrated data processing systems, 57–58
  general requirements for, 98–104
  intangible benefits of, 173
  management education for, 99
Production Engineering Research Association, 147
Programmers (*see also* Computer staff):
  qualifications and training, 227–230
Programming:
  amendments, 43
  description and function, 39–51
Programs, user (applications):
  definition, 40
  ownership of, 267
  package:
    in general, 75, 90, 267
    PERT (see separate entry)
    PROMPT, 103
    PROSPER, 129
    Wholesale IMPACT, 90–91
  sequencing of, 267
Punched cards:
  general description, 16
  as by-product of machine accounting, 16
  as a filing medium, 29, 193
  merits/demerits as an input medium, 193–194
Punched paper tape (*see* Paper tape)

Randax-EDP Ltd, 267, 271
Random access:
  definition, 12
  devices, 13–15
  evaluation, 177–178
  for hospital records, 69
  for stock control, 88
  interrogation, 31–32
Rank-Xerox Ltd, 280
Readers:
  card, general description, 17
  magnetic ink character, general
    description, 19
  optical, general description, 18–
    19
  paper tape, general description,
    17
  punched card, general descrip-
    tion, 17
Read-write head, 12
Real-time computing:
  description, 31–32
  impact on management, 53, 63–
    80
  in process control, 153
Redundancy, employee, 245–250
Remote terminals (see also Cath-
    ode-ray tube terminals, &c.)
  control of by software, 45, 48
  description and function, 34
  from service bureaux, 273–
    278
  use of in business, 188–189
Response time, 33
Rivett, Patrick, 134–135
Richemont, David A., 143–144
Return-on-Investment, 111, 209
Rolls-Royce Ltd, 167
Royal Aircraft Establishment,
    Farnborough, 147

Sales:
  analysis by service bureau, 270–
    272
  catalogues by computer, 107
  forecasting, 91, 112
  management methods, 95–98
  management responsibility,
    77

Salford University, 245
Satellite computers, 36–37
SCAN system, 277
Securicor Ltd, 269
Simulation, 120
Smith, K. L., 68
Snow, F. A., 155–159
Software (see also Operating sys-
    tems):
  description and function, 6,
    40
  evaluation of, 49, 191–192
Southern Television Ltd, 64
Stock control systems:
  at C.A.V. Ltd, 102–108
  general principles, 86–88
  in production, 101
  in retail stores, 111–115
  in warehouses, 87, 109, 111–115
Summers, John & Co. Ltd, 212
Supermarkets:
  as users of optical readers, 19
  sales analysis systems, 89, 109
Systems analysis and design:
  description and function, 230–
    235
  for service bureau applications,
    265–266
  from wrong premises, 83
  insufficient, 99, 257–258
  staff shortage, 233–234
  standardization of requirements,
    75
Systematics, 233
Systems analysts (see also Com-
    puter staff):
  qualifications and training, 230–
    235

Telecontrol system, 140–142
Telex system (for data transmis-
    sion), 37, 269
Terminals (see Remote terminals)
Time-sharing, 30
Timpson, William Ltd, 111–115
Total management system (see
    Management information)
Travelling salesman problem, 116
Tube Investments Ltd, 74–77

Univac computer applications, 32, 65, 69, 71–73, 84, 111, 115, 146, 184, 261, 274, 276

University Computing Company, 274, 276–277

Urwick-Diebold Ltd, 233

Vehicle routing, 116–117, 135
Verification:
  check-digit, 17
  other methods, 16

Weetabix Ltd, 261

Westinghouse Corporation:
  long-range planning, 130–133
  real-time order processing, 32, 88

West London traffic control system, 161

Wholesale IMPACT program, 90–91

Wiggin, Henry & Co. Ltd, 151

Wilkinson, J. V., 78–79

Wofac Corporation, 164

Wolvercote Paper Mill, 157

Wright, Pearce, 83

PRINTED BY COX AND WYMAN LTD.
LONDON, FAKENHAM AND READING